iPod touch

FOR

DUMMIES®

2ND EDITION

iPod touch®

FOR

DUMMIES®
2ND EDITION

by Tony Bove

WILEY

Wiley Publishing, Inc.

iPod touch® For Dummies®, 2nd Edition

Published by
Wiley Publishing, Inc.
111 River Street
Hoboken, NJ 07030-5774

www.wiley.com

Copyright © 2011 by Wiley Publishing, Inc., Indianapolis, Indiana

Published by Wiley Publishing, Inc., Indianapolis, Indiana

Published simultaneously in Canada

For general information on our other products and services, please contact our Customer Care Department within the U.S. at 877-762-2974, outside the U.S. at 317-572-3993, or fax 317-572-4002.

For technical support, please visit www.wiley.com/techsupport.

Wiley also publishes its books in a variety of electronic formats. Some content that appears in print may not be available in electronic books.

Library of Congress Control Number: 2010939500

ISBN: 978-0-470-88001-2

Manufactured in the United States of America

10 9 8 7 6 5 4 3 2 1

WILEY

About the Author

Tony Bove has written about every iPad, iPod, and iPhone model and every update to iTunes from the very beginning, and not only provides free tips on his Web site (www.tonybove.com) but also developed an iPhone application (*Tony's Tips for iPhone Users*). Tony has written more than two dozen books on computing, desktop publishing, and multimedia, including *iPod touch For Dummies, iPad Application Development For Dummies, iPhone Application Development All-In-One For Dummies* (all from Wiley), *Just Say No to Microsoft* (No Starch Press), The *GarageBand Book* (Wiley), *The Art of Desktop Publishing* (Bantam), and a series of books about Macromedia Director, Adobe Illustrator, and PageMaker. Tony also founded *Desktop Publishing/Publish* magazine and the *Inside Report on New Media* newsletter, and he wrote the weekly Macintosh column for *Computer Currents* for a decade, as well as articles and columns for a variety of publications including *NeXTWORLD,* the *Chicago Tribune* Sunday Technology Section, *Macintosh Today*, the Prodigy online network, and *NewMedia.* Tracing the personal computer revolution back to the 1960s counterculture, Tony produced a CD-ROM interactive "rockumentary" in 1996, *Haight-Ashbury in the Sixties* (which explains his taste in music in this book's examples). He also developed the Rockument music site, www.rockument.com, with commentary and podcasts focused on rock music history. As a founding member of the Flying Other Brothers, which toured professionally for a decade and released three commercial CDs (*52-Week High, San Francisco Sounds,* and *Estimated Charges*), Tony performed with Hall of Fame rock musicians.

Dedication

This book is dedicated to my sons, nieces, nephews, their cousins, and all their children . . . the iPod generation.

Author's Acknowledgments

I want to thank John and Jimi Bove for providing technical expertise and performing valuable testing. I also want to thank Rich Tennant for his wonderful cartoons, and Dennis Cohen for technical expertise beyond the call of duty. And let me not forget my Wiley editors, Jean Nelson and Brian Walls, for ongoing assistance that made my job so much easier. A book this timely places a considerable burden on a publisher's production team, and I thank the production crew at Wiley for diligence beyond the call of reason.

I owe thanks and a happy hour or three to Carole Jelen at Waterside, my agent. And finally, I have executive editor Bob Woerner at Wiley to thank for coming up with the idea for this book and helping me to become a professional dummy — that is, a Dummies author.

Publisher's Acknowledgments

We're proud of this book; please send us your comments at http://dummies.custhelp.com. For other comments, please contact our Customer Care Department within the U.S. at 877-762-2974, outside the U.S. at 317-572-3993, or fax 317-572-4002.

Some of the people who helped bring this book to market include the following:

Acquisitions, Editorial, and Media Development

Project Editor: Jean Nelson

Executive Editor: Bob Woerner

Copy Editor: Brian Walls

Technical Editor: Dennis Cohen

Editorial Manager: Kevin Kirschner

Media Development Project Manager: Laura Moss-Hollister

Media Development Assistant Project Manager: Jenny Swisher

Media Development Associate Producers: Josh Frank, Marilyn Hummel, Douglas Kuhn, and Shawn Patrick

Editorial Assistant: Amanda Graham

Sr. Editorial Assistant: Cherie Case

Cartoons: Rich Tennant (www.the5thwave.com)

Composition Services

Project Coordinator: Sheree Montgomery

Layout and Graphics: Samantha K. Cherolis

Proofreaders: John Greenoug, Betty Kish

Indexer: Glassman Indexing Services

Publishing and Editorial for Technology Dummies

Richard Swadley, Vice President and Executive Group Publisher

Andy Cummings, Vice President and Publisher

Mary Bednarek, Executive Acquisitions Director

Mary C. Corder, Editorial Director

Publishing for Consumer Dummies

Diane Graves Steele, Vice President and Publisher

Composition Services

Debbie Stailey, Director of Composition Services

Contents at a Glance

Table of Contents

Introduction

*T*his is the part in which I'm supposed to introduce the iPod touch and tell you why I wrote this book, but frankly, I'm so blown away by the iPod touch and all it can do that all *I* want to do is get you started with it.

Yes, I have a history with iPods: I wrote *iPod & iTunes For Dummies,* which I recommend for studying iTunes more closely. iTunes is the free software that controls the iPod touch from your computer. I even wrote an application for the iPhone and iPod touch, called Tony's Tips for iPhone Users. But enough about that: Obviously I'm a true fan of the iPod line, and I think you should be too! So, on with the book!

About This Book

The publishers are wise about book matters, and they helped me design *iPod touch For Dummies,* 2nd Edition, as a reference. With this book, you can easily find the information you need when you need it. I wrote it so that you can read from beginning to end to find out how to use your iPod touch from scratch. But this book is also organized so that you can dive in anywhere and begin reading the info you need to know for each task.

I didn't have enough pages to cover every detail of every function, and I intentionally left out some detail so that you won't be befuddled with techno-speak when it's not necessary. I wrote brief but comprehensive descriptions and included lots of cool tips on how to get the most out of your iPod touch.

At the time I wrote this book, I covered the most recent iPod touch model and the latest version of iTunes. Although I did my best to keep up for this print edition, Apple occasionally slips in a new model or new version of iTunes between book editions. If you've bought a new iPod touch with features not covered in the book, or if your version of iTunes looks a little different, be sure to check out the tips section of my Web site (www.tonybove. com) for updates on the latest releases from Apple.

Conventions Used in This Book

Like any book that covers computers, mobile devices, and information technology, this book uses certain conventions:

  ✔ **Choosing from a screen or menu:** When I write "Choose Settings⇨ General from the Home screen," you tap Settings on the iPod touch Home screen and then tap General on the Settings screen.

With iTunes, when I write "Choose iTunes⇨Preferences in iTunes," you click iTunes in the menu at the top of the display, and then click Preferences in the iTunes menu that appears.

✏ **Sliding, scrolling, and flicking on an iPod touch:** When you see "Scroll the screen" I mean you need to drag your finger to slide the screen slowly. When I write "scroll the list on the iPod touch Settings screen," I mean you should drag your finger over the list so that it slides horizontally or vertically. When I write "Flick the screen," you should flick the screen with your finger to slide it quickly.

✏ **Clicking and dragging on the computer:** When you see "Drag the song over the name of the playlist," I mean you need to click the song name (in iTunes), hold the mouse button down, and then drag the song — while holding the mouse button down — over to the name of the playlist before lifting your finger off the mouse button.

✏ **Keyboard shortcuts on the computer:** When you see ⌘-I, press the ⌘ key on a Mac keyboard along with the appropriate shortcut key. (In this case, after selecting a content item or app, press ⌘-I, which opens the Information window in iTunes.) In Windows, the same keyboard shortcut is Ctrl-I (which means press the Ctrl key along with the I key). Don't worry — I always tell you what the equivalent Windows keys are.

✏ **Step lists:** When you come across steps that you need to do in iTunes or on the iPod touch, the action is in bold, and the explanatory part follows. If you know what to do, read the action and skip the explanation. But if you need a little help along the way, check out the explanation.

✏ **Pop-up menus:** I use the term *pop-up menu* for menus on the Mac that literally pop up from dialogs and windows; in Windows, the same type of menu actually drops down and is called a drop-down menu. I use the term pop-up menu for both.

A Quick Peek Ahead

This book is organized into six parts, and each part covers a different aspect of using your iPod touch and iTunes. Here's a quick preview of what you can find in each part.

Part 1: Touching All the Basics

This part gets you started with your iPod touch: powering it up, recharging its battery, using its multi-touch interface and onscreen keyboard, and connecting it to your computer. You also find out all the techniques of an iPod touch road warrior: organizing apps into folders, setting your alarm and multiple clocks for time zones, keeping time with your stopwatch, changing your display settings, setting the passcode to lock up the device so others can't use it, and setting restrictions on content and the use of applications.

Part II: Filling Up Your Empty Cup

This part shows you how to download to your computer songs, albums, podcasts, audio books, movies, TV shows, and music videos from the iTunes Store, and applications from the App Store. You also find out how to buy music, podcasts, videos, and applications directly on your iPod touch. I also show you how to synchronize your iPod touch with your iTunes library on your computer, and with your personal contacts, e-mail accounts, Web bookmarks, and calendars.

Part III: Playing It Back with Interest

In this part, I show you how to locate and play all types of content on your iPod touch — music, audio books, podcasts, movies, TV shows, videos, and slideshows of your own photos. You discover how to control playback, adjust the volume and equalize the sound, and play YouTube videos. You also discover how to take photos and record videos.

Part IV: Touching the Online World

This part describes how to use your iPod touch and the Safari application to surf the Web. You also find out how to check and send e-mail, look at your stock portfolio, and check the weather in your city and other cities. I also show you how to display maps and driving directions.

Part V: Staying in Touch and Up-to-Date

In this part I explain how to use your iPod touch to locate and communicate with friends on Facebook, MySpace, Twitter, and other social networks, and use the FaceTime app to make and receive video calls. I also show you how to enter and edit calendar entries, and enter and sort contacts. You also find out how to update or restore your iPod touch, and reset its settings.

Part VI: The Part of Tens

In this book's Part of Tens chapters, I provide ten tips that can help make your iPod touch experience a completely satisfying one, and describe ten iPod touch apps that will rock your world.

Bonus Chapters

Lucky reader! You can take advantage of my previous forays into iPodland by checking out the online bonus chapters associated with my *iPod & iTunes For Dummies* book on the companion Web site at www.dummies.com/go/ ipod8e. Scattered through those chapters you'll find even more great informational nuggets. Topics include:

- ✒ Choosing audio encoding formats and quality settings for importing music

- ✒ Preparing photo libraries, videos, address books, and calendars for your iPod touch

- ✒ Managing multiple iTunes libraries and copying your library to other hard drives or computers

- ✒ Getting wired for playback and using accessories

Icons Used in This Book

 The icons in this book are important visual cues for information you need.

Remember icons highlight important things you need to keep in mind.

 Technical Stuff icons highlight technical details you can skip unless you want to bring out your inner technical geek.

 Tip icons highlight tips and techniques that save you time and energy — and maybe even money.

 Warning icons save your butt by preventing disasters. Don't bypass a Warning without reading it. This is your only warning!

 On the Web icons let you know when a topic is covered further online on a Web site. For example, I call your attention to specific areas within Apple's site (www.apple.com), and I refer to tips I provide on my site at www.tonybove.com.

Part I
Touching All the Basics

The 5th Wave   By Rich Tennant

"It's like any other pacemaker, but it comes with an internal iPod docking accessory."

In this part . . .

1 touch all the basics in this first part to get you started with your iPod touch as quickly as possible.

I start you out with a power punch in Chapter 1: opening the box, sorting out its contents, and then powering up the iPod touch and connecting it to iTunes (the software that synchronizes content with it). You also find out how to get the most from your battery.

Next, I show you how touch it — the multi-touch interface that drives the iPod touch. You get a quick tour of the Home screen, the icons, and the onscreen keyboard, including tricks like how to quickly type numbers, symbols, and accent marks.

Then, in Chapter 3, I set you up with the right time and date, clocks for different time zones, alarms, the timer, and the stopwatch. You discover how to set a passcode to lock your iPod touch so that no one else can use it. You also find out how to set the display's brightness, turn the sound effects and ringtone on or off, change the wallpapers that appear on the locked screen and behind the Home screen, and set restrictions so that your kids can't jump onto YouTube or download tunes or videos categorized as explicit in the iTunes Store.

Powering Your iPod touch

In This Chapter

▶ Looking inside the box

▶ Finding what your iPod touch is good for

▶ Connecting to your computer and iTunes

▶ Using and recharging your battery

*Y*ou hold in your hands the greatest pocket-sized music player in the world, which also happens to be a fantastic portable video and game player and video camera. But that's not all: With built-in wireless Internet connectivity, the iPod touch defines an entire new class of . . . things.

I want to call it a *device,* but it's so much more — the iPod touch puts the entire world in your pocket. It connects you to millions of songs as well as movies, TV shows, and other content on the iTunes Store, and lets you follow your stars on the Ping social network. It lets you communicate with your friends and family with FaceTime video calls, and participate in social and gaming networks like Facebook and the Game Center. It records stunning HD video as well as photos, and lets you edit them before sharing them. And, of course, it offers a library of hundreds of thousands of applications (known as *apps*) that offer everything from soup to nuts, including thousands of games — but I get into that later in this chapter.

Less than a third of an inch thick and weighing less than 4 ounces, the iPod touch is really a pocket computer — it uses a flash memory drive and the iOS operating system. It shares design characteristics and many of the features of its more famous cousin, the iPhone, with built-in speaker and volume controls, an accelerometer for motion detection (such as rotation and shaking), and Internet connectivity for surfing the Web and checking e-mail. Like the newest model iPhone, the newest model (4th generation) iPod touch sports a three-axis gyro for measuring or maintaining orientation (used extensively by games), and a 3.5-inch, widescreen, multi-touch Retina display that offers a stunning 960-x-640–pixel resolution at 326 pixels per inch — so many pixels that the human eye can't distinguish individual ones.

The newest iPod touch also offers a main camera on the back for recording HD (720p) video at up to 30 frames per second (with audio), and shooting photos at 960 x 720 pixel resolution. And you can use a front-facing video camera for taking VGA-quality photos and making FaceTime video calls over the Internet.

The newest model iPod touch can do nearly everything an iPhone can do, except make cellular-service phone calls or send text messages, or pinpoint its exact location with the Global Positioning System (GPS). Even so, the iPod touch can find its approximate location with Internet-based location services, and you can make the equivalent of a "phone call" using FaceTime, the Skype app, an Internet connection, and an external microphone. It also offers stereo Bluetooth for using wireless headphones and microphones.

So what's in the box and what can it do?

Thinking Inside the Box

Apple excels at packaging. Don't destroy the elegant box while opening it, and check to make sure that all the correct parts came with it, as shown in Figure 1-1. Keep the box in case, heaven forbid, you need to return the iPod touch to Apple — the box ensures that you can safely return it for a new battery or replacement.

The iPod touch is supplied with the following:

- Stereo earphones (often called *earbuds*) with remote control buttons and a microphone
- A quick-start guide
- A cable with a dock connector on one end and a USB connector on the other

The cable connects your iPod touch (or a dock for the iPod touch) to your computer or to the AC power adapter using a USB (Universal Serial Bus) connection — a way of attaching things to computers and bussing data around while providing power. The cable has a USB connector on one end and a flat dock connector on the other end to connect either to a dock or directly to an iPod touch.

Outside the box

You may want to have around a few things that are not in the box. For example, even though you don't really need an AC power adapter or dock (because you can connect the iPod touch directly to your computer to recharge your battery), a power adapter or dock is useful for keeping the battery charged without having to connect the iPod touch to your computer.

iPod touch — Earbuds

Dock connector to USB cable

Figure 1-1: Inside the box for the iPod touch.

The earbuds supplied with your iPod touch may not suit your tastes, but hundreds of other headphone and earphone products might. You can get all kinds of accessories, including headphones, earphones, speakers, the Apple Universal Dock, other docks, and AC power adapters, from the online Apple Store (www.apple.com/store), the physical Apple Store, or any electronics department or store (such as Amazon.com or Fry's).

Computer and software not included

You still need a computer and iTunes to manage your content and your iPod touch. These things are not in the box, obviously.

You've seen requirements before — lots of jargon about MB (megabytes), GB (gigabytes), GHz (gigahertz), and RAM (random access memory), sprinkled with names like Intel, AMD, and Mac OS X. Skip this section if you already know your iPod touch works with your computer and you already have iTunes. But if you don't know whether it will work, and you don't have iTunes yet, read on.

You need the following:

- **A PC or Mac to run iTunes:** On a PC, iTunes version 10 (version 10.0 as of this writing) requires Windows XP (with Service Pack 2) or a 32-bit edition of Windows 7 or Windows Vista. (You can use a 64-bit version of Vista if you also run the iTunes 64-bit installer — which you can download from the iTunes download page.) While you can run iTunes 10 on a PC with a 1GHz Intel or AMD processor with a QuickTime-compatible audio card and a minimum of 512MB of RAM, you need at least a 2GHz Intel Core 2 Duo or faster processor and at least 1 GB of RAM to play HD-quality videos, an iTunes LP, or iTunes Extras from the iTunes Store. You also need a DirectX 9.0–compatible video card with 32MB of video RAM (64MB recommended) to watch video.

  With a Mac, iTunes version 10 requires Mac OS X version 10.5 or newer (Leopard, Snow Leopard, or newer version). While you can run iTunes 10 on a Mac with an Intel, PowerPC G5 or G4 processor, and at least 512MB of RAM, you need at least a 1GHz PowerPC G4, G5, or Intel processor to play Standard Definition video, or at least a 2GHz Intel Core 2 Duo or faster processor and at least 1 GB of RAM to play HD-quality videos, an iTunes LP, or iTunes Extras from the iTunes Store.

- **USB connection:** You need a USB 2.0 connection (also called a *high-speed USB*) on your computer. All current-model Macs and many PCs provide built-in USB 2.0.

  For details about using USB, visit the companion Web site for *iPod & iTunes For Dummies,* 8th Edition, at www.dummies.com/go/ipod8e.

- **iTunes:** Make sure you have the current version of iTunes, which also includes QuickTime for playing video. You can download iTunes for Windows or the Mac from the Apple site (www.apple.com/itunes/download); it's free.

Discovering What Your iPod touch Can Do

Play music, videos, and games; get some "face time" communication with friends and relatives; participate in social and gaming networks; make travel reservations and see maps of the entire world; check the weather and your finances; record and edit videos; and keep track of all your appointments. You can do all this and much, much more by using apps and connecting to the Internet.

Whipping up a multimedia extravaganza

Portable DVD players are cute, but they don't come anywhere close to being as convenient as an iPod touch for a pocket video player. The iPod touch is the Swiss Army Knife of media: It plays music, music videos, TV shows, movies, audio books, photo slideshows, and *podcasts* (audio and video episodes designed to be downloaded to your iPod touch). With Apple's iBooks app or other book-reading apps, you can even read books.

The convenience of carrying content on an iPod touch is phenomenal. For example, the 32GB iPod touch can hold around 7,000 songs. That's more than a week of nonstop music played around the clock.

Apple offers the following sizes of iPod touch models as of this writing:

- ✔ **The 8GB model** holds about 1,750 songs, 10,000 photos, or about 10 hours of video.

- ✔ **The 32GB model** holds about 7,000 songs, 40,000 photos, or about 40 hours of video.

- ✔ **The 64GB model** holds about 14,000 songs, 90,000 photos, or about 80 hours of video.

All three models use the same battery that offers up to 40 hours of audio playback, or 7 hours of video playback.

How do you get 14,000 songs (or for that matter, any number of songs) onto your iPod touch quickly? If you have an iTunes library of songs, you can fill your iPod touch by connecting it to your computer (which I describe later in this chapter) and synchronizing it with iTunes (which I describe in Chapter 5). You can also download songs from the iTunes Store; see Chapter 4.

Audio books and videos — some of your favorite TV shows, plus music videos and full-length movies — are just a touch away on your iPod touch, or a click away in iTunes, as I show in Chapter 4. You can even rent movies and TV shows directly on your iPod touch. And you can organize your photos on your computer and then transfer them to your iPod touch using iTunes, as I describe in Chapter 9.

 You use iTunes to organize your content, make copies, burn CDs, and play disc jockey without discs. To find out more, see the latest edition of my other book, *iPod & iTunes For Dummies*.

Communicating with the world

Your iPod touch can sense Wi-Fi networks. (Wi-Fi, short for wireless fidelity, is a popular connection method for local area networks and the Internet; you can set up your home or office with Wi-Fi using a Wi-Fi hub such as Apple's AirPort Extreme.) After it finds one or more networks, the iPod touch lets you choose one to connect to the Internet, and it can remember the settings for that network so that it can automatically choose the same network again.

With a Wi-Fi connection, you can make FaceTime calls to other FaceTime users, browse the Web and interact with Web services, and send and receive e-mail. Stocks, Maps, and Weather are apps that show information from the Internet. You can also use the YouTube app to play YouTube videos on the Web. All these apps are supplied with your iPod touch.

You can download more apps to your iPod touch by connecting to Wi-Fi and the Internet, and tapping the App Store icon. You can also download music, videos, and podcasts by tapping the iTunes icon, as I describe in Chapter 4.

You also use apps to connect to the Internet in ways other than browsing. For example, popular social networks such as Facebook and MySpace offer apps to connect you with your friends on those services. Google offers an array of services through the Google Mobile app, including the ability to edit documents and spreadsheets, use the Gmail service, and share calendars and photos. The Twitter, Twitterific, and TweetDeck apps let you post tweets on Twitter, and the WhosHere and Loopt apps can connect you directly to other iPod touch and iPhone users for chatting.

Rolling the dice

Many of the apps you'll find listed at the App store are especially designed to take advantage of four distinct features of the iPod touch: the multi-touch display; the accelerometer (which detects acceleration, rotation, motion gestures, and tilt); the three-axis gyro (for detecting and measuring orientation); and Location Services for detecting its physical location.

For example, Motion X Poker — actually a dice game — uses the accelerometer to let you roll the dice by shaking the iPod touch. The Flick Fishing app senses motion so you can cast a fishing line with a flick of the wrist. And for really precise motion, try rolling a steel ball over a wooden labyrinth of holes in the free Labyrinth Lite app.

Sensing your iPod touch's location is a very useful feature. The Showtimes app uses your iPod touch's location to show the movie theaters closest to you. The Foursquare app provides a social city-guide of nearby places, offers rewards for checking into certain places regularly, and lets you see where your friends are. The Eventful app uses your location to display local events and venues, and the Lethal app can tell you the dangers which could surround you — the hostile animals, the likelihood of crimes, the prevalence of disease, and the potential accidents and disasters. And with the MobileMe service, you can find your iPod touch if it is lost, and even wipe its contents remotely (if it's stolen); see Chapter 6.

So now you know a bit about what the iPod touch can do. It's time to fire up this baby and start rockin' out.

Connecting to Power

Awaken your iPod touch by pressing the sleep/wake button, which is located on the top of the iPod touch, as shown in Figure 1-2. If you press the sleep/wake button again, it puts the iPod touch back to sleep and locks its controls to save battery power.

You can turn the iPod touch completely off by holding down the sleep/wake button for about two seconds, until you see the Slide to Power Off slider; then slide your finger across the slider to turn it off. You can then turn it back on by pressing and holding the sleep/wake button. To save battery power, you should plug the iPod touch into AC power or your computer before turning it back on from a completely off state. (For battery details, see the "Facing Charges of Battery" section in this chapter.)

You can supply power to your iPod touch (and charge your battery at the same time) by using the provided USB cable and your computer, or you can use the USB cable with an optional AC power adapter that works with voltages in North America and many parts of Europe and Asia.

On the bottom of the iPod touch, you find one large connection called the *dock connection,* and a smaller

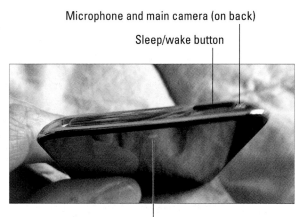

Microphone and main camera (on back)

Sleep/wake button

Front camera

Figure 1-2: The top of the iPod touch.

connection for head-phones and earbuds, as shown in Figure 1-3. To connect your iPod touch to your computer, plug the wide dock connector of the supplied USB cable into the iPod touch dock connection (see Figure 1-3), and then plug the USB connector on the other end of the cable into the USB port on your computer. You can con-nect the USB end of the supplied cable to either the Apple (or third-party USB) power adapter for power, or to the computer's USB port for power.

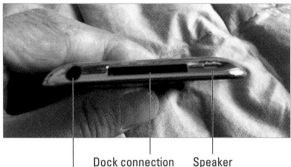

Dock connection   Speaker

Headphones/earbuds connection

Figure 1-3: The bottom of the iPod touch showing the dock connection.

 A dock can be convenient because you can slip your iPod touch into the dock without connecting cables. The dock connection on the back end of a dock mirrors the dock connection on the iPod touch. You can plug the supplied USB cable into the dock connection on the back end of the dock, and leave it that way on your desk. When you slip the iPod touch into the dock's cradle connector, the dock connects the iPod touch to the USB cable. You can pick up a dock at an Apple Store, order one online, or take advantage of third-party dock offerings. Some docks, such as the Apple Universal Dock, keep your iPod touch in an upright position while connected and also provide connections for a home stereo or headphones. Some docks offer built-in speakers.

 Most PCs and all current Macs already have USB 2.0 (high-speed USB), which is all you need to provide power and to sync an iPod touch with your com-puter. Although you can use a low-powered USB 1.0 or 1.1 connection to sync your iPod touch, it may not supply enough power to charge the iPod touch battery, and it's slower for syncing than molasses on a subzero morning.

 Don't use another USB device in a chain and don't use a USB 2.0 hub to con-nect your iPod touch unless the hub is a *powered* hub — a hub with a sepa-rate power source, in other words. Note that a USB keyboard typically acts like a USB 1.1 hub, but older ones can't provide power to the iPod touch.

After adding power, your iPod touch comes alive and displays the image of the USB cable and the iTunes icon. This is a simple message telling you to connect the iPod touch to iTunes on your computer.

iTunes is the software that manages your library of content and apps on your computer, and enables you to sync apps, content, and personal information with your iPod touch, as well as update the iPod touch software and restore it to original factory settings if you need to.

Macs already have iTunes, and setting up iTunes on a Windows PC is a quick and easy process. The most up-to-date version of iTunes as of this writing is version 10. However, software updates occur very rapidly. If you really want the latest version, go directly to the Apple Web site (www.apple.com/itunes) to get it. You can download iTunes for free.

For details on how to install iTunes, see the instructions on Apple's Web site or see my other book, *iPod & iTunes For Dummies*.

Be aware that, for your new iPod touch and iTunes to play nice with each other, you first have to get iTunes to recognize your new device; they have to be introduced, in other words. You do that by using the Register and Set Up screen, as spelled out in the following steps:

1. **With iTunes open, connect your iPod touch to the computer with a USB cable.**

   iTunes recognizes the iPod touch and opens the Register and Set Up screen to get you started.

   If the iPod touch isn't recognized in a few minutes, make sure it's charged. A lightning bolt battery icon appears when it's asleep and connected to power — if you don't see this icon, iPod touch isn't charging properly, and you may need to try a different cable or try a different USB 2.0 connection. (For more battery details, see the section "Facing Charges of Battery" in this chapter.) If the iPod touch is charged and still not recognized, try putting it to sleep and waking it again (see the preceding section). If that doesn't make your iPod touch recognizable by iTunes, try resetting your iPod touch as described in Chapter 14. If all else fails, try restarting your computer, and if that doesn't help, try reinstalling iTunes. Finally, contact Apple Support to return your iPod touch for repair (www.apple.com/support).

2. **Click Continue (or click Register Later to skip the registration process).**

   iTunes displays the License Agreement. You can scroll down to read it if you want. You must choose to accept the agreement, or the installer goes no further. (If you click Register Later, you skip a few screens in the set-up process, but you don't get to skip the License Agreement.)

   I don't recommend skipping the registration screens unless you intend to register the device later; registration helps you get better service from Apple in case you need it.

3. **Click the option to accept the terms at the end of the License Agreement and then click Continue.**

   After clicking Continue, iTunes lets you register your iPod touch with Apple online so you can take advantage of Apple support. You see a screen for entering your Apple ID; a membership ID for the MobileMe (formerly .Mac) service is also valid.

4. **Select the option (Use My Apple ID to Register My iPod or I Do Not Have an Apple ID) that applies to you and fill in the info beneath that option.**

   How you handle this step depends on how you purchased your iPod touch. Here's the scoop:

   • If you purchased your iPod touch directly from Apple and you have an Apple Store or MobileMe ID, select the Use My Apple ID to Register My iPod option and enter the ID and password to swiftly move through the registration process. Apple automatically recognizes your purchase so that you don't need to enter the serial number.

   • If you bought your iPod touch elsewhere or you don't have an Apple ID or MobileMe ID, select the I Do Not Have an Apple ID option. If needed, select your country from the pop-up menu below that. When you click Continue, iTunes displays a screen for entering your iPod touch serial number and your personal information. Fields marked with an asterisk (*) are required, such as your name and e-mail address.

   Got a magnifying glass? You can find the iPod touch serial number on the back of the device or on the side of its packaging.

5. **Click Continue to advance through each screen in the registration process and click Submit at the end to submit your information.**

   iTunes checks to see whether you've ever backed up an iPod touch, iPhone, or iPad before. If you've synced one of these devices previously, as I describe in Chapter 5 (and you haven't deleted its backup; see Chapter 14), iTunes displays the Set Up As a New iPod or Restore from the Backup Of choices, as shown in Figure 1-4. If you haven't backed up an iPod touch before, skip to Step 7.

6. **If you see the following choices (as shown in Figure 1-4), select one:**

   • **Set Up As a New iPod:** Select this option if you want to set the iPod touch up as new, and then click Continue. iTunes displays a screen that lets you enter a name for your iPod touch, as shown in Figure 1-5.

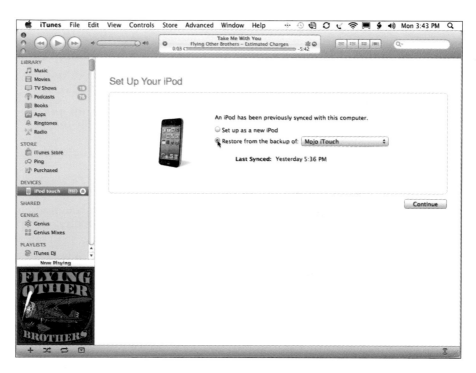

Figure 1-4: Choose whether to restore from a backup or set up the iPod touch as new.

• **Restore from the Backup Of:** Select this option, and pick an iPod touch from the pop-up menu, to restore the previous iPod's name and settings (you can also restore from the backup of an iPhone or iPad in order to use those settings). Then click Continue to finish setting up your iPod touch, and skip Step 7. Your automatic sync settings are restored from the previous backup, and you can change them how I show you in Chapter 5.

7. **Give your iPod touch a name, set the automatic sync options, and then click Done (on a Mac) or Finish (on Windows).**

   It's nice to give your iPod touch a name to give it more of a personality. And when it comes to setting automatic options (refer to Figure 1-5), here's the deal:

   • *Automatically Sync Songs and Videos to My iPod:* If you want to copy your entire iTunes music and video library onto your iPod touch, leave this option selected. If you want to control which portion of your library is copied to the iPod touch, deselect this option and turn to Chapter 5 for synchronization details.

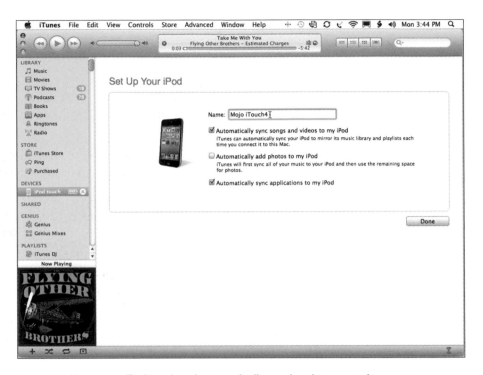

Figure 1-5: Name your iPod touch and automatically synchronize content in one step.

- *Automatically Sync Photos to My iPod:* Select this option to copy all the photos in your Pictures folder or photo library to your iPod touch, and select the photo library or folder in the Sync Photos From pop-up menu. (See Chapter 9 for information about synchronizing photo libraries.) Leave this option deselected if you want to transfer photos later.

- *Automatically Sync Applications:* Select this option to copy all iPod touch-compatible apps in your iTunes library to your iPod touch.

Don't want to add songs or videos now? If you deselect the option to automatically synchronize (refer to Figure 1-5), you can still add songs and videos later, along with podcasts and audio books — either manually or automatically, as I describe in Chapter 5.

After finishing setup, your iPod touch name appears in the iTunes source pane (the left column) under the Devices heading (refer to Figure 1-5). Click this name to display information about your iPod touch in the main iTunes window. The information you see also includes a message to update your iPod touch if Apple has an update for it. If you see this message, click the Update button to update your iPod touch (see Chapter 14 for details).

If you chose the option to automatically synchronize your songs and videos, or restored your iPod touch from a backup set to automatically sync your songs and videos, your iPod touch fills up with music and videos from your iTunes library.

You can leave your iPod touch connected to the computer, using the computer as a source of power — the iPod touch appears in iTunes whenever you start iTunes.

To disconnect it from iTunes and your computer, click the eject button next to the iPod touch name (refer to Figure 1-5) in the source pane. (The eject button shows a triangle with a line beneath it.)

After ejecting the iPod touch, wait for its display to show the Home screen or the slider to unlock it (which happens almost immediately after ejecting). You can then disconnect the iPod touch from the computer. Don't ever disconnect an iPod touch before ejecting it because such bad behavior might cause it to freeze up and require a reset. (If that happens, see Chapter 14 for instructions.)

Facing Charges of Battery

You can take a six-hour flight from New York City to California and watch a video on your iPod touch the entire time without recharging. The iPod touch uses a built-in, rechargeable lithium-ion (Li-Ion) battery that offers 40 hours of music playing time or 7 hours of video, browsing the Internet, or displaying photo slideshows with music.

Recharging your battery

The iPod touch battery recharges automatically when you connect it to a power source. For example, it starts charging immediately when you insert it into a dock that's connected to a power source (or to a computer with a powered USB connection). It takes only four hours to recharge the battery fully.

Need power when you're on the run? Look for a power outlet in the airport terminal or hotel lobby and plug in your iPod touch with your AC power adapter — the battery fast-charges to 80 percent capacity in two hours. After that, the battery receives a trickle charge for the next two hours until it's fully charged.

Maintaining battery mojo

There are ways to keep your battery healthy. I recommend a lean diet of topping off your battery whenever it is convenient.

Using and recharging 100 percent of battery capacity is called a *charge cycle.* You can charge the battery many times, but there is a limit to how many full charge cycles you can do before needing to replace the battery.

Each time you complete a charge cycle (100 percent recharge), it diminishes battery capacity slightly. Apple estimates that the battery loses 20 percent of its capacity (meaning it holds 80 percent of the charge) after 400 full charge cycles. Recharging your battery when it's only half empty does not count as a full charge cycle, but as half a charge cycle. That means you can use half its power one day and then recharge it fully, and then use half the next day and recharge it fully again, and this would count as one charge cycle, not two.

It's a good idea to *calibrate* the battery once soon after you get your iPod touch; that is, run it all the way down (a full discharge) and then charge it all the way up (which takes at least four hours). Although this doesn't actually change battery performance, it does improve the battery gauge so that the gauge displays a more accurate reading. This calibration occurs anyway if you fully recharge the battery, but if you've never done that, you can calibrate by disconnecting the iPod touch from any power for 24 hours to make sure the battery is empty and then fully recharging the battery.

Lithium-ion batteries typically last three years or more, but are vulnerable to high temperatures, which decrease their life spans considerably. Don't leave your iPod touch in a hot place, such as on a sunny car dashboard, for very long (don't leave it with the cake out in the rain, either — water can easily damage it).

For a complete description of how Apple's batteries work, see the Apple Lithium-Ion Batteries page at www.apple.com/batteries.

Don't fry your iPod touch with some generic power adapter. Use *only* the power adapter from Apple or a certified iPod adapter, such as the power accessories from Belkin, Griffin, Monster, XtremeMac, and other vendors.

When you awaken an iPod touch that's plugged into power, you see a large battery icon indicating how much juice you have. When you charge the battery, the large battery icon includes a lightning bolt.

You can also use your iPod touch while the battery is charging, or you can disconnect it and use it before the battery is fully charged. The small battery icon in the top-right corner of the iPod touch display indicates how much power is left. It's completely filled in when the battery is fully charged, and it slowly empties out into just an outline as the battery is used up. A lightning bolt appears inside it when recharging, and a plug appears inside when the iPod touch is connected to power.

The iPod touch built-in, rechargeable battery is, essentially, a life-or-death proposition. After it's dead, it can be replaced, but Apple charges a replacement fee plus shipping. If your warranty is still active, you should have Apple replace it under the warranty program (which may cost nothing except perhaps shipping). Don't try to replace it yourself because opening your iPod touch invalidates the warranty.

Keeping an iPod touch in a snug carrying case when charging is tempting but also potentially disastrous. You could damage the unit by overheating it and frying its circuits, rendering it as useful as a paperweight. To get around this problem, you can purchase one of the heat-dissipating carrying cases available in the Apple Store.

If you don't use your iPod touch for a month, even while it's connected to power and retaining a charge, it can become catatonic. Perhaps it gets depressed from being left alone too long. At that point it may not start — you have to completely drain and recharge the battery. To drain the battery, use it to play videos and surf the Web for about 7 hours, or leave it unconnected to power for 24 hours. Then, to fully recharge the battery, connect it to power for at least 4 hours without using it (or longer if you are using it).

Saving power

The iPod touch uses power accessing the Internet, using Bluetooth devices, and running apps. Keeping these activities to a minimum can help you save power.

The following are tips on saving power while using your iPod touch:

- ✔ **Pause.** Pause playback when you're not listening. Pausing (stopping) playback is the easiest way to conserve power.

- ✔ **Lock it.** Press the sleep/wake button on top of the iPod touch to immediately put it to sleep and lock its controls to save battery power. You can set your iPod touch to automatically go to sleep by choosing Settings⇨General⇨Auto-Lock from the Home screen, and choosing 1 Minute, 2 Minutes, 3 Minutes, 4 Minutes, or 5 Minutes (or Never, to prevent automatic sleep).

- ✔ **Back away from the light.** Turn down the brightness on an iPod touch by choosing Settings⇨Brightness and dragging the brightness slider to the left.

✔ **Don't ask and don't tell where you are.** Turn off Location Services if you aren't using apps that need it. Choose Settings⇨General from the Home screen, tap Location Services, and then tap On for the Location Services option at the top to turn it off (tap Off to turn it back on). See Chapter 3 for details.

✔ **Let the postman ring twice.** Check e-mail less frequently. You may want to turn off Push and change your Fetch settings. See Chapter 11 for details.

✔ **Put a cap on Bluetooth.** Turn off Bluetooth (choose Settings⇨General⇨ Bluetooth and tap the On button to turn it off) if you're not using a Bluetooth device.

✔ **Drop back in from the Internet.** Turn off Wi-Fi when not browsing the Internet: Choose Settings⇨Wi-Fi and tap the On button to turn it off.

✔ **Fasten your seat belt.** Turn on Airplane Mode to automatically turn off Wi-Fi and Bluetooth at once, before the flight attendant reminds you to do it: Choose Settings and tap Off to turn Airplane Mode on.

✔ **Turn it off completely.** You can turn the iPod touch completely off by holding down the sleep/wake button for about two seconds, until you see the Slide to Power Off slider; then slide your finger across the slider to turn it off. You can then turn it back on by pressing and holding the sleep/wake button.

Starting an iPod touch that was completely turned off takes quite a bit of power — more than if it woke from sleep. If you do turn it off, plug it into AC power or your computer before turning it back on.

✔ **You may continue.** Play songs continuously without using the iPod touch controls. Selecting songs and using the previous/rewind and next/ fast-forward buttons require more energy. Also, turn off your iPod touch equalizer (EQ) if you turned it on (see Chapter 7).

Always use the latest iPod touch software and update your software when updates come out. Apple constantly tries to improve how your iPod touch works, and many of these advancements relate to power usage.

2

Putting Your Finger On It

*W*ith an iPod touch, your fingers do the walking. The multi-touch display lets you make gestures to do things, such as flicking a finger to scroll a list quickly, sliding your finger to scroll slowly or to drag a slider (such as the volume slider), pinching with two fingers to zoom out of a Web page or photo, or pulling apart with two fingers (also known as *unpinching*) to zoom in to the page or photo to see it more clearly.

This chapter gives you a quick tour of the iPod touch Home screen and icons, and it describes all the touch-and-gesture tricks to make your iPod touch dance and sing. I also give you a complete tour of one of the most useful features of the iPod touch: the onscreen keyboard.

Touching and Gesturing

With the iPod touch, it's touch and go. It responds to tapping, flicking, and sliding your fingertip, among other gestures (such as shaking, tilting, two-finger tapping, and so on). One tap is all you need to run an app or select something, but sometimes you have to slide your finger to scroll the display and see more selections.

TIP Sticky fingers are not recommended. To clean your iPod touch, make sure to unplug all cables and turn it off. (See Chapter 1.) Use a soft, slightly damp, lint-free cloth to wipe your iPod touch clean — see Chapter 15 for cleaning tips.

Shake, rattle, and roll

Your iPod touch can sense motion with its built-in accelerometer, and orientation with its three-axis gyro. When you rotate it from a vertical view (portrait) to a horizontal view (landscape), the iPod touch detects the movement and orientation and changes the display accordingly. This happens so quickly that you can control a game with these movements.

For example, Pass the Pigs is a dice game in which you shake three times to roll your pigs to gain points. In the Labyrinth game, you tilt your iPod touch to roll a ball through a wooden maze without falling through the holes. And you can shake, rattle, and roll your way around the world in Yahtzee Adventures while you rack up high scores.

And if that's too tame for you, try Chopper, a helicopter game in which you need to complete your mission and return to base while avoiding enemy fire from tanks and bazooka-wielding madmen. You tilt the iPod touch to fly, and you touch the screen to drop bombs or fire the machine gun.

Xhake Shake lets you shake, flip, rub, and tap your iPod touch to challenge your hand-eye responses. And for scrolling practice, try Light Bike (loosely based on the Disney movie *Tron*) in which you scroll to maneuver a light bike from a third-person perspective against three computer-controlled light bikes. And infants can join the fun: Silver Rattle shows a screen that changes color and rattles with every shake. Big Joe Turner would be proud.

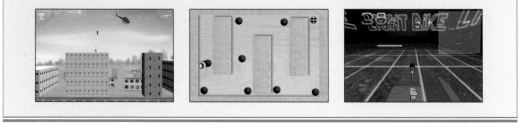

Here are the touches and gestures you need to know:

- ✔ **Drag with your fingertip:** Scroll up or down lists slowly.
- ✔ **Flick up or down:** Swipe your fingertip quickly across the surface to scroll up or down lists rapidly.
- ✔ **Touch and hold:** Touch and hold an object in order to drag it or, while scrolling, touch and hold to stop the moving list.
- ✔ **Flick from left to right or right to left:** Quickly swipe your fingertip across the screen to change screens or application panes (Home screens, Cover Flow view in Music, Weather, and other apps).
- ✔ **Single tap:** Select an item.

 ✔ **Double tap:** Zoom in or out with Safari, Maps, and other applications.

 ✔ **Two-finger single tap:** Zoom out in Maps.

 ✔ **Pinch:** Zoom out.

 ✔ **Unpinch:** Zoom in.

Need to practice your tapping? Try Tap Tap Revenge, a rhythm game that plays music while requiring you to tap each of the colored balls when they reach the line at the bottom of the screen. If you tap the ball on the beat, you gain points; if not, it counts as a miss. You can also activate a revenge mode to score more points by shaking the iPod touch after setting a winning streak of 50 beats.

Going on a Quick Tour of the iPod touch

The first message you see on an iPod touch display (besides the time of day and the date) is Slide to Unlock — to get started, you have to unlock the iPod touch by sliding your finger across the message. Once unlocked, your Home screen appears in all its glory.

Sliding to the Home screen

There's no place like Home — it's the screen where you start. Everything is available from the Home screen at the touch of a finger (see Figure 2-1). For example:

 ✔ Tap the Music icon to access your music.

 ✔ Tap the Videos icon to access your videos.

 ✔ Tap the Photos icon to access your photos.

 ✔ Tap the iTunes icon to access the iTunes Store.

 ✔ Tap the App Store icon to access the App Store.

Figure 2-1: The iPod touch Home screen.

After tapping an icon on the iPod touch screen, a new screen appears with selections and icons. (Touching Music, for example, brings up Playlists, Artists, Songs, and so on.) The multi-touch interface changes for each app. Press the physical Home button below the screen (not shown in Figure 2-1) at any time to go back to the Home screen.

Apps you download from the App Store (as I describe in Chapter 4) show up as icons on your Home screen. You can also save Web Clips to your Home screen as icons that take you directly to those Web pages (as I describe in Chapter 10). When you add enough apps and Web Clips so that they no longer fit on the first Home screen, the iPod touch automatically creates more Home screens to accommodate them. (See the section "Cleaning Up Your Home Screens," later in this chapter, to find out how to organize your icons into folders and rearrange icons on Home screens.)

The bottom row of the Home screen is called the *dock*. (Refer to Figure 2-1.) Icons in the dock remain on the screen when you switch from one Home screen to another. You can change the apps in the dock, as I show in "Cleaning Up Your Home Screens" later in this chapter.

The tiny dots above the dock indicate how many Home screens you have, and which Home screen you're viewing. To switch to another Home screen, flick with your finger left or right, or tap a dot in the row of dots (the far left dot is actually a magnifying glass icon for the Search screen).

Press the Home button under the screen to go to the first Home screen. To go to any other Home screen, tap one of the dots above the dock on any Home screen — for example, to go to Home screen 4, tap the fourth dot to the right of the magnifying glass icon.

Tapping the apps from Apple

The iPod touch Home screen (refer to Figure 2-1) offers the following apps supplied by Apple free:

- **FaceTime:** Make FaceTime video calls to other people that have FaceTime (currently fourth-generation iPod touch and iPhone 4 models) using Wi-Fi. See Chapter 13 for details.
- **Calendar:** View your calendar — see Chapter 13 for details.
- **Photos:** Select photos by photo album or select individual photos on the iPod touch, as I show in Chapter 9.
- **Camera:** Snap a photo or shoot video using either the main back camera or front camera, as I show in Chapter 9.

✔ **YouTube:** List and select videos from YouTube — see Chapter 8.

✔ **Stocks:** Check the prices for financial stocks, bonds, and funds. Chapter 12 shows you how.

✔ **Maps:** View maps and get driving directions, as I show in Chapter 12.

✔ **Weather:** View the weather in multiple cities — see Chapter 12.

✔ **Notes:** Add text notes — see the "Tickling the Keyboard" section, later in this chapter.

✔ **Utilities:** This is a folder containing the following apps:

 • **Clock:** View multiple clocks and use the alarm clock, timer, and stopwatch, as I show in Chapter 3.

 • **Calculator:** You can use your iPod touch as a regular calculator for adding, subtracting, multiplying, dividing, and so on. Also, if you hold the iPod touch horizontally, it becomes a scientific calculator.

 • **Voice Memos:** Record your voice, as I show in Chapter 13.

✔ **iTunes:** Go to the iTunes online store to purchase content — see Chapter 4 for details.

✔ **App Store:** Go to Apple's online App Store to download other Apple and third-party apps, as I show in Chapter 4.

✔ **Game Center:** Discover and play games online with your friends, as I show in Chapter 15.

✔ **Settings:** Adjust settings for Wi-Fi, sounds, brightness, Safari, and other apps, as well as other settings for the iPod touch itself.

✔ **Contacts:** View your contacts. To learn more about what you can do with your contacts, see Chapter 13.

Additionally, you can download Apple's free iBooks app to read electronic books (e-books) from Apple's iBook store.

There's one more icon for an app that you can activate in Settings, if you have the appropriate Nike shoes and the Nike+ iPod Sport Kit, sold separately. See Chapter 15 for details.

The following icons appear on the dock at the bottom of every Home screen:

✔ **Music:** Select music playlists, artists, songs, albums, and more (including podcasts, genres, composers, audio books, and compilations). Learn all about the Music app in Chapter 7.

✔ **Mail:** Check and send e-mail. The postman always beeps once — in Chapter 11.

> ✓ **Safari:** Browse the Web, as I show in Chapter 10.
>
> ✓ **Videos:** Select videos by type (movies, music videos, TV shows, or video podcasts) and play them, as shown in Chapter 8.

Searching for anything

The leftmost dot — actually a tiny magnifying glass — above the dock (refer to Figure 2-1) is the search icon. Tap the search icon (or flick the Home screen with your finger to the right) to show the Search screen (Figure 2-2). Search works just like the Spotlight Search feature of Mac OS X. You can type a search term and immediately see suggestions.

Search looks through contacts, calendars, e-mail (the To:, From:, and Subject: fields, but not the message content), the content (songs, videos, podcasts, and audio books), and even the text in the Notes app. Tap a contact, calendar entry, e-mail, or note suggestion to open it, or tap the song, video, podcast, or audio book suggestion to play it.

Figure 2-2: The iPod touch Search screen.

You can set which types of information to search through, and the order of information types to search first. Choose Settings➪General➪ Spotlight Search. Tap any information type (Contacts, Applications, Music, Podcasts, Video, Audiobooks, Notes, Mail, and Calendar) to remove the check mark, which removes that type of information from the search; tap the information type again to bring back the check mark and include it in the search. To change the order of information types to search, touch and hold an information type, and then drag it to a new position in the list.

Checking the status bar

The iPod touch shows its current state in the status bar at the top of the screen (refer to Figure 2-1). The icons mean the following:

> ✓ **iPod:** Just in case you forgot you had an iPod in your hands (very existential).
>
> ✓ **Airplane mode:** This icon shows if you turned on Airplane Mode on the Settings screen. When you turn Airplane Mode on, the iPod touch

automatically turns off Wi-Fi and Bluetooth. Note that you can turn Wi-Fi and Bluetooth back on while in Airplane Mode, so that you can use the airline's Wi-Fi (if offered).

✓ **Wi-Fi:** This icon says the iPod touch is connected to a Wi-Fi network. If the network offers Internet access (all commercial ones do), you're on the Internet. The more bars you see in the icon, the stronger the connection to the network. To find out more about setting up Wi-Fi with Internet in your home, see Chapter 4.

✓ **Network activity:** This icon twirls to show that data is traveling from the network to your iPod touch (or vice versa). (Not visible in Figure 2-1.)

✓ **VPN:** If you have special network settings that access a virtual private network (VPN), this icon shows up to tell you that you are connected to it. See Chapter 4 for details. (Not visible in Figure 2-1.)

✓ **Lock:** You see this icon whenever the iPod touch is locked. (The Slide to Unlock message also appears on the screen.) (Not visible in Figure 2-1.)

✓ **Play:** This icon tells you that a song, audio book, or podcast is playing (in case you didn't know — maybe you took your headphones off).

✓ **Portrait lock:** This icon appears if you locked the iPod touch in portrait orientation. See the section, "Switching orientation," later in this chapter for details.

✓ **Alarm:** This icon appears if you set an alarm. See Chapter 3 for details.

✓ **Location Services:** This icon appears if an app is using Location Services to determine the location of the iPod touch. See Chapter 3 for details. (Not visible in Figure 2-1.)

✓ **Bluetooth:** This icon appears only if Bluetooth is turned on. If Bluetooth is on and a device, such as a headset or keyboard, is connected, the icon is white; if it is on but nothing is connected, It turns gray.

✓ **Battery:** The battery icon shows the battery level or charging status. It's completely filled in when the battery is fully charged, and it slowly empties out into just an outline while the battery is used up. A lightning bolt appears inside the icon when the device is recharging, and a plug appears inside it when the iPod touch is connected to power.

Multitasking your apps

With fourth-generation iPod touch models, multiple apps can stay in memory and run simultaneously. Only one app runs in the *foreground* — where the action occurs — while all other apps hang out in the *background*. For example, audio services like Pandora work in the background to keep playing music from the Web while you run another app in the foreground. Other examples are voice-prompted navigation apps, Internet calling apps, and apps that perform long downloads — they keep working while you're using another app in the foreground.

You can quickly move the currently running app to the background, and switch to another background app, by double-clicking the Home button. The four most recently used apps in the background appear in the bottom row of the screen, as shown in Figure 2-3 (left side). Tap any app on this row to immediately switch to that app and move it to the foreground. You can also flick left to see more apps that are running in the background, and tap any one of them.

Figure 2-3: Switch to another app (left) and remove an app from the recent background (right).

While running any app, or while viewing any Home screen, you can double-click the Home button to see the bottom row of apps in the background. You can also remove an app from the bottom row, terminating the app so it no longer runs in the background — touch and hold the app icon until all the icons in the bottom row start wiggling as if they were doing the jailhouse rock, with a circled minus (-) sign in the top left corner of each app's icon, as shown in Figure 2-3 (right side). Tap the circled minus (-) sign to remove the app. You can free as many as you like. When finished, press the Home button once to stop the icons from wiggling. (The app appears again in the row of recently opened background apps the next time you run it and switch to another app.)

Switching orientation

The iPod touch Home screens appear in portrait orientation, as do most apps. However, many apps, including Safari and Mail, change the orientation to landscape when you quickly rotate the iPod touch. For example, to view a Web page in landscape orientation in Safari, rotate the iPod touch sideways. Safari automatically reorients and expands the page. To set it back to portrait, rotate the iPod touch again. You may prefer landscape for viewing Web pages or entering text with the onscreen keyboard, which is wider in landscape orientation.

You can lock the display of a third-generation or fourth-generation iPod touch in portrait orientation so that it doesn't jump to landscape even when you rotate the iPod touch. To lock the iPod touch in portrait orientation, double-click the Home button to see the bottom row of apps in the background, and then flick the bottom of the screen from left-to-right to show the Music player controls and portrait lock button, as shown in Figure 2-4. Tap the portrait lock button to lock the iPod touch into portrait orientation. The portrait lock icon appears in the status bar (refer to Figure 2-1) when the orientation is locked into portrait.

Portrait lock   Music app

Music player controls

Figure 2-4: Flick the background for the Music player controls and portrait lock button.

Cleaning Up Your Home Screens

It's easy to go crazy in the App Store and end up with a mess of apps across several Home screens. Fortunately, you can organize your apps into folders, and rearrange your app icons over your Home screens, and even create additional Home screens to hold them.

To rearrange your app icons within a Home screen or over several Home screens, or to organize them into folders, touch and hold any icon until all the icons begin to wiggle. (That's right, it looks like they're doing the Watusi.) Then follow the instructions in the sections that follow. After rearranging icons or organizing folders of icons, press the Home button to stop all that wiggling, which saves your new arrangement for your Home screens.

You can also delete apps you download from the App Store by tapping the circled X that appears inside the icon as it wiggles. A warning appears, telling you that deleting the app also deletes all the app's data. You can tap Delete to delete the app, or Cancel. You can then press the physical Home button to stop the icons from wiggling, or continue to rearrange icons and organize them into folders.

Rearranging icons on your Home screens

When you have your icons dancing how I describe earlier, you can drag a wiggling icon to a new position on the Home screen, and the other icons move to accommodate, creating a new arrangement.

To move a wiggling icon to the next Home screen, drag it to the right edge of the screen; to move it to the previous Home screen, drag it to the left edge. If you have no Home screen on the right, the iPod touch creates a new one. You can flick to go back to the first Home screen and drag more wiggling icons to the new Home screen. You can create up to eleven Home screens.

While the wiggling icons are doing their show, you can also change the icons in the dock. Although you are limited to four icons in the dock, you can drag any icon out of the dock and then drag another one in to replace it.

To stop all that wiggling, press the Home button, which saves your new arrangement.

To reset your Home screens to their default arrangements, thereby cleaning up any mess you may have made on them, tap Settings➪General➪Reset➪ Reset Home Screen Layout.

Organizing apps into folders

With the current version of iOS 4 (and you should update your iPod touch software when prompted to do so — see Chapter 14 for details), you can organize your app icons into folders on your Home screens so that you can find them more easily. The fourth-generation iPod touch comes with three apps already organized into a folder — the Utilities folder, which holds the Clock, Calculator, and Voice Memos apps. Folders also make it easier to find categories of apps — you can add all your social networking apps to a Social folder, or add all your news-gathering apps into a News folder.

While your icons are wiggling (as I describe previously), drag the first app icon you want to include in the folder onto the second app icon you want to include. The system creates a new folder, including the two app icons, and shows the folder's name, which is based on the first icon you dragged (for example, if you drag a "news" app like NYTimes (The New York Times app) over another "news" app, such as AP Mobile (the AP newswire app), the folder is called News, as shown in Figure 2-5, left side). You can then tap the folder's name field and use the keyboard to enter a different name, as shown in Figure 2-5 (right side).

Figure 2-5: Drag one icon over another to create a folder (left) and edit the folder name (right).

To close a folder, tap outside the folder, or press the Home button to stop rearranging your app icons.

To add another app icon to a folder, touch and hold an app icon to start the icons wiggling again (if they're not already wiggling), and drag the app icon onto the folder. To move an app icon out of a folder, start the icons wiggling again if they're not already, tap the folder to open it, and then drag the icon out of the folder. To delete a folder, move all the icons out of it. The folder is deleted automatically when empty.

You can put up to 12 app icons into a folder. Like individual icons, folders can be rearranged by dragging them around the Home screens. You can also drag folders to the dock.

Tickling the Keyboard

One trick that's sure to amaze your friends is the ability to whip out your iPod touch and type notes, contact information, calendar entries, map locations, stock symbols, and even the addresses for Web sites. You can also make selections for pop-up menus. You can do all this with the onscreen keyboard.

You may want to start practicing on the keyboard with just one finger, and as you get used to it, try also using your thumb. Tap a text entry field, such as the URL field for a Web page in Safari (as I describe in Chapter 10) or the text of an e-mail message (as I describe in Chapter 11), and the onscreen keyboard appears.

Typing text, numbers, and symbols (using Notes)

You can practice your technique using the Notes app. Tap Notes on the Home screen, and the onscreen keyboard appears with letters of the alphabet, as shown in Figure 2-6 on the left. (If you've already saved notes, a list of notes appears — tap the + button in the upper-right corner to type a new note.)

The following list provides helpful tips to enter text, numbers, punctuation, and symbols on your iPod touch:

- **To enter letters,** tap the keys, and while you type, each letter appears above your thumb or finger. If you tap the wrong key, slide your finger to the correct key. The letter isn't entered until you lift your finger from the key.

- **To enter numbers, symbols, or punctuation,** tap the .?123 key at the bottom-left corner of the keyboard (refer to Figure 2-6, left side), which changes the keyboard layout to numbers (refer to Figure 2-6, right side). After tapping the .?123 key, you can then tap the #+= key to change the keyboard layout to symbols. To return to the alphabetical keys, tap the ABC key.

- **To quickly start a new sentence,** double-tap the spacebar. The iPod inserts a period followed by a space. The keyboard automatically capitalizes the next word after you type a period, a question mark, or an exclamation point.

- **To switch to the numeric keyboard layout and back to alphabetical layout automatically** (in order to type a number and continue typing letters): Touch and hold the .?123 key and then slide your finger over the keyboard to the number you want. Release your finger to select the number. The onscreen keyboard reverts immediately to alphabetical keys so that you can continue typing letters.

✏ **To type a letter with an accent mark,** touch and hold your finger on a letter (such as *e*) to show a row of keys offering variations on the letter. Slide your finger over the row to highlight the variation you want and then release your finger to select it. For instance, the word *café* should really have an accent mark over the *e,* and there may even come a day when you need to include a foreign word or two in a note — lycée or Autowäsche or también, for example. Although you can switch the language for the keyboard (as I describe in Chapter 15), you can also include variations of a letter by using the English keyboard.

Figure 2-6: Type characters (left) and numbers (right).

To save your note, tap Done in the upper-right corner. A list of Notes appears with the last-modified date attached to each note. You can also delete a note by choosing the note and tapping the trash icon at the bottom of the note.

You can transfer notes you type in Notes to your computer by e-mailing them to yourself. Choose the note from the Notes screen and tap the envelope icon at the bottom of the note to display a ready-made e-mail message containing the text of your note — all you need to do is enter the e-mail address. See Chapter 11 for details on sending the message.

Editing text and handling word suggestions

Yes, you can edit your mistakes. To edit text in an entry field, touch and hold to see the magnifier, which magnifies portions of the text view, as shown in Figure 2-7 (left side).

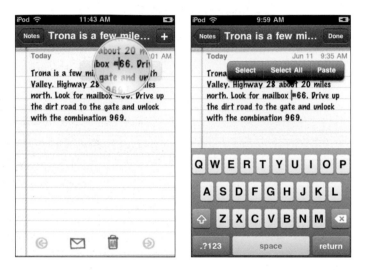

Figure 2-7: Touch and hold for the magnifier (left) and release when positioned correctly (right).

Before releasing your finger, slide the magnifier to the position for inserting text. After releasing, the Select/Select All/Paste bubble appears above the insertion point, as shown in Figure 2-7 (right side), which is useful for selecting, copying, and pasting text (as I describe in the next section). You can then tap keys to insert text, or you can use the delete key — the key sporting the X — to remove text.

The intelligent keyboard automatically suggests corrections while you type, as shown in Figure 2-8 (some languages only). You don't need to accept the suggested word — just continue typing. If you do want to accept it, tap the spacebar, a punctuation mark, or the Return key. iPod touch fills in the rest of the word.

To reject the suggested word, finish typing the word or tap the *x* next to the suggestion to dismiss it. Each time you reject a suggestion for the same word, your iPod touch keeps track and eventually adds the word you've been using to its dictionary. The iPod touch includes dictionaries for English, English (UK), French, French (Canada), German, Japanese, Spanish, Italian, Dutch, and other languages. The appropriate dictionary is activated automatically when you select an international keyboard. (See Chapter 15 for details about international keyboards.)

You can turn off suggestions by choosing Settings⇨General⇨Keyboard from the Home screen and tapping On for Auto-Correction. (On changes to Off when you tap it.)

Copying (or cutting) and pasting

You can copy or cut a chunk of text and paste it into another app — for example, you can copy a paragraph from a note in Notes and paste it into an e-mail message in Mail, or vice-versa. You can even copy paragraphs from a Web page and paste them in Notes or an e-mail message, as I show in Chapter 10.

Figure 2-8: The keyboard suggests the correct word for a typo.

To select the nearest word (or even the entire text) for copying or cutting, touch an insertion point to bring up the magnifier, then release to show the Select/Select All/Paste bubble. (Refer to Figure 2-7, right side.) You can then tap Select to select the nearest word or tap Select All to select all the text. The Cut/Copy/Paste bubble appears above the text, which is selected with handles on either end, as shown in Figure 2-9 (left side). Tap Cut to cut the selection, or Copy to copy it.

Figure 2-9: Copy or cut the selected text (left), and paste into a message (right).

To paste the cut or copied text somewhere new, open a note (or create a new note) in Notes, or start a new e-mail message, or open any app that lets you enter text. Touch and hold to magnify the text view so that you can mark an insertion point precisely. After you remove your finger, the Cut/Copy/Paste bubble appears, or if the message or note already contains text, the Select/ Select All/Paste bubble appears, as shown in Figure 2-9 (right side). Either way, you can then tap Paste to paste the text at the insertion point.

You can also double-tap a word to select it for copying (or cutting) and pasting. You can also make a more precise selection by dragging one of the handles. A rectangular magnifier appears for dragging the handle precisely. After you remove your finger to stop dragging, the Cut/Copy/Paste bubble appears for copying (or cutting) the selection.

Setting keyboard options

To set keyboard options, choose Settings⇨General⇨Keyboard from the Home screen. The Keyboard settings screen appears, with options for Auto-Correction, Auto-Capitalization, Enable Caps Lock, and the shortcut for inserting a period.

Tap On to turn off Auto-Correction if you don't want the keyboard to suggest typing corrections.

Auto-Capitalization automatically capitalizes the next word after you type a period, question mark, or exclamation point (punctuation that ends a sentence). It also automatically capitalizes after you tap the Return key. The assumption is that you're starting a new sentence or new line of text that should begin with a capital letter. Tap On to turn this feature off if you want; tap Off to turn it back on.

To turn on caps lock (locking the keyboard to uppercase letters), tap the Off button next to Enable Caps Lock. (Tap it again to turn it off.) You can then double-tap the Shift key to turn on caps lock (uppercase letters). The Shift key turns blue, and all letters you type are uppercase. Tap the Shift key again to turn caps lock off.

The shortcut for inserting a period is to double-tap the spacebar, which inserts a period followed by a space. The assumption is that you want to finish a sentence and start the next one. Tap On to turn this feature off if you want; tap Off to turn it back on.

3

Clocking, Locking, and Personalizing

In This Chapter

▶ Setting the time, date, clock, alarm, timer, and stopwatch

▶ Locking your iPod touch with a passcode

▶ Changing the brightness, wallpaper, sound effects, and restrictions

---

*Y*ou may think Apple designed the iPod touch just for listening to music or watching videos, but those thoughtful engineers crammed a lot more features into their invention. You can use your iPod touch as a time-keeper to help you keep track of your personal life — setting alarms, using the stopwatch, and displaying clocks of different time zones for traveling. And, if you worry that your iPod touch might fall into the wrong hands, consider setting a passcode to lock it. This chapter shows you how to do all this and more with your iPod touch: Find out how to set the brightness of the display, set the *wallpaper* (a stylin' background when your iPod touch is locked), turn on its capability to know your location, and set restrictions on downloading and playing content.

There's No Time Like the Right Time

Your iPod touch may already be set to the correct time, date, and time zone, depending on where you bought it. If you need to change the time zone, time, or date, you can do that at any time (sorry for the pun), and even set how the time appears in the status bar at the top of the screen. To set the date and time, follow these steps:

1. **Choose Settings⇨General⇨Date & Time from the Home screen.**

   The Date & Time screen appears with the 24-Hour Time, Time Zone, Set Date & Time options, and time zone support for your calendar.

2. **(Optional) If you'd rather see military time, tap the Off button for the 24-Hour Time option to turn it on.**

   With 24-hour display, 11 p.m. displays as 23:00:00 and not 11:00:00. To turn off the 24-Hour Time option, tap the On button.

3. **Tap the Time Zone option to set the time zone.**

   The onscreen keyboard appears; see Chapter 2 for instructions on how to use it. Type the name of the city you're in (or, if you're in the middle of nowhere, the nearest big city in your time zone) and tap the Return button on the keyboard, and your iPod touch looks up the time zone for you.

4. **Tap the Date & Time button in the upper-left corner of the display to finish and return to the Date & Time menu.**

5. **Tap the Set Date & Time option.**

   Tapping the Date field brings up a slot-machine-style Date wheel, as shown in Figure 3-1 (left).

6. **Slide your finger over the wheel to select the month, day, and year.**

   Slide until the selection you want appears in the gray window on the slot-machine wheel.

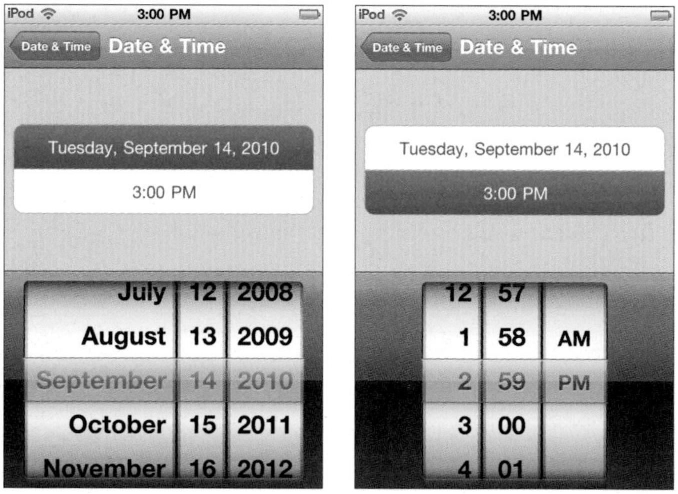

Figure 3-1: Slide the wheel of fortune to set the month, day, year (left) and time (right).

7. **Tap the Time field to bring up a Time wheel, as shown in Figure 3-1 (right). Slide your finger over the wheel to set the hour, minutes, and AM or PM.**

8. **Tap the Date & Time button in the upper-left corner of the display (refer to Figure 3-1) to finish and return to the Date & Time menu.**

9. **Tap the General button in the upper-left corner to return to the General screen.**

Rock Around the Clocks

You can always know what time it is with your iPod touch — just look at the time on the Home screen. However, you can also know what time it is in other time zones by displaying multiple clocks. Your iPod touch even lets you set alarms and run a stopwatch.

Checking the time in Paris and Bangkok

You can display clocks with different time zones, which is useful for traveling halfway around the world (or calling someone who lives halfway around the world).

To add clocks, tap the Clock icon on the Home screen and tap the World Clock icon along the bottom of the display. It takes only two steps to add a clock:

1. **Tap the plus (+) button in the upper-right corner of the display.**

   The onscreen keyboard appears with a text entry field.

2. **Type a city name on the keyboard and tap Return (or tap Cancel next to the text entry field to cancel).**

   The iPod touch looks up the city's time zone to display the clock. (For details on how to use the onscreen keyboard, see Chapter 2.)

The initial clock and any clocks you add sport a daytime face (white background and black hands) from 6 a.m. to 5:59 p.m., as shown in Figure 3-2, and a nighttime face (black background with white hands) from 6 p.m. to 5:59 a.m. If you add more clocks than can fit on the screen, you can flick to scroll the screen to see them.

Figure 3-2: Add a clock for any time zone.

To remove a clock, tap the Edit button in the upper-left corner of the display (refer to Figure 3-2) and then tap the circled minus (–) button next to the clock to delete.

Getting alarmed

Time is on your side with your iPod touch. You can set *multiple* alarms to go off on different days and set a variety of tones and sounds for your alarms that play through its speaker. Follow these steps:

1. **Tap the Clock icon on the Home screen and tap the Alarm icon along the bottom of the display.**

2. **To add an alarm, tap the plus (+) button in the upper-right corner of the display.**

   The Add Alarm screen appears, as shown in Figure 3-3, with options and a slot-machine-style wheel for setting the alarm time.

3. **Slide your finger over the wheel to set the hour, minute, and AM or PM.**

   Slide until the selection you want appears in the gray window on the slot-machine wheel.

   Now you can set some optional features, or you can skip to Step 8 and be done with it.

4. **(Optional) Tap the Repeat option to set the alarm to repeat on other days.**

Figure 3-3: Add an alarm.

   You can set it to repeat every Monday, Tuesday, Wednesday, Thursday, Friday, Saturday, or Sunday.

5. **(Optional) Tap the Sound option to select a sound for the alarm.**

   A list of sounds appears; touch a sound to set it for the alarm.

6. **(Optional) Tap the On button to turn off the Snooze option, or tap it again to turn it back on.**

   With the Snooze option, the iPod touch displays a Snooze button when the alarm goes off, and you tap Snooze to stop the alarm and have it repeat in 10 minutes (so that you can snooze for 10 minutes).

7. **(Optional) Tap the Label option to enter a text label for the alarm.**

   The label helps you identify the alarm in the Alarm list.

8. **Tap the Save button in the upper-right corner to save the alarm.**

When the alarm goes off, your iPod touch displays the message You Have an Alarm (and the date and time), along with the Snooze button if the Snooze option is turned on (refer to Step 6). Slide your finger to unlock the iPod touch to stop the alarm's sound, or tap the Snooze button to stop the alarm temporarily and let it repeat 10 minutes later. (When it goes off again, slide the unlock slider to turn it off — don't tap the Snooze button again, you're late for work!)

To delete an alarm, tap the Clock Icon on the Home screen and tap the Alarm icon along the bottom of the display. In the Alarm list, tap the alarm you want to trash and then tap the Edit button in the upper-left corner of the display. The alarm appears with a circled minus (–) button next to it; tap this button and then tap the red Delete button that appears to delete the alarm.

Timing your steps

You can set an hour-and-minute timer for anything — baking cookies, baking CDs, baking a speech for a timed presentation, or baking in the sun on the beach. The timer built into the Clock app will continue running even when playing music and videos or running other iPod touch apps. You might want to use a timer to see whether a set of activities — playing songs, playing videos, selecting from menus, and running apps — occurs within a specific time. (If you need to use seconds as well as minutes and hours, try the stop-watch, which I describe in the following section.)

To use the timer, follow these steps:

1. **Tap the Clock icon on the Home screen.**

   The Clock display appears.

2. **Tap the Timer icon along the bottom of the Clock display.**

   The Timer wheel for minutes and hours appears, along with the Start button.

3. **Flick the timer wheel to set the timer in hours and minutes.**

4. **Tap the When Timer Ends button and tap a sound to use when the timer is up.**

5. **Tap Set in the upper-right corner of the display to set the sound (or Cancel in the upper-left corner to cancel the sound).**

6. **Tap Start to start the timer.**

The timer runs backward. You can touch Cancel to cancel the timer or wait until it runs out. When it runs out, the iPod touch plays the sound (if a sound is set) and presents an OK button. Tap OK to stop the sound.

Let the good times roll

Many games use the iPod touch clock to measure time. Some use it against you: Super Horsey (see the vertical figure with the chess piece) is a very challenging game that puts you in the role of the traditional chess knight who must complete the labyrinth before the time elapses.

If speed is the issue, SlotZ Racer lets up to four people race slot cars on a single iPod touch. You can compete for laps or against the clock in Time Trials and drive an endurance race (with simulated days and nights). SlotZ Track Editor lets you create the slot-car track of your dreams, with huge and detailed tracks that you can trick out with jumps, bridges, and scenery.

If you enjoy role-playing games that take you on a journey with humor and storytelling (like Zelda, Pokémon, Dragon Quest, or Final Fantasy), try Arvale: Journey of Illusion, which offers over 20 hours of game-play, six immense continents, 280 maps (see the horizontal figure with a map), 200 monsters, hundreds of items (including wheelbarrows), and thousands of laughs. And in Rock'n'Roll, you've messed up your enemy's music game, and all the notes have scattered over an island — it's up to you to roll through each level to collect these notes. Once all the notes are collected, you move on to the next level. But in Rock the Clock mode, there are another 15 levels that must be beaten in the time provided. Good luck with that!

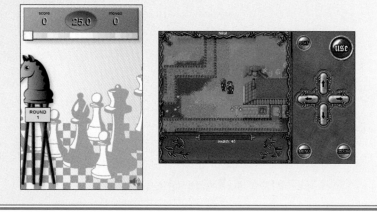

Using the stopwatch

You can use a stopwatch with a lap timer for timing exercises, jogging, race laps, how long it takes the bus to travel across town, or how long your friend takes to recognize the song you're playing. Whatever you want to measure with accurate time to the tenth of a second, the stopwatch is ready for you.

Even while you're running the stopwatch, you can still use the iPod touch to play music, videos, audio books, and podcasts. When you play a video, the stopwatch continues to count as usual; when you switch back to the stopwatch display, the video automatically pauses.

To use the stopwatch, follow these steps:

1. **Tap the Clock icon on the Home screen and tap the Stopwatch icon along the bottom of the display.**

   A stopwatch appears with Start and Reset buttons and 00:00.00 (minutes, seconds, and fractions of seconds) as the stopwatch counter, as shown in Figure 3-4 (left side).

2. **Tap the Start button to start counting.**

   The stopwatch starts counting immediately, while the left button changes to Stop, and the right button changes to Lap, as shown in Figure 3-4 (right side).

Figure 3-4: Tap Start (left) and tap Lap for each lap or Stop (right).

3. **(Optional) Tap the Lap button to mark each lap.**

   Tap the Lap button to record each lap. Repeat this step for each lap.

4. **Tap the Stop button to stop counting.**

   The counter stops counting. The left button changes to Start and the right button changes to Reset. You can resume the count from where you left off by tapping Start, or you can start the count again from zero by tapping Reset.

Setting the Passcode for Your Lock

Your iPod touch locks itself when it goes to sleep, and, as you already know, you have to slide your finger over the unlock message to wake it up. However, you can also set a passcode that keeps the iPod touch from waking up unless you supply the passcode. Setting a passcode also turns on data protection so that your iPod touch uses your passcode as the key for encrypting mail messages and their attachments. (Data protection may also be used by some apps.) *Note:* The lock-up works only when your iPod touch is not attached to a computer.

If you're playing music when you lock your iPod touch, the music continues playing — and you can even use the play/pause button to pause and resume playback — but if you set a passcode, no one can navigate the iPod touch or even change the volume without providing the passcode.

To conserve power, you can force your iPod touch to go to sleep by pressing the sleep/wake button, but it won't unlock. When it awakens, it remembers everything — including the passcode you need to provide.

Don't bother to call Apple to see whether the company can unlock your iPod touch for you. If you can't attach it to the proper computer or enter the correct passcode, your only recourse is to restore the iPod touch to its factory conditions — see Chapter 14.

To set a passcode, follow these steps:

1. **Choose Settings⬄General⬄Passcode Lock from the Home screen.**

   The Passcode Lock screen appears with the Simple Passcode and Turn Passcode On options.

2. **To use a four-number passcode, leave the Simple Passcode option turned on; if you want to use a more complex alphanumeric password as your passcode, tap On for Simple Passcode to turn it Off.**

3. **Tap Turn Passcode On at the top and then enter the passcode.**

   If you left the Simple Passcode option turned on in Step 2, you see a calculator-style keypad — enter a four-number passcode by touching numbers in the keypad. If you turned off the Simple Passcode option in Step 2, you see a full keyboard — enter an alphanumeric password as your passcode, using the keyboard. If you change your mind, tap the Cancel button to cancel the operation.

4. **Enter the same passcode again to confirm the passcode.**

   After reentering the passcode, the Passcode Lock screen appears with the Turn Passcode Off, Change Passcode, Require Passcode, and Erase Data options.

5. **Choose Passcode options:**

   • You can choose Turn Passcode Off to turn it off or choose Change Passcode to change it. You need to enter the passcode to do either.

   • You can set the Require Passcode option to Immediately, After 1 Minute, After 5 Minutes, After 15 Minutes, After 1 Hour, or After 4 Hours.

   • You can turn On or Off the Erase Data option. This option erases all the information and content on the iPad, iPod touch, or iPhone after 10 successive failed passcode attempts.

6. **When you're done, tap General to return to the General menu.**

Don't forget this passcode! Use one that's easy to commit to memory.

The passcode screen appears immediately after you slide the Slide to Unlock message. After correctly entering the passcode, the iPod touch unlocks.

To unlock a passcode-locked iPod touch, you must enter the same combination, or restore your iPod touch to its original factory settings. As I describe in Chapter 14, this erases everything in the process. After correctly entering the combination, the iPod touch unlocks and returns to the last viewed screen.

With the Erase Data option turned on, If anyone (including you) tries ten times to enter the passcode and fails each time, your iPod touch settings are reset to their defaults and all your information and media are removed by overwriting the data. It's as if the Mission: Impossible force had set it to self-destruct. Your iPod touch is restored to factory conditions, so you might as well go to Chapter 14 to see what that means.

Getting Personal

Your future might be so bright that you gotta wear shades, but your iPod touch display might not be bright enough. And it still needs that personal touch that only wallpaper can bring.

And of course, there are the keyboard clicks and alert sounds you can use to indicate that e-mail has arrived, that something in your calendar needs attention, and so on. Screen brightness, wallpaper, and sound effects are a lot to keep track of, but your iPod touch makes customizing each feature so doggone easy.

If you share your iPod touch with children or adults that act like children, you may want to place restrictions that prevent explicit music from the iTunes Store from being displayed in playlists, or prevent the use of apps such as YouTube, or stop any access to the iTunes Store or App Store. Your iPod touch can let you do that, too.

Brightening and wallpapering

To adjust the brightness, tap the Settings icon on the Home screen and then tap Brightness, which is near the top of the Settings screen. The Brightness screen appears with a slider that shows the brightness setting, which ranges from low (a dim sun icon) to high (a bright sun icon). Slide the brightness slider's knob with your finger to the right to increase the brightness (toward the bright sun) and to the left to decrease the brightness (toward the dim sun). Of course, the brighter the screen, the more power it draws from the battery.

While you're at it, why not wallpaper your display? You can make your iPod touch display different stylish wallpaper backgrounds for your lock screen and Home screen (or use the same wallpaper for both). You can also put up photos or other images stored in your iPod touch as your wallpaper. One wallpaper image appears on the lock screen and another appears behind the icons on your Home screens.

To set these wallpapers, choose Settings⇨General⇨Wallpaper, and then tap the lock screen and Home screen thumbnail that appears, to show a menu of wallpaper options. On the wallpaper options menu, you can choose from among stylish built-in wallpaper images by tapping the Wallpaper button at the top. You can also choose from the photos you synchronized with your iPod touch by tapping Photo Library or a photo album, or you can choose photos saved on your iPod touch by tapping Camera Roll. (For more about photos, see Chapter 9.)

Tap a thumbnail to select the image for your wallpaper or tap the Wallpaper button in the upper-left corner to return to the Wallpaper menu. After tapping an image, your iPod touch displays the Move and Scale screen, which lets you optionally pan the image by dragging your finger, and optionally zoom in or out of the image by pinching and unpinching with your fingers. Tap the Set button to set the image as your wallpaper or tap Cancel to cancel.

You can then tap Set Lock Screen to set the image for the lock screen only, Set Home Screen to set it for the Home screen only, or Set Both to set the image to both at once (or Cancel to cancel).

Sound effects and ringtones

Don't want to hear the keyboard click while you type, or hear the snap noise as you swipe your finger over the unlock message? You can set which events can trigger sound effects and set the volume of the sound effect.

Choose Settings⇨General⇨Sounds from the Home screen. You can then turn the alert on or off and tap sounds for new mail, sent mail, calendar alerts, locking and unlocking, and using the onscreen keyboard. Tap On to turn off each option, or vice versa.

When someone calls you with FaceTime (see Chapter 13 for details), your iPod touch plays a ringtone just like a cell phone.

You can decide what the ringtone sound should be by choosing a built-in ringtone, or downloading ringtones based on popular songs from the iTunes Store, or making them yourself using a sound-editing program such as GarageBand on a Mac. After downloading ringtones from the iTunes Store, or importing the ringtones to the Library section of the iTunes source pane, you can sync the ringtones with your iPod touch as I show in Chapter 5.

You can also assign individual ringtones to people in your Contacts list, so that you can tell by the ringtone who's calling — see Chapter 13 for details.

To set the ringtone, choose Settings⇨General⇨Sounds from the Home screen, and tap Ringtone. You can then select a built-in ringtone, or if you synced ringtones from iTunes, you can select a synced ringtone.

Drag the Ringer and Alerts volume slider above the Ringtones setting to adjust the volume of the ringtone and alert sounds. If you turn on the Change with Buttons option under the volume slider, you can also use the volume buttons on the side of the iPod touch to set and change the volume.

Location, location, location

Perhaps nothing is more personal than your physical location. Your iPod touch can triangulate its location with scary precision, even though it has neither a cell phone nor the location-determining technology known as GPS. (The iPod touch's cousin, the iPhone, does have both a cell phone and GPS.) The iPod touch does this by leveraging the most extensive Wi-Fi reference database in the world.

With Location Services, the Maps app can find your location on the map, which is very useful for getting directions (see Chapter 12). Other apps (such as Google Earth, SkyORB, Foursquare, and various travel apps) can grab this physical location information and use it to help you find things closer to you.

You can turn Location Services on or off by choosing Settings⇨General⇨ Location Services from the Home screen, and then tapping the Off button for Location Services at the top of the screen to turn it on, or the On button to turn it off.

The Location Services setting at the top of the screen turns on the services for all apps. You can also decide which apps can use Location Services. Each app you used that requested your location within the last 24 hours appears in the Location Services screen, showing whether Location Services has been turned on or off for that app. Tap the On button for each app to turn it off for that app.

After turning it off, your iPod touch prompts you to turn it back on if you run an app that makes use of Location Services (such as Maps).

To conserve battery power, turn off Location Services if you aren't using apps that make use of it.

Setting notifications

The Notifications setting appears in the Settings menu if you've installed an app in your iPod touch that uses the Apple Push Notification service. Push notifications are used by apps to let you know about new information, such as messages, even when the app isn't running (see Chapter 11 for more about the Push feature).

Notifications differ depending on the app — some notify you with alerts (text or sound), and some also display a numbered badge on the app icon (for example, to show that you have messages on Facebook or MySpace, or unread e-mails). You can control what type of notification you receive from each app, and you can also turn notifications off or on.

It's a good idea to turn notifications completely off if you are trying to conserve battery life.

To turn notifications on or off, choose Settings⇨Notifications to see the Notifications screen. Tap On next to Notifications to turn it off, or tap Off to turn it on. You can also specify the type of notification for each app: select the app and then tap the options on or off for alerts, sounds, or icon badges.

Setting restrictions

Are you lending your iPod touch to a youngster (or an adult acting like one)? You may want to set restrictions that

- Prevent access to explicit music, podcasts, and videos according to ratings.
- Prevent the use of apps such as YouTube and FaceTime.
- Prevent installation of new apps.
- Disallow in-app purchases.
- Stop any access to the iTunes Store or App Store.

Choose Settings⇨General from the Home screen and then tap Restrictions to see the Restrictions screen. Tap Enable Restrictions and then set up a restrictions passcode (which is separate from your Passcode Lock passcode). Enter a four-number passcode by touching numbers in the calculator-style keypad. If you change your mind, tap the Cancel button to cancel the operation. Then enter the same passcode number again to confirm the passcode, and the Restrictions are enabled and appear ready for you to change.

Set the restrictions you want by tapping each control's On switch to turn it off. By default, all controls are on, which means usage is allowed (not restricted). Turn off a control to restrict its use.

To turn off all restrictions, choose Settings⇨General⇨Restrictions and then enter the passcode. Tap Disable Restrictions and then reenter the passcode. Your iPod touch is now free. Be careful out there!

Part II
Filling Up Your Empty Cup

The 5th Wave By Rich Tennant

"Why can't you just bring your iPod touch like everyone else?"

In this part . . .

This part shows you how to fill up your iPod touch with extreme content and killer apps.

First, in Chapter 4, you find out all about iTunes and how to set yourself up with an account for the iTunes Store and App Store. You're then given free rein to browse the stores online from iTunes or browse for content and apps directly from your iPod touch. You also find out how to connect to a Wi-Fi network.

Next, in Chapter 5, I show you how to synchronize your iPod touch with your iTunes library, which you can fill up with songs, videos, and other content and apps from Apple's online stores and other sources. You can match your iPod touch library content item for content item with your iTunes library, or you can be more selective about what you copy to your iPod touch. You can also make sure your iPod touch downloads, including apps, are backed up in your iTunes library.

Then, in Chapter 6, I show you how to organize and synchronize your personal information with your iPod touch — your contacts, calendars, notes, Web bookmarks, and e-mail accounts.

After all that, your iPod touch should be filled to the brim!

4

Exploring iTunes and the Online Store

In This Chapter

▶ Finding out all about iTunes

▶ Setting up an account with the iTunes Store

▶ Previewing and buying songs, TV shows, movies, and apps

▶ Choosing Wi-Fi to go online

▶ Downloading music, podcasts, and apps directly to your iPod touch

*I*f the iPod touch were a spaceship, iTunes would be the space station it docks with to get its supplies. iTunes is the central repository of all content and iPod touch apps, and it's the gateway to the online iTunes Store and App Store from your computer.

The iTunes Store offers millions of songs — many for $0.69, $0.99, or $1.29, although album prices may vary. Some of these albums offer an immersive visual experience (called iTunes LP) that includes liner notes, pictures, video, animation, and lyrics. You can also buy audio books, TV episodes, and first-run movies, as well as rent TV shows and movies. On top of that, iTunes offers tons of free content in the form of *podcasts,* which are similar to syndicated radio and TV shows. You can download podcasts into iTunes and play them at your convenience on your computer and on your iPod touch. iTunes even offers free lectures, language lessons, and audio books with educational content in its iTunes U section.

The iTunes Store includes the App Store, which offers free and commercial iPod touch applications by the hundreds of thousands. You can find apps in just about every category you can think of, including gaming, social networking, sports, business, and more.

You can download and organize your content and apps in your iTunes library on your computer, and then put items on your iPod touch to carry around with you. You can also download content from the iTunes Store and apps from the App Store *directly* to your iPod touch and then synchronize these items with your iTunes library on your computer later.

This chapter gives you an overview of what you can do with iTunes, and it shows you how to sign in and take advantage of what the iTunes Store and App Store have to offer.

Discovering What You Can Do with iTunes

iTunes (a.k.a. iTunes Player in some Apple documents) is the free software for Mac and Windows that manages content on my iPod touch, all my other iPods, my iPhone and iPad, and even my Apple TV. Whether I download content from the iTunes Store or App Store through my iPod touch, my iPhone, my iPad, or my computer running iTunes, it all ends up in my iTunes library on my computer, where I can make backup copies on another hard drive. I can also parcel the content from my computer out to various iPads, iPods, and iPhones for playback, and burn music CDs.

Although you can download content and apps directly from the iTunes Store or App Store to your iPod touch, you can't edit the content information (such as the artist and album title) directly — not like you can in iTunes. iTunes also lets you import music from CDs, convert media files to play on your iPod touch, and make a backup of your content library. iTunes does all this and more, and provides a quick and easy browsing experience for accessing the iTunes Store and App Store from your computer.

You can import CD music and downloaded MP3 song files into iTunes. You can also add videos to your iTunes library in a couple of ways: by choosing content from the iTunes Store (such as TV shows, feature-length high-definition movies, music videos, and even free movie trailers), or by downloading video files in a standard MPEG-4 format from other sources on the Internet and other applications that capture video. You can even transfer video from camcorders (using applications such as iMovie on a Mac), or from cameras built-in to computers (such as the iSight camera included with MacBooks and iMacs) and import them into your iTunes library.

Although you can't use iTunes to transfer video content from a DVD, you can use other software to convert DVDs to digital video files, and you can transfer video content from older VHS players by using a digital video camcorder. Visit the tips section of my Web site at www.tonybove.com for more details.

As if that weren't enough, iTunes gives you the power to organize content into playlists. A *playlist* is a list of the items that you want in the sequence that you want to play them. For example, you can make a playlist of love songs from different albums to play the next time you need a romantic mood, or you can compile a playlist of surf songs for a trip to the beach. You can even combine videos and music in a playlist.

If you organize songs into playlists in iTunes, you can then easily synchronize those playlists with your iPod touch to be more selective about the music you copy. See Chapter 5 for sync details. (Also, see my other book, *iPod & iTunes For Dummies,* to find out all about iTunes.)

iTunes even connects you to other iTunes Store buyers with its Ping social network for music. You can follow artists, follow your friends to learn what music interests them, and learn about concerts and events near you. Ping makes it easy to discover and download new music in the iTunes Store and keep up on your friends' tastes in music. To find out more about Ping, see the latest edition of my other book, *iPod & iTunes For Dummies.*

What's that you say? You're still not satisfied with what iTunes can do for you? Well, iTunes also has a built-in equalizer with preset settings for all kinds of music and listening environments, with the added bonus of being able to customize and save your own personalized settings with each item of content.

You can run iTunes anytime (with or without your iPod touch attached to your computer) to build and manage your library. You don't have to connect your iPod touch until you're ready to sync it (as I describe in Chapter 5).

Browsing your iTunes library

The Mac and Windows versions of iTunes look nearly identical and offer the same functions and viewing options, including the *cover browser* (also known as Cover Flow) and the *column browser*. In Figure 4-1, the iTunes window on the Mac shows the Album List view and the column browser.

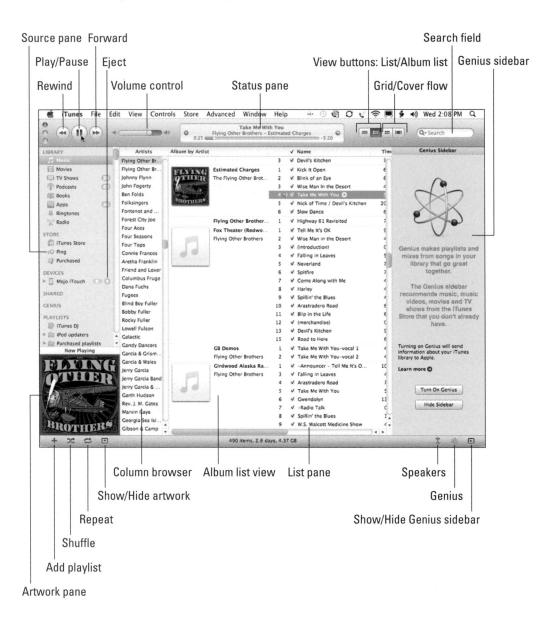

Source pane Forward

Play/Pause Eject

Rewind Volume control Status pane

Search field

View buttons: List/Album list Genius sidebar

Grid/Cover flow

Column browser Album list view List pane Speakers

Show/Hide artwork Genius

Repeat Show/Hide Genius sidebar

Shuffle

Add playlist

Artwork pane

Figure 4-1: iTunes Album List view and the column browser.

iTunes offers a view of your library and your sources for content, as well as controls for organizing, importing, and playing content, as follows:

- **Source pane:** Displays the source of content, handily divided into the following sections:

  - *Library:* Includes your music, movies, TV shows, podcasts, books (audio books and e-books), apps, ringtones, educational lessons from iTunes U, and all available radio stations.

  - *Store:* Includes the iTunes Store, the Ping social network for iTunes users, and your Purchased or Downloads list (if you've purchased or recently downloaded items).

  - *Devices:* Includes audio CDs and any iPads, iPods (such as *Mojo iTouch* in Figure 4-1), iPhones, and Apple TV devices that are connected to your computer.

  - *Eject button:* This button appears next to the name of an audio CD or device in the source pane (refer to Figure 4-1). Clicking the eject button, um, *ejects* a CD or removes *(unmounts)* the device from the system so that you can disconnect it.

  - *Shared:* Includes iTunes libraries on your home network that you can share. (To learn more, see my other book, *iPod & iTunes For Dummies.*)

  - *Genius:* Includes Genius mixes and your Genius playlists, which I describe in Chapter 7.

  - *Playlists:* Includes iTunes DJ and your playlists.

- **List pane:** Depending on the source that's selected in the source pane, the list pane displays a list of items.

- **View buttons:** The four buttons in the upper-right corner change your view of the list pane to show a list (List view), an album list with cover art (Album List view), a grid of cover art images (Grid view), or the cover browser (Cover Flow).

- **Cover browser:** Also called Cover Flow, the cover browser lets you flip through your cover art to choose songs. You can use the slider to move swiftly through your library, or you can click to the right or left of the cover in the foreground to move forward or backward in your library.

- **Column browser:** To see the column browser, choose View⇨Column Browser⇨Show Column Browser. To hide the column browser, choose View⇨Column Browser⇨Hide Column Browser.

- **Player buttons — forward/next, play/pause, and previous/rewind:** Use these buttons to control the playback of content in iTunes.

- **Volume control:** You can change the volume level in iTunes by dragging the volume control slider in the upper-left section of the iTunes window to the right to increase the volume, or to the left to decrease it.

✔ **Status pane:** When content is playing, you can see the artist name, piece title (if known), and the elapsed time displayed in this pane.

✔ **Search field:** Type in this field to search your library. You can also use the Search field to peruse a playlist or to look within the iTunes Store.

✔ **Playlist buttons — add, shuffle, and repeat:** Use these buttons to add playlists and shuffle or repeat playback of playlists.

✔ **Show/hide artwork button:** Use this button to display or hide artwork associated with your music or videos (either your artwork or the artwork supplied by the iTunes Store).

✔ **Speakers:** Click this icon in the lower-right corner of the iTunes window to reveal the Speakers pop-up menu and select a different speaker system than the computer's speakers. This icon appears only if you choose Preferences (from the iTunes menu on a Mac or the Edit menu in Windows), click the Devices tab, and turn on the Look for Remote Speakers Connected with AirTunes option. If iTunes locates remote speakers connected to an Airport Express or Apple TV using AirTunes (the technology for streaming music over a Wi-Fi or Ethernet local area network), the pop-up menu appears.

✔ **Genius button:** The Genius button, located in the lower-right corner of the iTunes window to the left of the show/hide Genius Sidebar button, generates a playlist of songs from your library that go great with the song you selected. The genius button appears only when you've selected music, movies, TV shows, or a playlist. (See Chapter 7 for details about creating Genius playlists.)

✔ **Show/hide Genius Sidebar button:** Use this button to display or hide the Genius Sidebar (refer to Figure 4-1). The Genius Sidebar makes suggestions for what to get from the iTunes Store based on what you've selected.

Setting up an iTunes Store account

One important task that you must do is set up your iTunes Store account. You can set it up in iTunes on your computer or directly on your iPod touch (as I describe in "Shopping with Your iPod touch," later in this chapter). You need an account to purchase content or apps on your computer as well as to use the iTunes Store and App Store apps on your iPod touch. You can create as many accounts as you need — perhaps one for each family member. To create an iTunes Store account using iTunes on your computer, follow these steps:

1. **In iTunes, click the iTunes Store option in the Store section of the source pane.**

   The iTunes Store home page appears, as shown in Figure 4-2, replacing the list pane.

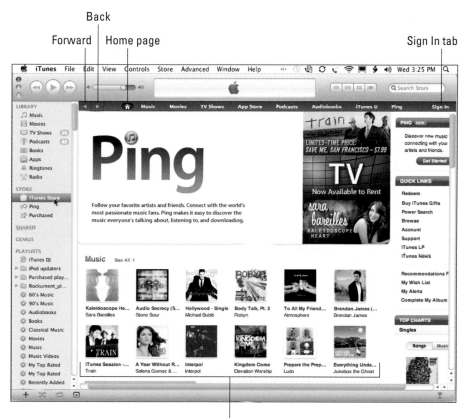

Figure 4-2: The iTunes Store home page.

2. **Click the Sign In tab in the upper-right area of the window (refer to Figure 4-2) to either create an account or sign in to an existing account.**

   When you're logged in to an iTunes account, the account name appears in place of the Sign In tab.

   After you click the Sign In tab, iTunes displays the account sign-in dialog.

   If you already set up an account with the iTunes Store with the MobileMe (formerly .Mac) service or with other Apple services (such as the Apple Developer Connection or Apple's online store), you're halfway there. Type your ID and password and then click the Sign In button.

Apple remembers the personal information that you put in previously, so you don't have to re-enter it every time you visit the iTunes Store. If you forgot your password, click the Forgot Password? button; iTunes provides a dialog so that you can answer your test question. If you answer correctly, iTunes e-mails your password to you.

3. **Click the Create New Account button.**

   iTunes displays a new page that welcomes you to the iTunes Store.

4. **Click Continue on the iTunes Store welcome page.**

   After you click Continue, the terms of use appear with the option at the end to agree to the terms. If you don't select the option to agree, iTunes continues to display the terms until you agree or click Cancel.

5. **Select the I Have Read and Agree to the iTunes Terms and Conditions option to agree with the legal terms. Then click Continue.**

   iTunes displays the next page of the setup procedure.

6. **Fill in your personal account information.**

   You need to enter your e-mail address, password, test question and answer (in case you forget your password), birth date, and privacy options. *Don't forget your password* — you need it to access the store from your iPod touch.

7. **Click the Continue button to go to the next page of the account setup procedure and then enter your credit card information.**

   The entire procedure is secure, so you don't have to worry. The iTunes Store keeps your personal information (including your credit card information) on file, and you don't have to type it again.

8. **Click Continue to finish the procedure.**

   The account setup finishes and returns you to the iTunes Store home page. You can now use the iTunes Store to purchase and download content to play in iTunes and use on any iPod, iPhone, or Apple TV.

Shopping at the iTunes Store

If you have an iTunes Store account set up (see the previous section), you can buy and download content immediately, including movies and TV shows for rent. I don't know of a faster way to purchase or rent content from the comfort of your home.

If you already have your iTunes program open, click iTunes Store in the Store section of the source pane. The iTunes Store home page opens (refer to Figure 4-2).

Cruising in the multimedia mall

The iTunes Store home page is loaded with specials and ads to peruse. To look at music in more depth, click the Music tab in the dark gray bar above the list pane (refer to Figure 4-2). You can also pick a music genre by clicking the down-arrow button that appears next to the Music tab when your pointer is over the tab.

Besides Music and other tabs, iTunes Store offers buttons on the dark gray bar just above the advertised content in the list pane (refer to Figure 4-2). The left and right triangle buttons work just like the back and forward buttons of a Web browser, moving back a page or forward a page, respectively. The button with the Home icon takes you to the iTunes Store home page.

After clicking an album or selecting an advertisement for an album, the album's page appears with a description and other links, as shown in Figure 4-3. You can then click the Buy Album button, or the Buy buttons for individual songs, as I describe in the "Buying and downloading items" section, later in this chapter.

Figure 4-3: An iTunes Store page showing an iTunes LP album.

You can preview any song in the iTunes Store for up to 30 seconds. Some movies offer one-minute previews and movie trailers you can view free, and TV shows and audio books can offer up to 90 seconds. To preview a song, TV show, movie, or music video, click the title in the list and then click the play button (or press the spacebar). Click the iTunes player buttons to control playback, and use the iTunes volume slider to control the volume.

A video preview plays in the iTunes window, in the artwork pane in the lower-left corner of the iTunes window, in a separate window, or full-screen, depending on your playback settings. To set your playback settings, choose iTunes⇨Preferences (Mac) or Edit⇨Preferences (Windows), and click the Playback tab. You can then choose the video playback option for movies/TV shows and music videos separately: In the Artwork Viewer (artwork pane), In the iTunes Window, In a Separate Window, or Full Screen, which fills the entire computer display.

To browse the iTunes Store, choose View⇨Column Browser⇨Show Column Browser, or click the Browse link in the Quick Links column on the right side of the iTunes Store home page. iTunes displays the store's offerings categorized by type of content (such as Music), and it displays music by genre and subgenre — and within each subgenre, by artist and album. Select a genre in the Genre column, then a subgenre in the Subgenre column, then an artist in the Artist column, and finally an album in the Album column, which takes you to the list of songs from that album that are available to preview or purchase, as shown in Figure 4-4.

You can play music in your iTunes library while browsing the iTunes Store, as I do in Figure 4-4 — I'm playing Elvis while searching for more Elvis.

Buying and downloading items

While you browse items in the iTunes Store, you can purchase and download them to your computer immediately. All you need to do is click the Buy button on an album or movie page or in the far-right column of the song or other content item — you may have to scroll your iTunes Store window to see the far-right column (refer to Figure 4-3 for an album page, or Figure 4-4 for the column browser).

The iTunes Store may prompt you to log in to your account after you click the Buy button (unless you just recently logged in). Then, a warning dialog displays to make sure that you want to buy the item; you can continue by clicking the Buy button, or Cancel. After you click the Buy button, iTunes downloads the item and, after downloading, it appears in your iTunes library. You can continue buying items while downloading, and because you already logged in, the iTunes Store complies immediately without asking again for a password. The iTunes Store keeps track of your purchases over a 24-hour period and charges you for a total sum rather than for each single purchase.

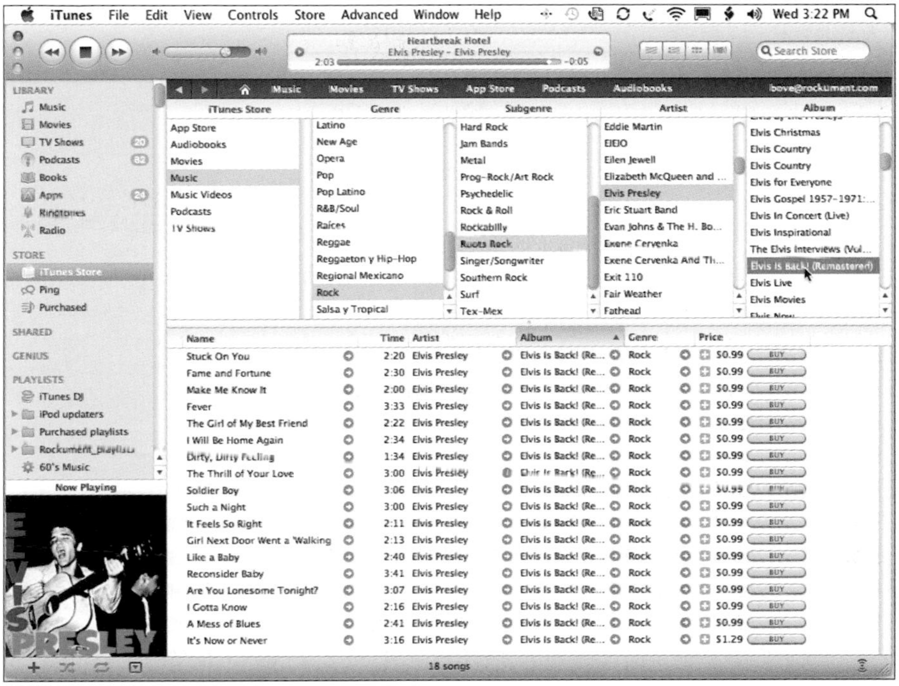

Figure 4-4: Browse the iTunes Store for music by genre, artist, and album.

You can see the list of all the items that you purchased (no matter which shopping method you used at the time) by selecting the Purchased playlist under the iTunes Store option in the source pane. The list pane changes to show the items you purchased.

Each time you buy content, you get an e-mail from the iTunes Store with the purchase information. It's nice to know right away what you bought.

You can change iTunes Store preference settings by choosing iTunes⇨ Preferences on the Mac or by choosing Edit⇨Preferences in Windows. In the Preferences window, click the Store tab. The Store preferences pane appears, and you can set the following features:

✔ Automatically check for available downloads from the iTunes Store, such as downloads that were not completed and new episodes for a podcast subscription.

✔ Automatically download prepurchased content, such as an iTunes Pass for TV show episodes. As the episodes become available, iTunes automatically downloads them.

✔ Automatically download missing album artwork from the iTunes Store for albums and songs you import from other sources (such as audio CDs).

✔ Use the full iTunes window for the iTunes Store (rather than just the list pane) so that you can see more of the store choices.

Appearing at the App Store

You can get loads of free and commercial apps that run on your iPod touch just like the built-in apps such as Map and Weather. (To no one's big surprise, many of the apps are games.) To find hundreds of thousands of apps, click the App Store tab in the center of the dark gray bar at the top of the Store page (refer to Figure 4-2). The App Store page appears, as shown in Figure 4-5.

Figure 4-5: Find iPod touch apps in the App Store section of the iTunes Store.

Click an app's icon to go to the information page for that app, which may also contain reviews and a slideshow depicting the app in all its glory. The information page offers the Buy App button (to purchase and download a commercial app), or the Free App button (to download a free app). Click the Buy App or Free App button to download the app to your iTunes library.

Downloaded apps appear in the Apps section of your iTunes library — click Apps in the Library section of the source pane to see their icons.

When an app you downloaded is updated, iTunes informs you — the message Update Available appears at the bottom of the Apps section with an arrow that links you to the My Apps Update page in the iTunes Store, with icons of the apps to update. Click the Get Update button next to each app to download the update, which automatically replaces the previous version of the app. (You also get notified in the App Store app on your iPod touch — see the later section, "Updating apps you've downloaded," for details.)

Going Online with Your iPod touch

As with many other iPod touch apps, you need to connect to the Internet to use the iTunes Store and App Store apps. The iPod touch can join any Wi-Fi network (such as one you set up at home, or a Wi-Fi network at work, or Wi-Fi hotspots around the world). Wi-Fi networks connect to an Internet Service Provider (such as your cable or DSL service at home or work). Although some public Wi-Fi networks are free, others require logging in first, and still others require logging in and supplying a credit card number. Still others are detected but locked — if you select a locked network, a dialog appears asking for a password.

If you don't have Wi-Fi at home but you do have a broadband Internet connection (such as cable or DSL), I recommend buying an AirPort Express or AirPort Extreme, available in the Apple Store — you can then connect your Internet connection to the AirPort to extend Internet access over Wi-Fi throughout your home.

Turning Wi-Fi on or off

To turn on Wi-Fi, choose Settings➪Wi-Fi from the Home screen to display the Wi-Fi Networks screen, and tap the Off button for the Wi-Fi setting (tap it again to turn it off).

When Wi-Fi is turned on, your iPod touch detects and automatically acquires a Wi-Fi signal you've used before, or it can detect one or more signals in the area and present them in a list for you to choose. The list of available Wi-Fi networks appears below the Wi-Fi setting, as shown in Figure 4-6.

If your iPod touch isn't already connected to Wi-Fi, it's set by default to look for networks and ask whether you want to join them whenever you use something that requires the network (such as Safari, Weather, YouTube, Mail, and so on). You can stop your iPod touch from looking and asking: Scroll down to the end of the list of Wi-Fi networks on the Wi-Fi Networks screen and then tap the On button for the Ask to Join Networks option to turn it off. You can still join networks manually, but you won't be interrupted with requests to join networks.

Figure 4-6: Enable Wi-Fi and then choose a Wi-Fi network.

You should turn off Wi-Fi if you're not using it to save battery power and to keep your iPod touch from automatically receiving e-mail. Choose Settings➪Wi-Fi and then tap the On button for the Wi-Fi setting to turn it off.

Choosing a Wi-Fi network

You can scroll the list of networks in the Wi-Fi Networks screen to choose one. (Refer to Figure 4-6.) You can scroll quickly by flicking your finger or scroll slowly by dragging up or down, but however you scroll, you choose a Wi-Fi network by tapping its name. Networks are named by their administrators. (If you set up your own home Wi-Fi, you get to name yours whatever you want.)

When connected to a Wi-Fi network, your iPod touch displays the Wi-Fi icon in the status bar at the top of the display, which also indicates the connection strength — the more bars you see, the stronger the connection.

If a lock icon appears next to the Wi-Fi network name (refer to Figure 4-6), it means the network is locked and you need a password. When you select a locked network, the iPod touch displays an Enter Password screen and the onscreen keyboard. Tap out the password using the keyboard. (For details on how to use the onscreen keyboard, see Chapter 2.) Tap Join to join the network or tap Cancel in the upper-right corner to cancel joining.

To join a Wi-Fi network that requires either a credit card or an account for you to log in, select the network and then use Safari to open the network's Web page. (For more on using Safari, see Chapter 10.) The first Web page you see is typically the log-in page for the service (for example, a commercial Wi-Fi service or a hotel service).

Your iPod touch remembers most Wi-Fi connections and their passwords, and automatically uses one when it detects it within your range. If you've used multiple Wi-Fi networks in the same location, it picks the last one you used.

You can also *forget* a network — such as a paid or closed Wi-Fi service that somehow got hold of your iPod touch and won't let you move on to other Web pages without typing a password. See Chapter 15 for the details about how to forget a network.

Shopping with Your iPod touch

The entire iTunes Store and App Store are available right at your fingertips on your iPod touch. You can search for, browse, and preview content; make purchases; and download content and apps directly to your iPod touch.

Whatever you buy on your iPod touch is automatically copied to your iTunes library the next time you synchronize it with your computer, as I describe in Chapter 5.

Be sure to set up an iTunes Store account first if you don't already have one, as I describe earlier in this chapter — and you'll need to remember your password. To download content and apps directly to your iPod touch, you can set up your iPod touch with iTunes, which basically means signing in to your iTunes Store account in iTunes on your computer, and then syncing your iPod touch to iTunes as I describe in Chapter 5. After doing that once, you shouldn't have to bother with it again, and you'll be able to download items from the iTunes Store and App Store on your iPod touch from then on. All you need to do is enter the password for your iTunes Store account when prompted.

You can also create or sign into one or more iTunes Store accounts directly from your iPod touch, and view your account information: choose Settings⇨Store from the Home screen. To sign into an existing account, tap Sign In and type your account name and password. If your iPod touch is already synced with your account, the View Account button appears in place of Sign In — tap View Account to see account information. To create one or more accounts directly on your iPod touch, tap Create New Account. Confirm your country or region and touch Next. Tap Agree to the terms of service and then enter the information on the New Account screen with the onscreen keyboard. (The information you need to supply is the same information shown in the "Setting up an iTunes Store account" section, earlier in this chapter.) Tap Next to continue through the setup screens to finish setting up your account.

Browsing and downloading content

To go to the iTunes Store on an iPod touch, tap the iTunes icon on the Home screen. The store screen appears with Music, Videos, Ping, Search, and More icons along the bottom. Here's the lowdown on the icons:

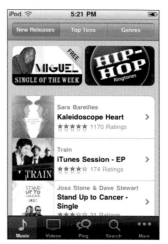

Figure 4-7: Browse the iTunes Store on an iPod touch.

- ✔ **Tap the Music icon** to see featured music, new releases, and store recommendations, as shown in Figure 4-7. The screen displays New Releases, Top Tens, and Genres buttons along the top. To search through genres, tap the Genres button and choose a genre. Tap the Top Tens button to see a list of the top ten choices in different genres. Choose iTunes in the Top Tens list to see the top ten songs throughout the iTunes Store. Tap Music in the top-left corner to return to the previous Music screen.

- ✔ **Tap the Videos icon** and the screen displays Movies, TV Shows, and Music Videos buttons along the top. Tap Movies to see new movie releases; TV Shows to see new and noteworthy TV shows; or Music Videos to see the hottest music videos in the iTunes Store.

- ✔ **Tap the Ping icon** to sign in and use the Ping social network for music. To find out more about Ping, see the latest edition of my other book, *iPod & iTunes For Dummies.*

- ✔ **Tap the Search icon** to search the store and then tap the entry field to bring up the onscreen keyboard. Type the search term and tap the Search button to search the store.

- ✔ **Tap the More icon** and then either select Podcasts to select podcasts, Audiobooks to buy audio books, iTunes U to download learning content, or Downloads to see the progress of your downloads from the store.

If this is your first time to the store on your iPod touch, the Music section appears with New Releases in a scrollable list. Tap any song to hear a preview. To buy and download a song, tap the button with the price tag. Enter your password and tap OK.

You can similarly preview and buy videos — tap the video, then tap the Preview button to see a preview, and tap the Buy (with price tag) button to buy it and download it.

After selecting a podcast, a list of episodes appears. Tap the Free button (or Buy button for paid podcasts) next to an episode, enter your password, and then tap OK to start downloading the podcast episode.

Purchased and downloaded items are added to a Purchased playlist on your iPod touch, and they're included in your Purchased playlist in iTunes as well as in a special Purchased on *YourDeviceName* playlist. iTunes automatically syncs items downloaded on your iPod touch to your iTunes library when you connect it to your computer so that you have a backup.

Some albums offer bonus content, such as liner notes, which are downloaded to your iTunes library on your computer, but not to your iPod touch. Also note that an alert appears on your iPod touch if you've previously purchased one or more songs from an album. Tap Buy if you want to purchase the entire album, or tap Cancel if you want to buy the remaining songs on the album individually.

If you lose your network connection or turn off your iPod touch while downloading, the download pauses and then resumes when you reestablish Wi-Fi. If you go back to your computer, iTunes can complete the download operation to your iTunes library. To make sure you received all downloads to your iPod touch, use iTunes on your computer and choose Store⇨Check for Available Downloads.

Browsing and downloading apps

Tap the App Store icon on the Home screen to grab some apps. The Store screen appears with Featured, Categories, Top 25, Search, and Update icons along the bottom of the screen. The following list tells you what's what when it comes to the icons:

  ✔ **Tap the Featured icon** for featured apps. You can see what's hot, based on downloads, by tapping the What's Hot button at the top. For the newest apps, tap the New button, as shown in Figure 4-8. To see App Store recommendations based on apps you already own, tap the Genius button in the top-right corner, tap Turn On Genius if it isn't already on, and then tap Use Existing Account (meaning your iTunes Store account), or Create New Account (to set up an account), or Cancel. See Chapter 7 for details about using the Genius feature.

✔ **Tap Categories** to browse by category, and then tap a category, such as Games, to see a list of all games by popularity.

✔ **Tap the Top 25 icon** and then tap Top Paid to see the top 25 paid apps by popularity, or tap Top Free to see the top 25 free apps.

✔ **Tap the Search icon** to search the store, and tap the entry field to bring up the onscreen keyboard. Type the search term and tap Search to search the store. Suggestions pop up right away; for example, if you search for *Tony's Tips* in the App Store, my app, Tony's Tips for iPhone Users Manual, appears in the list of suggestions.

Figure 4-8: Browse featured apps in the App Store on an iPod touch.

✔ **Tap the Updates icon** . . . wait, forget I said that. I cover that icon in the *next* section, so check that out if you want details.

To view information and download an app, tap the app in the list that appears after tapping the Featured, Categories, Top 25, or Search icon. You can then scroll the display to see more information about the app.

To download an app, tap the Price button (for a paid app) or Free button (for a free app). The Price or Free button changes to the Install button. Tap Install and then enter your password and tap OK.

The iPod touch displays the Home screen with the icon for the new app as it loads. As soon as the Loading message is replaced by the name of the app, the icon is ready to be tapped.

Updating apps you've downloaded

The App Store on your iPod touch notifies you if any of your apps have been updated — a number appears in the App Store icon. You should update an app when an update is available because updates fix bugs and introduce new features you may want.

Tap the More icon at the bottom–right corner of the App Store screen, and then tap Updates to see the list of updated apps. To update an app, tap the app in the list to see the app's information screen and then tap the Update button. The Update button changes to the Install button. Tap Install and then enter your password and tap OK.

The update replaces the previous version of the app as it loads into your iPod touch. As soon as the Loading message is replaced by the name of the app, the app is ready to be tapped.

Capacity								Capacity							
29.38 GB	Audio	Video	Photos	Apps	Other			8 GB	Audio	Video	Photos	Apps	Other	Free
	23.07 GB	2.92 GB	96.9 MB	381.9 MB	337.2 MB				23.07 GB	2.92 GB	96.9 MB	381.9 MB	337.2 MB	2.61 GB

5

Syncing Your Content and Apps

In This Chapter

▶ Synchronizing your iPod touch with your iTunes Store account

▶ Synchronizing your iTunes library with your iPod touch

▶ Copying songs and videos directly to, or deleting them from, your iPod touch

*S*ynchronizing your iPod touch with iTunes means automatically copying content and iPod touch-compatible apps to your iPod touch. Syncing also keeps your iPod touch up-to-date with your iTunes library, so that if you change song information or a playlist in iTunes, the changes are also made to your iPod touch if you sync that song or playlist with the iPod touch.

The sync operation also keeps your computer's iTunes library up-to-date with items downloaded from the iTunes Store or App Store directly to your iPod touch. Not only that, but the content you obtain from the online stores with one Apple account — either using iTunes or downloading directly to your iPod touch — can be synced with all the iPads, iPods, and iPhones you have set up with that account, at no extra cost.

If you make changes to your iTunes library after syncing the iPod touch, those changes are automatically made in the iPod touch when you sync again. Your iPod touch mirrors as much of the content of your iTunes library as will fit, making assumptions if the entire library won't fit.

The full, everything-but-the-kitchen-sync approach works well if your combined iTunes library and photo library are small enough to fit in their entirety on your iPod touch. For example, if your iTunes and photo libraries combined are less than 60GB and you have a 64GB iPod touch, sync everything. (You can see the size of your iTunes library in GB, or *gigabytes*, at the bottom of the iTunes window in the center.) Syncing everything copies your entire library, and it's just as fast as copying individual items (if not faster) because you don't have to select the items to copy.

If your libraries are larger than your iPod touch, or you want to leave room in your iPod touch for new downloads, you can make decisions about which parts of your iTunes and photo libraries to sync. You can select options to synchronize music, TV shows, movies, and so on. For example, you can copy all your songs and audio books, but only some of your TV shows, none of your movies, and only the podcasts you haven't heard yet.

This chapter also describes how to copy songs, videos, podcasts, and audio books directly to your iPod touch using the manual method. You can even combine automatic syncing with manual methods to build your iPod touch library as you see fit.

Syncing with Your iTunes Library and Account

You can automatically sync your iPod touch with your iTunes Store account information using iTunes (you can also set the account up by hand with your iPod touch, as I describe in Chapter 4). To make sure your iPod touch is set with your iTunes Store account information, sign in first to the iTunes Store, and then sync your iPod touch.

After syncing your iPod touch, iTunes copies anything you downloaded from Apple's online stores to your iPod touch back to your iTunes library — that way you don't lose any media if, heaven forbid, something happens to your iPod touch.

Follow these steps to sync your iPod touch with iTunes:

1. **With iTunes running, visit the iTunes Store and sign in to your account.**

   You don't have to buy anything; just signing in to the store provides all the info you need to sync your iPod touch with the iTunes Store account. (If you haven't set up your iTunes Store account yet, flip back to Chapter 4, do the deed, and then sign in by clicking the Sign In tab in the upper-right area of the iTunes window.) When you're signed in to an iTunes Store account, the account name appears in place of the Sign In tab.

2. **Connect the iPod touch and select Its name when it appears in the Devices section of the source pane.**

   iTunes displays the iPod touch sync options to the right of the source pane, with the Summary tab selected. (The other tabs are Apps, Ringtones, Music, Movies, TV Shows, Podcasts, Books, Photos, and Info.) The Summary page shows the iPod touch capacity — how much space is occupied, and how much is still free. The capacity changes as you change sync options to reflect how much space would be occupied after syncing. (See Figure 5-1.)

Figure 5-1: The iPod touch Summary page in iTunes offers sync options.

3. **If the iPod touch isn't already synchronizing, click the Sync button in the bottom-right corner to synchronize it.**

   Most likely your iPod touch is already set to automatically synchronize with iTunes after connecting it. After clicking the Sync button (or if iTunes is automatically syncing), the iTunes status pane tells you that iTunes is syncing the iPod touch. If you haven't made any sync selections, the default is to copy everything in your iTunes library to your iPod touch.

   If your iPod touch isn't set to automatically synchronize, or even if synchronization is going on, you can select content to sync, as I describe later in this chapter.

4. **Wait for the synchronization to finish and then click the eject button next to the iPod touch name in the source pane.**

   Wait until the status pane (at the top) displays that the sync is complete.

5. **Disconnect your iPod touch from your computer.**

   That's it. Your iPod touch is now synchronized.

Syncing Everything

After connecting the iPod touch to iTunes, you can copy everything at once by following Steps 2–5 in the previous section (refer to Figure 5-1).

Photo albums you've organized in a photo library (using a program such as iPhoto on a Mac or Adobe Photoshop Elements in Windows) can also be synced. See Chapter 9 for details.

If your iTunes library is too large to fit on your iPod touch, iTunes decides which songs and albums to include by using the ratings that you set for each song. (To find out how to set ratings, see Chapter 15.) If your iPod touch already has photos on it, iTunes asks whether you want to delete them to gain more space. After clicking Yes or No, iTunes tries its best to fit everything. If it has to cut something, though, it skips copying new photos and displays the message Some Photos Were Not Copied.

If you're still short of space even after skipping photos, iTunes displays a warning about the lack of free space, and it asks whether you want to disable podcast synchronization and let iTunes create a selection of songs in a playlist based on ratings and playback counts in iTunes. (A *playlist* is a list of the items that you want in the sequence that you want to play them — you can use playlists to organize your music playback experience.)

- ✔ **If you click Yes,** iTunes creates a new playlist (titled "*Your device name* Selection," as in "My iPod touch Selection") and displays a message telling you so. Click OK, and iTunes synchronizes your iPod touch using the new playlist. iTunes also sets your iPod touch to synchronize music automatically by playlist, as I describe in the next section.
- ✔ **If you click No,** iTunes updates automatically until it fills your iPod touch without creating the playlist.

From that point on, your iPod touch synchronizes with your iTunes library automatically, right after you connect it to your computer. If you add or delete content in your iTunes library, that content is added or deleted in the iPod touch when you sync again.

You can squeeze more songs onto an iPod touch if you convert them to a lower-bit-rate format — and you can do this on the fly while syncing (although it can dramatically increase sync time; large libraries might need to be synced overnight). Select the Convert Higher Bit Rate Songs to 128 kbps AAC option (refer to Figure 5-1). As a result, the songs take up less space on the iPod touch than they occupy in your iTunes library.

By the way, to find out more about importing music from CDs, setting the music format and bit rate, and creating playlists, consult the latest edition of *iPod & iTunes For Dummies* (by yours truly).

During the synchronization process, iTunes also performs a backup of the sync settings and other settings for your iPod touch from the last time you synchronized it.

To prevent an iPod touch from automatically synchronizing, press ⌘-Option (Mac) or Ctrl-Alt (Windows) while you connect the device, and then keep pressing until the iPod touch name appears in the iTunes source pane. You can then change the iPod touch sync setting to manually manage music and videos, as I describe later in this chapter.

If you connect an iPod touch previously linked to another computer to *your* computer, iTunes displays a message warning you that clicking Yes replaces the iPod touch content with the content from your computer's library. If you don't want to change the iPod's content, click No. If you click Yes, iTunes erases the iPod touch and synchronizes it with your computer's library. To avoid this warning, first set the iPod touch sync settings to manually manage music and videos.

Choosing What to Sync

If you have a massive music library, one that would never fit on even the most capacious of iPod touches, you can go the selective route, choosing which content to automatically sync with your iTunes library. By synchronizing selectively, you can still make your iPod touch match at least a subset of your iTunes library. If you make changes to that subset in iTunes, those changes are automatically made in the device when you synchronize again.

Syncing everything but the kitchen

You can decide which items you *don't* want to synchronize and simply not include them by first *deselecting* them one by one in your iTunes library. (If you have a large iTunes library, this may take some time — you may find it easier to synchronize by playlists, artists, and genres, as I show you later in this section.)

By default, all content items are selected — a check mark appears in the check box next to the item. To deselect an item in your iTunes library, click the check box next to the item so that the check mark disappears. To reselect an item, just click the check box again.

You can quickly select (or deselect) an entire album by showing the Browser (choose View➪Column Browser➪Show Column Browser) and selecting the album. Then press ⌘ (Mac) or Ctrl (Windows) while selecting (or deselecting) a single song in the album in the list pane.

After you deselect the items you don't want to transfer, connect your iPod touch to your computer and select its name when it appears in the Devices section of the source pane (refer to Figure 5-1). Then select the Sync Only Checked Songs and Videos option. After selecting a new option, iTunes replaces the Sync button in the bottom-left corner with the Revert and Apply buttons (for a sneak preview of these buttons, see Figure 5-2). Click Apply and continue with Steps 3–5 in the earlier section, "Syncing with Your iTunes Library and Account," or click Revert to go back to the original setting.

iTunes restarts synchronization and deletes from the iPod touch any items in the library that are deselected, to save space, before adding back in the items in the iTunes library that are selected. That means the items you deselected are now *gone* from your iPod touch — replaced by whatever items were selected. Of course, the items are still in your iTunes library.

Getting picky about playlists, artists, and genres

You can include just the items that are defined in playlists, including Genius playlists, and/or just specific artists. Syncing by playlists, artists, and genres is a great way of syncing vast amounts of music without syncing the entire library.

To find out more about creating smart and Genius playlists, consult *iPod & iTunes For Dummies* by yours truly.

For example, you can include all rock, folk, blues, and/or jazz albums (selecting by genre) and select some playlists you've created in advance, along with everything by specific artists (such as Frank Zappa, who doesn't fit into these genres).

After connecting your iPod touch to your computer, select its name when it appears in the Devices section of the source pane (refer to Figure 5-1). Then click the Music tab of the sync options. (You may have to click Apply first to apply the changes you made to other sync options pages.) The Music sync options page appears, as shown in Figure 5-2.

Figure 5-2: Synchronize your iPod with only selected playlists, artists, and genres (scroll down to see genres).

By default, the Entire Music Library option is selected, unless you're manually managing music, as I describe later in this chapter. To change your sync options, select the Sync Music check box. If you are manually managing music, a message appears asking if you're sure that you now want to sync music — and stating that all content already on your iPod touch will be replaced. Click the Sync Music button to go ahead (or Cancel to cancel), which returns you to the Music sync options page.

To choose playlists, artists, and genres to sync, click the Selected Playlists, Artists, and Genres option at the top of the Music sync options page (shown in Figure 5-2). You can then select each playlist from the Playlists list, each artist from the Artists list, and (if you scroll down) each genre from the Genres list. You can choose any number of playlists, artists, and genres. (In Figure 5-2, I selected the `Donovan_trips`, `Doobie_bros_albums`, and `driving south` playlists, along with Joe Cocker and Ry Cooder in the Artists column.)

Finally, click the Apply button to apply changes (or Revert to cancel), and then click the Sync button if synchronization hasn't already started automatically. iTunes copies only what you've selected in the Playlists, Artists, and Genres sections of the Music sync options page.

You can also automatically fill up the rest of your iPod touch free space with random songs (after syncing your selected playlists, artists, and genres) by selecting the Automatically Fill Free Space with Songs option. iTunes randomly chooses the music, as I describe in the "Syncing Everything" section, earlier in this chapter.

Picking podcast episodes and books

You can get picky about which podcast episodes should be copied over during synchronization, and even which parts of audio books. If you've installed Apple's iBooks app, you can also choose which electronic books (e-books) to sync and use with it.

After syncing podcast episodes, audio books, or e-books, you can continue listening or reading on your iPod touch from where you left off on your computer or other synchronized device. For example, if you were reading an e-book using the iBooks app on an iPad, and synced the iPad with iTunes, and then synced your iPod touch with iTunes, you can continue reading with the iBooks app on your iPod touch from where you left off on the iPad.

Clicking the Podcasts tab of the sync pages presents options for choosing podcast episodes to include.

Connect your iPod touch to your computer, and select its name when it appears in the Devices section of the source pane (refer to Figure 5-1). Then click the Podcasts tab. The Podcasts sync options page appears, as shown in Figure 5-3. Click the Sync Podcasts option at the top.

The Podcast sync options let you choose unplayed or recently added episodes (as shown in Figure 5-3). Select the Automatically Include _____ Episodes Of _____ check box; choose a modifier from the first pop-up menu, such as All Unplayed or 10 Most Recent; and then choose All Podcasts or Selected Podcasts from the second pop-up menu. If you choose Selected Podcasts, you can select a podcast in the Podcasts column below these options and then select specific episodes in the Episodes column (which may already be selected depending on your choices in the pop-up menus).

Figure 5-3: Sync the ten most recent episodes of selected podcasts and a few episodes of another podcast.

When you're set, click the Apply button to apply changes, and then click the Sync button if synchronization hasn't already started automatically. (If you're done syncing, wait for the sync to finish and then click the eject button next to the iPod touch name in the source pane to eject the iPod touch.)

Clicking the Books tab of the sync pages presents options for choosing audio books. If you have the iBooks app installed on your iPod touch, you also have options for choosing e-books. To sync books, follow these steps:

1. **Connect your iPod touch to your computer and then select its name when it appears in the Devices section of the source pane (refer to Figure 5-1).**

2. **Click the Books tab.**

   The Books sync options page appears with options for syncing audio books, and additional options for syncing e-books if you have iBooks installed on your iPod touch.

3. **To sync audio books, click the Sync Audiobooks option, and then click one of the following sync options:**

   - Choose All Audiobooks to sync all of them.

   - Choose Selected Audiobooks, and then choose entire audio books in the Audiobooks column on the left, or select an audio book on the left and then choose specific parts of the audio book in the right column.

4. **To sync e-books for use with iBooks, click the Sync Books option, and then click one of the following sync options:**

   - Choose All Books to sync all of them.

   - Choose Selected Books and then click the check boxes next to the books you want to sync.

5. **After choosing sync options, click Apply to apply changes, and then click the Sync button if synchronization hasn't already started automatically.**

6. **Wait for the sync to finish and then click the eject button next to the iPod touch name in the source pane to eject the iPod touch.**

   Always wait until the iTunes status pane (at the top) tells you that the sync is completed.

Choosing movies and TV shows

Movies and TV shows take up a lot of space, so if you limit the movies and TV episodes you synchronize with your iPod touch, you gain extra space for more music, audio books, podcasts, and photos.

To get choosy about movies, connect your iPod touch to your computer and select its name when it appears in the Devices section of the source pane (refer to Figure 5-1). Then click the Movies tab of the sync options. The Movies sync options page appears, as shown in Figure 5-4.

Select the Sync Movies check box (as shown in Figure 5-4). Select the Automatically Include ____ Movies check box and then choose a modifier from the pop-up menu, such as All, 1 Most Recent, All Unwatched, or 10 Most Recent Unwatched. If you choose any option other than All, you can then select specific movies from the list below the option.

To pick only the TV episodes you want, click the TV Shows tab of the sync options. (You may have to click the Apply button first, to apply the changes you made to other sync options pages.) The TV Shows sync options page appears, as shown in Figure 5-5.

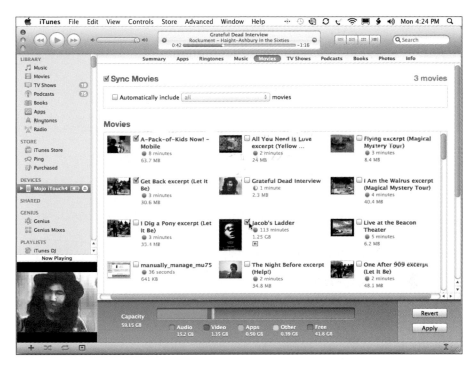

Figure 5-4: Sync the most recent movie and the selected movie.

Select the Automatically Include ____ Episodes Of ____ check box, choose a modifier from the first pop-up menu, such as All, All Unwatched, or 5 Most Recent, and then choose All Shows or Selected Shows from the second pop-up menu. If you choose Selected Shows, or deselect the Automatically Include option (as I do in Figure 5-5), you can select shows in the Shows column below these options, and then select specific episodes in the Episodes column.

When you're set, click the Apply button to apply changes, and then click the Sync button if synchronization hasn't already started automatically. (If you're done syncing, wait for the sync to finish and then click the eject button next to the iPod touch name in the source pane to eject the iPod touch.)

To find out about converting videos for use in iTunes and the iPod touch, visit the tips section of my Web site at www.tonybove.com.

Figure 5-5: Sync selected TV show episodes.

Syncing and arranging apps

Your iPod touch is set by default to sync all the iPod touch-compatible apps in your iTunes library. iTunes automatically skips any app that doesn't belong on the device (such as an iPad app when you are syncing an iPod touch), and displays a warning about any other app it skips for other reasons (such as not having a proper authorization code). Because most apps don't take up a lot of space, I recommend simply letting iTunes do its thing, syncing all the apps that belong on the device.

However, you can selectively choose apps to synchronize. Follow these steps:

1. **Connect your iPod touch to your computer, and select its name when it appears in the Devices section of the source pane (refer to Figure 5-1).**

2. **Click the Apps tab of the sync options.**

   The Apps sync options page appears, as shown in Figure 5-6.

Figure 5-6: Sort the list of apps and then select apps to sync.

3. **Click the Sync Apps option if it is not already turned on.**

4. **From the list box on the left (refer to Figure 5-6), click the app's check box for each app that you want to synchronize.**

   You can scroll the list box to see all your apps — and you can click the Sort button at the top to toggle sorting the list by Name, Kind, Category, Date, or Size. For example, in Figure 5-6, I am switching from Sort by Kind to Sort by Category.

Although you can rearrange and delete apps on your iPod touch Home screens directly, as I describe in meticulous detail in Chapter 2, you can also do this in iTunes while syncing. Click the thumbnail image of any Home screen on the far-right side of the Apps sync options page to view the app icons on that Home screen, and then click and drag the app icons to the positions you want. You can even drag an app from the list box to its precise position on a Home screen to sync that app.

To organize apps into folders, drag an app icon on top of another in the Home screen on the right side of the Apps options page. For example, in Figure 5-7, I dragged the NPR Addict app over the NY Times app in Home screen 5 to create the News folder, which I can then rename if I want to.

Figure 5-7: Organize apps into folders on Home screens.

After choosing sync options, click the Apply button to apply changes, and then click the Sync button if synchronization hasn't already started automatically. (If you're done syncing, wait for the sync to finish and then click the eject button next to the iPod touch name in the source pane to eject the iPod touch.)

Syncing ringtones

You can purchase ringtones from the iTunes Store using iTunes on your computer, and synchronize them with your iPod touch to use with FaceTime calls. To selectively choose ringtones for your iPod touch, follow these steps:

1. **Connect your iPod touch to your computer, and select its name when it appears in the Devices section of the source pane (refer to Figure 5-1).**

2. **Click the Ringtones tab of the sync options.**

   The sync options appear for ringtones.

3. **Click Sync Ringtones at the top of the page if the option is not already turned on.**

4. **Click the All Ringtones option, or click the Selected Ringtones option, and then select each ringtone to synchronize in the Ringtones box.**

   You can scroll the list box to see all your ringtones. Click the check box to select one.

5. **Click Apply to apply changes, and then click the Sync button if synchronization hasn't started automatically.**

6. **Wait for the sync to finish, and then click the Eject button next to the iPod touch name in the source pane to eject the iPod touch.**

   iTunes erases any previous ringtones in the iPod touch and copies only the ringtones you selected in Step 4.

Manually Managing Music and Videos

If your entire library is too big for your iPod touch, you may want to copy individual items directly. By setting your iPod touch to manually manage music and videos, you can add content to your iPod touch directly via iTunes, and you can delete content as well. You can even copy some songs or videos from another computer's iTunes library without deleting any content from your iPod touch.

To set your iPod touch to manually manage music and videos, first connect your iPod touch to your computer. Then follow these steps:

1. **Select the iPod touch name in the Devices section of the iTunes source pane.**

   After selecting the name, the Summary page appears, displaying the iPod touch sync options (refer to Figure 5-1).

2. **Select the Manually Manage Music and Videos option near the bottom of the Summary page.**

   iTunes displays a message warning you that manually managing music and videos also requires manually ejecting the iPod touch before each disconnect.

3. **Click OK for the warning and click the Apply button to apply the change.**

Don't disconnect your iPod touch while managing music and videos manually. You have to eject it first, as spelled out in the next section. If you don't, you may find that it doesn't work properly and needs to be restored, as I describe in Chapter 14.

That album is just a drag

After turning on the option to manually manage music and videos, you can select and drag music and video to your iPod touch name in the source pane. You can drag the media from its section in the iTunes library or from an existing playlist, or drag an entire playlist. To do so, follow these steps:

1. **In the iTunes source pane, select the source of your media.**

   You might select Music in the Library section, for instance, or a playlist in the library.

   You can select music in your library using List, Album List, Grid, or Cover Flow view (see Chapter 4 for browsing details), or select songs in a playlist.

2. **Drag items (such as an album) directly from your iTunes library or playlist over the iPod touch name in the Devices section of the source pane.**

   You can drag individually selected songs (as I do in Figure 5-8) or an entire album from Cover Flow view, Grid view, Album List view, or List view. When you drag an album cover from the Album List view, or drag the album title from the column browser, all the songs in the album are copied. You can even drag a playlist name from the Playlists section of the source pane to the iPod touch name in the Devices section, and all the songs associated with the playlist copy along with the playlist itself.

3. **Wait for the copying to finish, and then click the eject button next to the iPod touch name in the source pane to eject the iPod touch.**

   Always wait until the iTunes status pane (at the top) tells you that the copying is completed, then click the eject button

4. **Disconnect your iPod touch from your computer.**

Delete to make room for more

When you manually manage music and videos, you can also delete content from the iPod touch. Set the option to manually manage music and videos (if it isn't set that way already) and then follow these steps:

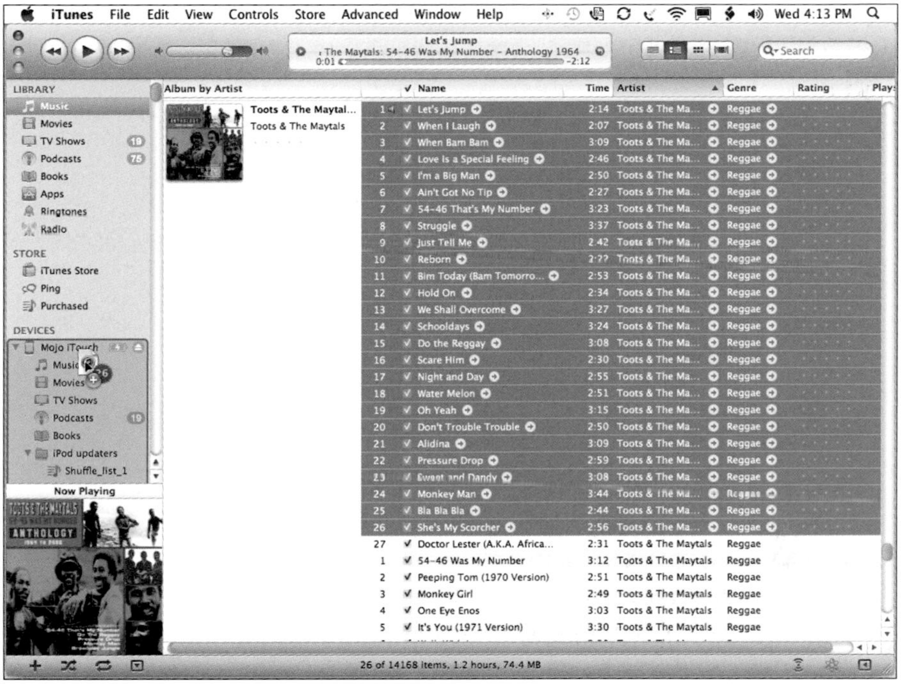

Figure 5-8: Drag songs to an iPod touch (Mojo iTouch).

1. **In the source pane, click the triangle to the left of the iPod touch name to expand its library.**

   The iPod touch library appears in the source pane with Music, Movies, TV Shows, and other sections, followed by playlists. The library is indented underneath the iPod touch name.

2. **Click any content type in the iPod touch library to see the items.**

   The content items appear in the iTunes list pane to the right of the source pane.

3. **Select an item and press Delete/Backspace or choose Edit⇨Delete.**

   iTunes displays a warning to make sure you want to do this; click OK to go ahead or Cancel to stop. If you want to delete a playlist, select the playlist underneath the iPod touch name in the source pane and then press Delete or choose Edit⇨Delete.

Like in the iTunes library, if you delete a playlist, the songs listed in the play-list aren't deleted. They're still on your iPod touch unless you delete the songs directly from the iPod touch library.

Autofill it up

You can also automatically fill your iPod touch while managing music and videos manually: Autofill randomly picks songs from your entire iTunes library or from a playlist you select in the iTunes Source pane.

Set the option to manually manage music and videos (if it isn't set that way already). Then follow these steps:

1. **In the source pane, click the triangle to the left of the iPod touch name to expand its library.**

   The iPod touch library appears in the source pane (Music, Movies, TV Shows, and other sections), followed by playlists. The library is indented underneath the iPod touch name.

2. **Select Music under the iPod touch name in the Devices section of the source pane.**

   The music on your iPod touch appears in the list pane, along with the Autofill pane along the bottom, as shown in Figure 5-9.

3. **Choose your source of music in the Autofill From pop-up menu.**

   Choose either one of your playlists, or choose Genius (as I did in Figure 5-9 for my Genius selections — for details about Genius, see Chapter 7), Purchased (for all purchased music), or Music for the entire music library. If you choose a playlist, Autofill uses only the playlist as the source to pick random songs. After choosing your source of music, iTunes creates a playlist and displays it in the list pane.

4. **(Optional) Click the Settings button to set options and then click OK.**

   After you click the Settings button, the Autofill Settings dialog appears. You can choose to replace all the songs on the iPod touch, to pick songs randomly, and to pick only the best songs (if choosing randomly). If you don't select to replace all songs, iTunes adds the songs without replac-ing existing songs. Click OK to close the Autofill Settings dialog.

5. **Click the Autofill button to start copying songs.**

   iTunes copies the contents of the Autofill playlist to your iPod touch.

6. **Wait for the copy operation to finish and then click the eject button.**

   Always wait until the iTunes status pane (at the top) tells you that the copying is finished before clicking the eject button.

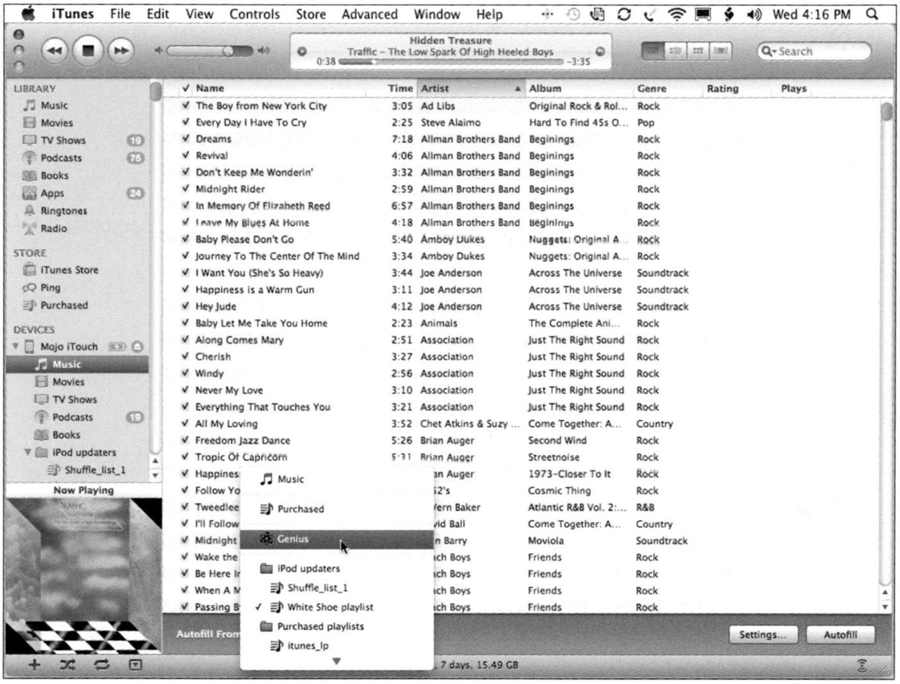

Figure 5-9: Autofill your iPod touch from an iTunes playlist.

You can click the Autofill button over and over to create different random playlists. When you get one you like, select all its contents and choose File⇨ New Playlist From Selection to create a new playlist that contains the songs generated by Autofill. The next time you connect your iPod touch, select this new playlist from the Autofill From pop-up menu and then click the Autofill button to load the music from the playlist to your iPod touch.

Exchange   **mobile**_me_   **6**   **YAHOO!**   **G**ᴍ**ail**

Syncing Your Day in the Life

* * *

In This Chapter

▶ Synchronizing e-mail, calendars, contacts, and bookmarks

▶ Using MobileMe to sync over the Internet

▶ Setting up e-mail accounts on your iPod touch

* * *

*Y*our iPod touch can take care of all aspects of your digital life: It can send and receive e-mail, keep track of your calendar and notes, sort your contacts, and save bookmarks to all your favorite Web sites while you browse them.

If you're a road warrior, you may want to fill up your iPod touch with your personal information. You can then go out into the world, conquer it, and bring back new or edited contacts, new events, and new Web site bookmarks, which you can then synchronize with your computer.

Organizing Your Personal Info

Where do I start? First, your iPod touch has no problem sending and receiving e-mail using the Mail application (as I describe in Chapter 11). It also offers the Contacts app to store contact info, the Calendar app to store events (see Chapter 13), the Notes app to take notes (see Chapter 2), and the Safari app to surf the Web with your bookmarks (see Chapter 10).

You can use iTunes to synchronize your iPod touch apps with the calendars, contacts, notes, e-mail accounts, and bookmarks you've already organized on your computer. With a little help from these apps, you'll soon have your schedule whipped into such shapc that it will be humming along like a finely tuned German automobile.

If you're a Mac user, you have it easy: You can use the free iCal and Address Book applications to manage your calendars and contacts, the free Mail application to manage e-mail and notes, and the free Safari Web browser to manage your bookmarks. All these applications are provided with Mac OS X. You can also sync contacts from Microsoft Entourage, Yahoo! Address Book, and Google Address Book, as well as sync calendars from Entourage.

If you're a Windows user, you can sync your contacts and e-mail accounts with Microsoft Outlook 2003 or 2007, Yahoo! Address Book and Yahoo! Mail, Google Address Book and Gmail, Windows Address Book (Outlook Express), AOL (e-mail only), or Vista Contacts. You can sync calendars and notes with Outlook and use Microsoft Internet Explorer or Apple Safari to manage bookmarks. The iPod touch can also use the Exchange ActiveSync protocol to sync e-mail, calendars, and contacts with Microsoft Exchange Server 2003 Service Pack 2, or Exchange Server 2007 Service Pack 1. For many e-mail accounts, the settings automatically appear, like magic.

If you signed up for Apple's MobileMe service (formerly the .Mac service, now www.me.com), you can automatically keep your iPod touch synchronized along with several computers, iPads, and iPhones, all at once, with the latest e-mail, bookmarks, calendar entries, and contacts, as I describe in the "Going MobileMe to Sync Your iPod touch" section, later in this chapter.

What's cool about cloud computing Web services like MobileMe, Microsoft Exchange, and Yahoo! Mail is that their e-mail services *push* e-mail messages to your computer and your iPod touch so that they arrive immediately and automatically. Other types of e-mail account services let you *fetch* e-mail from the server — you must first select the account in Mail on your iPod touch before your iPod touch can actually retrieve the e-mail. I show you how to use your push and fetch settings in Chapter 11.

You probably already know how to manage your calendar activities and your contacts on your computer. In fact, you're probably knee-deep in contacts, and your calendars look like they were drawn up in the West Wing. If not, visit the tips section of my Web site (www.tonybove.com) for advice on using MobileMe and on adding and editing contacts and calendar information on your Mac (with Address Book and iCal) or Windows computer (with Outlook).

Syncing Your Personal Info Using iTunes

You can sync your personal information between your computer and your iPod touch using iTunes, or using a push service such as MobileMe (if you purchase the MobileMe service) or Microsoft Exchange. Please note that you're not wedded to one method or the other — you can switch between iTunes and the push service any time you want.

MobileMe and Exchange get their write-ups in the next section, while this section tackles the iTunes method. To sync your iPod touch with contacts, calendars, e-mail accounts, notes, and bookmarks by using iTunes, follow these steps:

1. **Connect the iPod touch and select its name when it appears in the Devices section of the source pane.**

   iTunes displays the iPod touch sync options to the right of the source pane, with the Summary page (under the Summary tab) open.

2. **Click the Info tab in the top-right corner of the sync options.**

   The Info sync options page appears as shown in Figure 6-1, offering the Contacts, Calendars, Mail Accounts, Other (bookmarks and notes), and Advanced sections, which you have to scroll the page to see. (Only Contacts and part of Calendars are visible in Figure 6-1.)

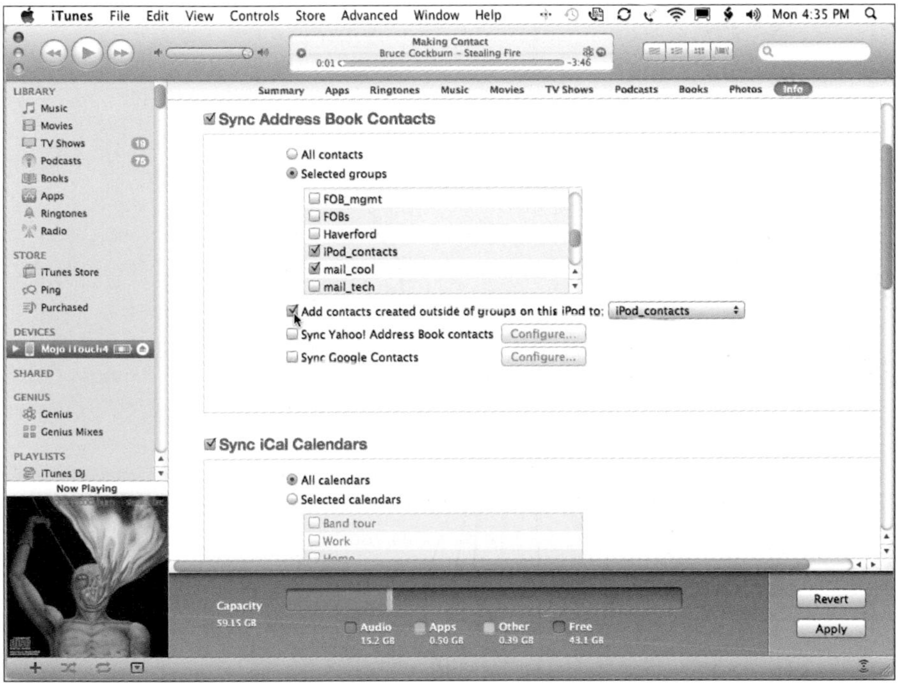

Figure 6-1: Sync contacts and calendars.

3. **Select the option to sync contacts:**

   - *On a Mac:* Select the Sync Address Book Contacts check box (refer to Figure 6-1). You can also sync with Yahoo! Address Book or Google Contacts — click the Configure button to enter your login information. An option to sync with Microsoft Entourage appears if you have the application on your Mac.

   - *On a Windows PC:* Select the Sync Contents With option and choose Yahoo! Address Book, Windows Address Book, Google Contacts, or Outlook from the pop-up menu.

4. **Select the All Contacts option or select the Selected Groups option and choose which groups to sync.**

   You can synchronize all contacts or just selected groups of contacts. To choose groups, select the check box next to each group in the list; scroll the list to see more groups.

   If you select groups, you can also select the Add Contacts Created Outside of Groups on this iPod To option, and choose a group for the new contacts you create on your iPod touch.

5. **Scroll the page and select the option to sync calendars.**

   - *On a Mac:* Select the Sync iCal Calendars check box (refer to Figure 6-1); an option to sync with Entourage also appears if you have it on your Mac.

   - *On a Windows PC:* Select the Sync Calendars With option and choose Outlook from the pop-up menu.

6. **Select the All Calendars option. (Alternatively, if you're using iCal with Mac OS X, select the Selected Calendars option and choose the calendars to synchronize.)**

   In Windows, you can synchronize all calendars with Outlook, but not selected calendars. With iCal on Mac OS X, you can synchronize all calendars or just those you select. To choose specific calendars, select the check box next to each calendar in the list.

   You can also set the Do Not Sync Events Older Than *xx* Days option, in which you can set the *xx* number of days (see the top of Figure 6-2 for this option, which is at the very bottom of the Calendars section).

7. **To sync e-mail accounts, scroll down to the Mail Accounts section and select the Sync Mail Accounts option.**

   Mail Accounts, as shown in Figure 6-2, appears below the Calendars section on the Info sync options page. On a Mac, select the Sync Mail Accounts option. On a Windows PC, choose Outlook or Outlook Express from the pop-up menu for the Sync Mail Accounts From option. After selecting the sync option, a list of e-mail accounts appears in the box below the option.

Figure 6-2: Sync e-mail accounts.

8. Choose the e-mail accounts you want to sync.

To choose accounts, select the check box next to each account in the list; scroll the list to see more e-mail accounts.

9. To sync Web bookmarks, scroll down to the Other section and select the Sync Bookmarks With option.

On a Mac running OS X, the option is Sync Safari Bookmarks; on a Windows PC, iTunes offers a pop-up menu to choose Internet Explorer or Safari.

10. To sync notes, select the Sync Notes With option in the Other section.

You can sync the notes you create in the Notes app (see Chapter 2) with the Mail application on a Mac, or with Outlook on a Windows PC. On a Mac, select the Sync Notes option; on a Windows PC, choose Outlook from the pop-up menu for the Sync Notes With option.

11. Click the Apply button to apply the changes. (Alternatively, click Revert to revert to the original settings.)

iTunes starts to synchronize your iPod touch.

12. **Wait for the sync to finish and then click the eject button next to the iPod touch name in the source pane to eject the iPod touch.**

Wait until the iTunes status pane (at the top) displays the message Sync is Complete before clicking the eject button.

After setting the sync options, every time you connect your iPod touch, iTunes automatically synchronizes it with these settings. Synchronizing an e-mail account to your iPod touch copies *only* the e-mail account setup information; the messages are retrieved by the iPod touch over the Internet.

If you select a calendar or a group of contacts to be synchronized and later want to remove that particular calendar or group of contacts, deselect the calendar (see the preceding Step 6) or the group (see the preceding Step 4) and then click Apply to resynchronize. iTunes synchronizes only the group of contacts and calendars selected, removing from the iPod touch any that aren't selected.

iTunes also offers Advanced options at the bottom of the Info page for syncing your iPod touch from scratch to replace all contacts, calendars, notes, or mail accounts. You can choose which ones you want to replace by selecting the check box next to each option. iTunes replaces the information once, during the next sync operation. After that operation, these Advanced options are automatically turned off.

Going MobileMe to Sync Your iPod touch

MobileMe synchronizes MobileMe e-mail accounts along with contacts, calendars, and bookmarks, on a Web server on the Internet — also known as *the cloud.* You can then keep your iPod touch synchronized to the cloud wirelessly, without having to connect it to your computer.

Your iPod touch can receive pushed e-mail, contacts, calendars, and bookmarks from the MobileMe cloud as long as your iPod touch is awake (meaning that the screen is on or it is connected to your computer or to a power adapter).

The place to start organizing your information is usually your computer. However, if you've already entered contacts and calendars on your iPod touch, sync the contacts and calendars on your iPod touch with iTunes first, as I describe earlier in the section "Syncing Your Personal Info Using iTunes." Then sync your computer with MobileMe, and then your iPod touch with MobileMe.

Make sure the information you synchronize the very first time to MobileMe is the correct, complete information. You should synchronize your primary source with MobileMe — typically your computer, which has the newest info — *before* synchronizing your iPod touch with MobileMe.

MobileMe first makes its appearance when you set up your iPod touch: An advertisement appears with buttons to try MobileMe. If you skipped the ad (like many people do), you can go to the Apple MobileMe setup page (www. apple.com/mobileme) and sign up for a free trial. After setting up your MobileMe account on a Mac or Windows PC, as described in the next sections, you turn on your MobileMe account on your iPod touch, as I describe in the section "Setting Up Mail Accounts on Your iPod touch."

Setting up on a Mac

Setting up MobileMe is easy on a Mac: When you sign in to MobileMe for the first time, MobileMe automatically configures Mac OS X Mail on your Mac to send and receive e-mail from your MobileMe account and to synchronize contacts from Address Book and calendars from iCal. If you already set up your iPod touch with a Mac and MobileMe service, automatic synchronization should already be set up on that Mac.

If not, you can set up a Mac to sync with MobileMe at any time. Follow these steps:

1. **Choose System Preferences from the Apple menu, choose MobileMe, click the Account tab, and sign in.**

2. **Click the Sync tab.**

   The Sync options for MobileMe appear, as shown in Figure 6-3.

3. **Select the Synchronize with MobileMe check box and then choose a sync interval from the pop-up menu. (Refer to Figure 6-3.)**

   For the most frequent updates, choose Automatically to sync with MobileMe every 15 minutes. You can instead choose Manual to sync only when you click the Sync Now button.

4. **Click the check boxes to select information to sync with MobileMe.**

   You can choose to sync just contacts, calendars, bookmarks, mail accounts, notes, or all of them.

5. **Click the Sync Now button if you chose Manual (otherwise syncing begins automatically).**

   The sync commences. (If you don't want to sync now, click Cancel Sync.) After it finishes, you can make sure your data has synced by going to www. me.com, logging in, clicking the MobileMe icon, and clicking the Contacts icon to see contacts and clicking the Calendar icon to see calendars.

Figure 6-3: Sync options for MobileMe on a Mac.

Setting up on Windows

Download and install on your PC the latest version of MobileMe Control Panel for Windows, available from `http://support.apple.com/ downloads`. MobileMe Control Panel is required to set up and manage MobileMe syncing and manage iDisk settings on a Windows PC.

To set up a Windows PC to sync with MobileMe or to check your sync settings or sync immediately, follow these steps:

1. **From the Windows Start menu, open Control Panel and choose MobileMe Control Panel.**

   The MobileMe panel appears with tabs along the top.

2. **Click the Account tab for the Account pane (if it isn't already visible) and log in with your MobileMe member name and password if you aren't already logged in.**

3. **Click the Sync tab.**

   The sync options appear, as shown in Figure 6-4.

4. Select the Sync with MobileMe check box and then select a sync interval.

For the most frequent updates, choose Automatically to sync with MobileMe every 15 minutes. You can instead choose Manual to sync only when you click the Sync Now button.

5. Select the check boxes to sync your contacts, calendars, and bookmarks, and then use the drop-down lists to choose which Windows applications you want to use when syncing with these items.

6. Click the Sync Now button.

The sync starts up. After it finishes, you can make sure your data has synced — go to www.me.com, log in, click the MobileMe icon, and click the Contacts icon to see contacts and click the Calendar icon to see calendars.

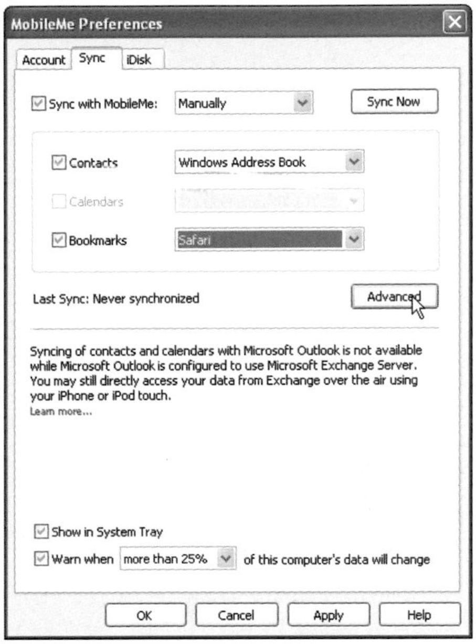

Figure 6-4: Sync options for MobileMe on a Windows PC.

When you sync upon a cloud

If your contacts or calendar entries show up in duplicate or triplicate on your iPod touch or computer, as if they were stuck inside of MobileMe with the memory blues again, you probably need to overwrite the data in the MobileMe cloud.

Selecting items to synchronize may not overwrite all the data in the cloud. To overwrite the data stored in the cloud with the data on your computer, open MobileMe (in System Preferences on a Mac, or Control Panel in Windows), click the Sync tab, and then click the Advanced button. (Refer to Figure 6-3 for a Mac, or Figure 6-4 for Windows.) Select the computer you are syncing from in the list at the top and then click Reset Sync Data.

In the dialog that appears, choose an option from the Replace pop-up menu:

- ✔ **On a Mac,** you can choose All Sync Info, Bookmarks, Calendars, or Contacts. (The other choices in the pop-up menu — Key Chains, Mail Accounts, and so on — don't copy over to the iPod touch, but are useful for keeping other computers synchronized.)

- ✔ **In Windows,** you can choose All Sync Info, Bookmarks, Calendars, or Contacts.

After choosing an option from the Replace pop-up menu, click the arrow underneath the Cloud icon to change the animation so that the data arrow points from the computer to the cloud. Finally, click Replace.

This action replaces the data in the MobileMe cloud with the data on your computer. You can also use these steps to go in reverse — replace the data on your computer with the data in MobileMe. To do this, click the arrow so that the animation points the arrow from the cloud to the computer.

Changes you make to contacts, calendars, and bookmarks in your iPod touch are synchronized to the Web server at www.me.com. You can also go to www.me.com and access your information directly with your Web browser.

Setting Up Mail Accounts on Your iPod touch

To set up a Mail account on your iPod touch — including a MobileMe e-mail account (with contacts, calendars, and bookmarks) or a Microsoft Exchange account — follow these steps:

1. **Choose Settings⇨Mail, Contacts, Calendars from the Home screen.**

   The Mail, Contacts, Calendars settings screen appears, with the Accounts section at the top, as shown in Figure 6-5 (left side).

2. **Tap the Add Account button and then tap the account type from the list of account types that appears.**

   Your choices are Microsoft Exchange, MobileMe, Gmail, Yahoo! Mail, AOL, or Other, as shown in Figure 6-5 (right side). After tapping the account type, the New Account screen appears for Exchange, MobileMe, Gmail, Yahoo! Mail, and AOL accounts, and the Other screen appears for Other accounts.

3. **Enter your account information as follows:**

   - *MobileMe, Gmail, Yahoo! Mail, or AOL:* Enter your name, user-name, password, and optional description in the New Account screen, and then tap Save in the upper-right corner. If the account is verified, you're done for a Gmail, Yahoo! Mail, or AOL account and you can skip the rest of these steps — the Mail, Contacts, Calendars settings screen appears with the new account listed in the Accounts section. For MobileMe, your iPod touch displays account's settings screen. (If your account doesn't verify, try Steps 2 and 3 again.)

- *Exchange:* Enter your name, username, domain (optional), password, and optional description in the New Account screen, and then tap Next in the upper-right corner to move on to the Exchange account's settings screen. Microsoft's Autodiscovery service kicks in to check your user name and password to determine the address of the Exchange server. If it can't find the server's address, a dialog appears for you to enter it — enter the complete address in the Server field and tap Save.

- *Other:* Tap Add Mail Account on the Other screen for an IMAP (Internet Message Access Protocol) or POP (Post Office Protocol) account. The New Account screen appears; enter your name, username, password, and an optional description, and then tap Save in the upper-right corner to save account information. The iPod touch searches for the account on the Internet and displays the New Account settings screen.

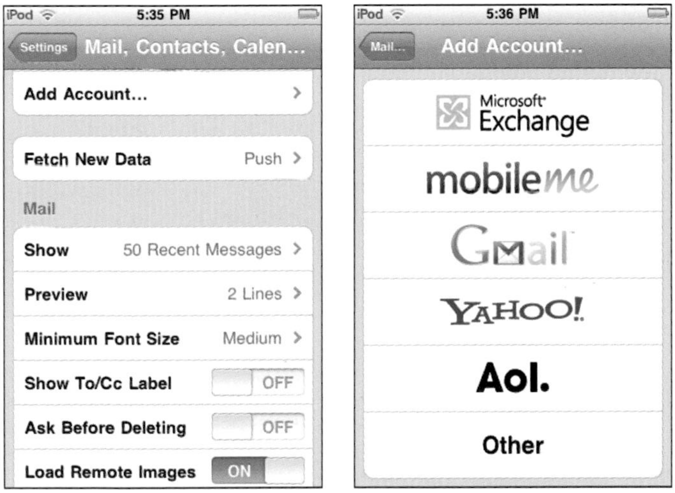

Figure 6-5: Tap Add Account (left) to see the list of account types (right).

4. **Set your mail account settings in the New Account settings screen as follows:**

   • *MobileMe or Exchange:* Turn on any or all of the items you want to sync: Mail, Contacts, Calendars, and Bookmarks (MobileMe only). If you sync these items using your MobileMe or Exchange account, syncing them in iTunes is turned off, and they are replaced by the MobileMe or Exchange account versions in your iPod touch. You can always return to the account setting's screen to turn them off in order to enable syncing with iTunes. For Exchange, you can set how many days of e-mail you want to sync. Tap Save in the upper-right corner to finish and save your settings.

   • *Other:* Tap IMAP or POP on the New Account settings screen, depending on the type of e-mail account you have — ask your e-mail service provider if you don't know. Then enter or edit the existing account information (also get this information from your service provider if you don't know). Tap Save in the upper-right corner to finish and save your settings. The Mail, Contacts, Calendars settings screen appears with the new account listed in the Accounts section.

5. **When the Sync or Cancel warning appears for MobileMe or Exchange accounts, tap Sync (or Cancel).**

   When you tap the Sync button, MobileMe or Exchange overwrites any existing contacts, calendars, and bookmarks on your iPod touch (or the subset of these that you chose in Step 4). After syncing, the Mail, Contacts, Calendars settings screen appears with the new account listed in the Accounts section.

6. **Tap Fetch New Data on the Mail, Contacts, Calendars settings screen (refer to Figure 6-5, right side), and tap Off for Push to turn it on (if it isn't already on).**

That's it! Your iPod touch syncs automatically from this point on, with data pushed or fetched from the e-mail account depending on your Push and Fetch settings (see Chapter 11 for details on Push and Fetch).

Whether the messages in your inbox appear on your iPod touch *and* on your computer depends on the type of e-mail account you have and how you've configured it. For example, if you delete on your computer an e-mail message from a push account (such as MobileMe), or from an account set up to delete messages on the server as soon as you delete them on your computer, the message also disappears from your iPod touch.

Changing and Deleting Mail Accounts

You can temporarily turn off a Mail account on your iPod touch, as well as change its settings or delete it. To turn off a Mail account in your iPod touch temporarily or change account settings, choose Settings⇨Mail, Contacts, Calendars from the Home screen, and then touch the account in the Accounts section to see that account's settings screen. You can then change your account's settings, including the items that are synced with a MobileMe or Exchange account.

To delete the account, scroll down and tap Delete Account. Deleting a Mail account from iPod touch doesn't affect the e-mail account or its settings on your computer.

Changes you make to accounts are *not* transferred back to your computer when you synchronize, so it's safe to make changes without affecting e-mail account settings on your computer.

It's way beyond the scope of this book to explain all of the e-mail account and advanced options. Grab your network administrator or Internet service provider and offer free coffee in exchange for help. If you don't have anyone to turn to, visit the tips section of my Web site (www.tonybove.com) for tips on using MobileMe and other e-mail accounts, and changing e-mail account settings on your iPod touch.

Part III
Playing It Back with Interest

The 5th Wave   By Rich Tennant

RICHTENNANT

"I could tell you more about myself, but I think the playlist on my iPod says more about me than mere words can."

In this part . . .

*H*ere's the big playback for your efforts. This part shows you how to play music, TV shows, movies, podcasts, audio books, and slideshows on your iPod touch.

Chapter 7 is all about playing songs. I show you how to find songs, control the playback and volume, shuffle and repeat songs and albums, and create playlists right on your iPod touch.

Next, Chapter 8 shows you to how to locate and play videos, including movies, TV shows, and YouTube videos. You can skip forward or backward, scale the picture to fit the display, and bookmark your favorite sections. I also show you how to play podcasts and audio books.

Then, in Chapter 9, you find out all about synchronizing photo albums with your iPod touch, taking pictures and videos, zooming into photos, sharing pictures with friends, and putting on a slideshow.

The Songs Remain the Same

In This Chapter

▶ Locating songs by artist, album, or playlist

▶ Repeating and shuffling a song list

▶ Creating and saving playlists on your iPod touch

▶ Adding a touch of Genius

▶ Changing the volume level and volume limit

*E*ven though the iPod and iTunes have irrevocably changed the entertainment industry and how you enjoy music, one thing remains the same: You still play songs. You just play them with more *panache* on your iPod touch.

You can pick any song that you want to hear at any time. You can also shuffle through songs to get an idea of how wide your music choices are or to surprise yourself or others. Browse by artist and album, select a playlist, and even create playlists on-the-fly — this chapter explains it all.

Locating "A Song for You"

With thousands of songs on your iPod touch, finding a particular song by its title may turn your finger into a scrolling stone. It may be faster to locate albums by cover art or to find songs by searching for artist (or composer), genre, album, or playlist. You can browse your music any number of ways without interrupting the music you're playing.

Going with the Cover Flow

Cover Flow (also called the *cover browser*) lets you flip through your cover art to select music alphabetically by artist. Choose Music from the Home screen and then turn the iPod touch quickly to view it horizontally. This movement changes the display to landscape mode and displays the cover browser, as shown in Figure 7-1.

Slide your finger across the album covers to scroll swiftly through the music library, or tap to the right or left of the cover art in the foreground to move forward or backward an album cover at a time. Tap the play button in the lower-left corner (shown in Figure 7-1) to start playing the first song in the foreground album; the play button turns to a pause button so that you can tap it again to stop playback. Tap the *i* button in the lower-right corner (or tap the foreground cover art) to list the songs in that album. Then you can tap a song to start playing it.

Figure 7-1: Cover Flow: the cover browser.

Finding artists, albums, and songs

You can quickly and easily locate a song by browsing or searching for the song, or looking up either the song's artist or its album. First, tap the Music icon on the Home screen if the Music app is not already running.

To browse music by artist, tap the Music icon on the Home screen and tap the Artists icon along the bottom row of the Music screen. A scrollable list of artists appears, with an alphabet listed vertically along the right side, as shown in Figure 7-2 — flick your finger down to see the very top, which shows the search field.

Tap any letter in the alphabet shown on the right to scroll the list directly to that letter. Tap an artist name to see a list of albums or songs by that artist. (You see multiple albums if more than one album is available.) Tap an album title or its cover art to see a list of songs in the album. Tap a song title to start playing the song.

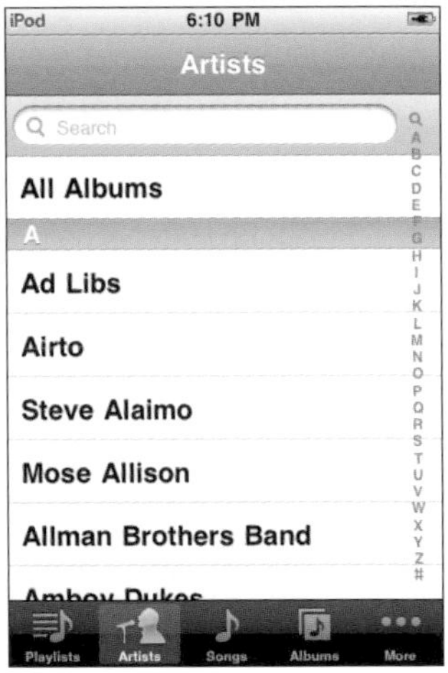

Figure 7-2: Locate an artist.

To search, tap inside the search field and start typing on the onscreen keyboard that appears. Suggestions appear below matching what you type — tap a suggestion to go to it.

To browse music by album title, tap Albums in the bottom row of icons. To locate songs by title, tap Songs in the bottom row of icons. In either case, a scrollable list appears — after tapping Albums, album titles appear in a scrollable list with the album cover on the left side and an alphabet along the right side, as shown in Figure 7-3. Just like the artists list, you can slide to scroll the list, tap a letter to go directly to that letter, and use the search field at the top.

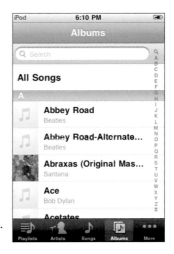

Figure 7-3: Browse by album title.

If you sync Genius mixes (along with other music) to your iPod touch, or if you sync your entire music library (which includes Genius mixes), the Genius button appears in the lower-left corner of the Music screen, shifting the other buttons to the right (Albums moves to the More menu). In that case, in order to browse by albums on an iPod touch, tap More, and then tap Albums. To learn more about Genius mixes, see the "Playing Genius Mixes" section, later in this chapter).

You can also find music by composer or genre by tapping the More icon along the bottom row of the Music screen, and then tapping either Composers or Genres.

Choosing a playlist

When you sync your iPod touch with your entire iTunes library, your iTunes playlists are included (along with any Genius playlists and Genius mixes). Well, that makes sense, doesn't it?

To browse music by playlist on your iPod touch, tap the Music icon on the Home screen and tap the Playlists icon along the bottom row of the Music screen. A scrollable list of playlists appears. Tap a playlist title to see a list of songs in the playlist and tap a song title to start playing the song.

The songs in the playlist are in the order defined for the playlist in iTunes. But don't despair for lack of something new — not only can you edit your playlist to change the song order and add and delete songs, but also you can create entirely new playlists — right in your iPod touch, as I describe later in this chapter.

Controlling Song Playback

To play a song, tap the song title (or the play button in Cover Flow).

When the song finishes, the iPod touch plays the next song in the sequence that appeared in the list you chose it from. For example, if you chose a song in the Songs screen, the next song would be the next one in sequence in the Songs screen. If you chose the last song on an album in the Albums screen, the iPod touch stops after playing it. If you chose a song from a playlist on the Playlists screen, the next song would be the next one in the playlist, and after playing the last song it also stops playing, as with an album. (See the "Repeating songs" section later in this chapter to find out how to repeat albums and playlists.)

Whenever you play a song, you see the album cover associated with the song on the Now Playing screen. You also see the buttons for playback control — previous/rewind, play/pause, and next/fast-forward. (See Figure 7-4.) Slide your finger along the volume slider at the bottom of the display to change the volume.

Figure 7-4: The Now Playing screen.

Tap the next/fast-forward button once to play the next song in sequence, and tap the previous/rewind button once at the beginning of a song, or twice during the song, to play the previous song. You can fast-forward through a song by touching and holding down the next/fast-forward button, and you can rewind a song by touching and holding down the previous/rewind button.

You can tap the bullet-list button in the upper-right corner if you want to display a list of the album's contents. You can then tap the title of another song on the album to start playing that song.

To return to menus and make other selections when playing a song, tap the left-arrow button in the upper-left corner of the display.

Tap underneath the left-arrow button or the album title while a song is playing to show more buttons and the scrubber bar for navigating through the song, as shown in Figure 7-5 — and if lyrics are available in the iTunes information, lyrics also appear. (To learn how to add lyrics to your song information, see *iPod & iTunes For Dummies* by yours truly.)

To skip to any point in a song, drag the playhead along the scrubber bar. To start a song over from the beginning, drag the playhead on the scrubber bar all the way to the left, or tap the previous/rewind button once.

TIP

If you're viewing another content menu on the iPod touch, tap Now Playing at the top-right corner of the display to go directly to the Now Playing display.

TIP

You can control music playback while using another app, or while the iPod touch is locked. Double-click the physical Home button, and then flick left to right along the bottom row to see the Music app's music controls. Tap the Music icon to go back to the Music app. See Chapter 2 to find out more about using the Home button double-click to multitask your apps and lock the display orientation to portrait.

Figure 7-5: Tap under the album title to show more buttons, the scrubber bar, and lyrics.

Repeating songs

If you want to drive yourself crazy repeating the same song over and over, your iPod touch is happy to oblige. (You might want to try repeating "They're Coming to Take Me Away, Ha-Haaa" by Napoleon XIV, a favorite from the old *The Dr. Demento Show* radio broadcasts — and perhaps they will come to take you away.) More than likely, you'll want to repeat a playlist or album, which you can easily do.

Tap underneath the left-arrow button or the album title while a song is playing. The repeat and shuffle buttons appear, along with the scrubber bar and lyrics, directly below the top row of buttons. (Refer to Figure 7-5.)

Ordinarily when a song finishes, the iPod touch plays the next song in the sequence that appeared in the list on the screen you chose it from. When it reaches the end of that list, it stops — if you chose the last song on an album in the Albums screen, the iPod touch stops after playing it. But if you tap the repeat button once while the songs are playing, the entire sequence repeats. If you chose an album, the album repeats; if you chose a playlist, the playlist repeats.

After you tap the repeat button once to repeat the sequence of songs, the repeat button shows blue highlighting. Tap the repeat button again to repeat only the current song — the button changes to include a blue-highlighted numeral 1. Tap it once more to return to normal playback.

Shuffling song order

Maybe you want your song selections to be surprising and unpredictable, or you just want your iPod touch to mess with your mind. You can *shuffle* song playback to play in random order, just like an automated radio station without a disk jockey or program guide.

You can just shake your iPod touch, and it shuffles the songs in the album you are playing. By default, your iPod touch is set to shuffle when shaken (not stirred). To turn this off, choose Settings⇨Music from the Home screen, and touch On for the Shake to Shuffle option to turn it off.

You can also set your iPod touch to shuffle songs across your library. The shuffle algorithm is as random as it gets (not taking into account a fundamental tenet of chaos theory that says a pattern will emerge). When an iPod touch creates a shuffle, it reorders the songs (like shuffling a deck of cards) and then plays them in the new order.

To turn your iPod touch into a random song player, choose Music from the Home screen and tap the Songs icon at the bottom of the display. The song list appears, with Shuffle at the top of the list. Tap Shuffle to turn on Shuffle.

You can also shuffle songs within an album or playlist, which gives you some control over random playback. For example, you can create a playlist for all jazz songs and then shuffle the songs within that jazz playlist. To shuffle songs in an album or playlist, start playing a song in the album or playlist and then tap underneath the left-arrow button or the album title while a song is playing. The repeat and shuffle buttons appear, along with the scrubber bar, directly below the top row of buttons (refer to Figure 7-5). Tap the shuffle button to shuffle songs within the currently playing album or playlist.

You can also set an iPod touch to shuffle any album or playlist *before* playing it. First, select the playlist or album; then tap Shuffle at the top of the list of songs for that playlist or album.

Want to repeat an entire album or playlist but still shuffle the playing order each time you hear it? Start playing a song in the album or playlist and then set your iPod touch to repeat all the songs in the album or playlist as described in the preceding section, "Repeating songs." Then set the iPod touch to shuffle the songs as described in this section.

Creating and Editing Playlists on Your iPod touch

If you don't like the playlists copied over from your iTunes library, go out and make some of your own! You can edit the playlists you synced from your library, and create new ones, queuing the songs in the order you want, right on your iPod touch. You can give these new playlists names, and sync them back to your iTunes library. This option is particularly useful for picking songs to play right before a long drive. (Hel-*lo!* You shouldn't be messing with your iPod touch while driving.)

Creating a new playlist

Follow these steps to select songs for your On-The-Go playlist:

1. **Choose Music from the Home screen.**

   The Music screen appears with the Playlists and other icons along the bottom of the display.

2. **Tap the Playlists icon and tap Add Playlist near the top of the Playlists list.**

   The New Playlist dialog appears and the onscreen keyboard pops up, as shown in Figure 7-6 (left side).

3. **Type a name for the playlist and tap Save.**

   The Songs list appears with a plus (+) sign next to each song, as well as an Add All Songs option at the top, as shown in Figure 7-6 (right side). If you have only several dozen albums, this list isn't too long, and you can skip to Step 5. If you have a lot more music, narrow your search with Step 4.

4. **(Optional) Narrow your search for songs to add to the playlist.**

   Tap an icon along the bottom row (see Figure 7-6, right side) to browse your iPod touch library — for example, tap Playlists to select songs from playlists or entire playlists; tap Artists to browse artists to select songs; and so on.

5. **Tap the plus (+) sign next to a song you want to add to the playlist, or tap the plus sign next to Add All Albums to add all the albums of an artist found in Step 4.**

   When you tap the plus sign for a song, that song is included in the play-list, and it turns gray in the list so that you know it has already been selected. You can tap Add All Albums as an alternative if you want to add all the songs for a particular artist — first browse for that artist in Step 4.

Figure 7-6: Give the playlist a name (left) and add songs (right).

6. **Repeat Steps 4 and 5, adding songs in the order you want them to play.**

   You can continue to add songs to the list.

7. **Tap the Done button when you're finished adding songs.**

   The Done button appears at the top while you select songs, just waiting for you to finish. After tapping Done, to finish selecting songs, your iPod touch saves the playlist and displays it with Edit, Clear, and Delete buttons, as shown in Figure 7-7 (left side).

8. **To start playing the playlist, tap any song.**

   Scroll up or down the list to choose a song, and tap the song title to play the playlist starting from that song. You can tap Shuffle to shuffle the songs in the playlist.

Editing or deleting a playlist

The songs in a playlist are in *playlist order* (the order you added them, either in iTunes, or on your iPod touch as I described in the previous section). You can change that order, or delete songs from the playlist, by tapping the Edit button (see Figure 7-7, left side). The Edit screen appears with a circled minus (–) sign on the far left side of each song, and a Move icon (three horizontal bars, like half of an I-Ching symbol) on the far right side (see Figure 7-7, right side).

To rearrange songs in the playlist, drag the Move icon for a song to move it up or down the list. To delete a song from the playlist, tap the circled minus (–), and then tap the Delete button that appears. After rearranging or deleting, tap the Done button at the top of the Edit screen to finish.

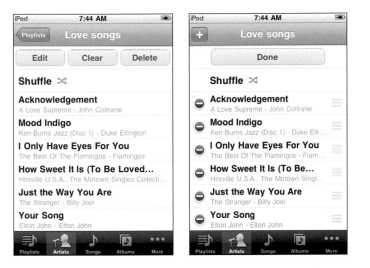

Figure 7-7: Play the playlist (left) or edit the playlist (right).

To delete the *entire* playlist at once, tap Delete (refer to Figure 7-7, left side). To clear the contents of a playlist but save its name (so that you can add more songs without naming it again), tap Clear.

When you delete songs from a playlist, they disappear from the playlist but they are still in your iPod touch; only the playlist is changed.

Consulting the iTunes Genius

Your iPod touch can also be a genius about picking songs. If you don't want to go through the process of selecting songs, just select one song and tap the Genius button. Your iPod touch takes a look at whatever song you select and creates a playlist of songs already on the iPod touch that go along with it.

Giving Genius a lesson in your tastes

The Genius button and its sidekick, the Genius Sidebar in iTunes, work with the iTunes Store to match up your tastes to other iTunes users using a technique called *collaborative filtering*. The "genius" software working behind the scenes in the store analyzes the music and video in other people's iTunes libraries — people who also have the same song or video you selected (if they also turn on the Genius feature in iTunes). The Genius Sidebar appears next to the list pane in iTunes whenever it's open and informs the online store about the items you select. It then shows you music and video that other listeners purchased when they purchased the items you're playing. All of this information is shared anonymously.

For the Genius feature to work in your iPod touch, you must first give iTunes permission to scan your music library and catalog your iTunes collection, and then you need to sync your iPod touch (as I describe in Chapter 5). The scanning process may take a few minutes or (for very large collections) a few hours, but you can continue using iTunes while it scans your music. To do this, open the sidebar by clicking the show/hide Genius Sidebar button in the lower-right corner of the iTunes window. (Refer to Chapter 4.) Then click the Turn on Genius button in the sidebar, enter your Apple ID and password for your iTunes Store account, and click Continue.

If you don't have an iTunes Store account yet, select the Create a New iTunes Store Account option and see Chapter 4 for further instructions on creating an account.

After you have enabled the Genius Sidebar, you can turn off the Genius feature in iTunes by choosing Store⇨Turn Off Genius, and turn it back on by choosing Store⇨Turn On Genius. If you add new music to your iTunes library, you can tell iTunes to immediately update the Genius feature with new information by choosing Store⇨Update Genius.

When you have the Genius Sidebar open, iTunes transmits information to the store about the selection you're playing. To hide the Genius Sidebar (and stop transmitting this information), click the show/hide Genius Sidebar button in the bottom-right corner of the iTunes window.

Creating a Genius playlist

In your iPod touch, the Genius feature recognizes the song or video you selected, but you must have enough songs or videos on your iPod touch that match the Genius collaborative filtering technique (such as songs purchased by other people who also played the song you are playing).

To create a Genius playlist on your iPod touch, choose Music from the Home screen and follow these steps:

1. **Locate and start playing a song to base the Genius playlist on.**

   The Now Playing screen appears when the song is playing.

2. **Tap the Now Playing screen to see the control buttons.**

   Tap underneath the left-arrow button or the album title while a song is playing. The Repeat, Genius, and Shuffle buttons appear underneath the scrubber bar directly below the top row of buttons. (Refer to Figure 7-5.) The Genius button is the one in the center sporting the atom icon.

3. **Tap the Genius button.**

   The Genius Playlist screen appears as shown in Figure 7-8, with New, Refresh, and Save buttons at the top. You can flick your finger to scroll the list. Tap any song to start playing the playlist from that song. If you navigate to other screens, you can return to the Genius playlist by tapping Genius Playlist in the Playlists menu.

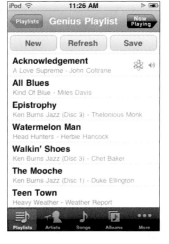

Figure 7-8: The Genius playlist.

4. **(Optional) Refresh the Genius playlist by tapping Refresh.**

   Refreshing a playlist changes it to include different songs based on the same song you played (depending on how many similar songs you have in your iPod touch).

5. **Save the Genius playlist by tapping Save.**

   The playlist is saved in the Playlists section of your iPod touch using the title of the song it is based on. The playlist is copied back to your iTunes library when you sync your iPod touch. That's all you need to do — the next steps are optional.

   If you subsequently refresh a saved Genius playlist before syncing, the saved playlist is refreshed and you lose the previous version of it.

6. **(Optional) Create a new Genius playlist by tapping New and then selecting a new song to base it on.**

   After tapping New, the song list appears for selecting a song. Choose a song, and your iPod touch creates a new Genius playlist and starts playing the song, displaying the Now Playing screen.

7. **(Optional) After Step 6, return to the Genius playlist by tapping the left-arrow button in the top-left corner of the Now Playing screen.**

You can refresh any Genius playlist, whether you created it in iTunes and synced to your iPod touch or you created it directly on your iPod touch. Select the playlist and tap Refresh at the top of the list (or tap Delete to delete the list).

In search of the lost chord

If you don't like the music, go out and make some yourself! You can look for the chord the guitar player is playing in a song, and you can try to play it yourself with PocketGuitar (available in the App Store), an app that turns your iPod touch into a virtual guitar. You can press and strum strings with your fingers on the iPod touch screen.

For anyone who plays guitar or wants to play one, you can't beat the value of GuitarToolkit, an iPod touch app (available in the App Store) that provides a chromatic tuner, a chord finder, a metronome, and pitch reference tones. The tuner itself (see figure with the meter) is worth the price ($9.99 as of this writing) and is far more convenient than carrying a separate tuner. The chord finder lets you quickly cycle through chords and see the fingering for each chord. Slide your fingers across the iPod touch screen to strum the chord. The scales feature offers a playable fretboard (see figure with the guitar fretboard) to hear what each note sounds like, and the metronome lets you dial in an exact count in beats per minute (BPM) or tap along to a song to get the tempo.

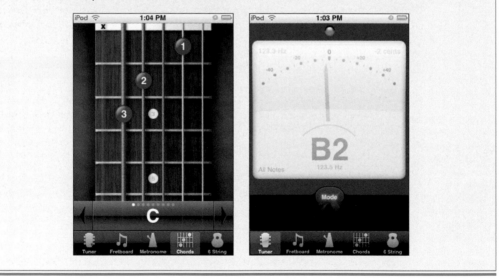

Playing Genius mixes

Genius mixes are playlists that are put together by iTunes based on songs in your library. The songs are supposed to go great together, although the choices may be surprising. Simply select Genius Mixes in the Genius section of the source pane to see the mixes. Genius mixes are synced automatically if you sync everything to your iPod touch, or you can sync specific mixes as playlists, as I describe in Chapter 5. (To learn more about Genius mixes, consult *iPod & iTunes For Dummies* by yours truly.)

If you sync Genius mixes to your iPod touch, the Genius button appears in the lower left corner of the Music screen, shifting the other buttons to the right (Albums moves to the More menu).

To play your Genius mixes on your iPod touch, tap the Genius icon in the lower-left corner. Flick left or right to browse the mixes. The dots at the bottom of the Genius Mixes screen indicate how many mixes are synced. To start playing a mix, tap the play button that appears in the middle of the screen for every Genius mix.

Adjusting and Limiting the Volume

Because an iPod touch can be quite loud when set to its highest volume, I recommend turning down the volume before using headphones.

To adjust volume, play something on the iPod touch, and then press the volume button on the left side of the iPod touch at the top (to increase the volume) or bottom (to lower the volume). You can also slide your finger on the volume slider that appears on the Now Playing screen underneath the playback controls. (Refer to Figure 7-4.) Use your finger to slide the knob to the right to increase the volume or to the left to decrease the volume.

You may want to limit the highest volume for your iPod touch to be lower than the actual maximum. This limit can help protect your hearing while you're listening to content from sources with different volume levels. Follow these steps:

1. **Choose Settings⇨Music from the Home screen.**

2. **Choose Volume Limit from the Music settings screen.**

   A volume slider appears with a silver knob.

3. **Slide your finger on the volume slider to limit the volume.**

   Slide the knob with your finger to the right to increase the volume or to the left to decrease the volume.

4. **Tap the Music button in the upper-left corner of the display to set the limit and return to the previous menu, or, if you want, tap the Lock Volume Limit button to lock the volume limit.**

   If you accept the new limit without locking it, you get to skip the next step; you're done. The lock is useful for locking the volume limit so others can't change it (such as your children). However, it also means that you have to enter the volume limit code to unlock the iPod touch in order to change the volume limit.

5. **Set the Volume Limit Code for locking the volume limit.**

   If you tapped the Lock Volume Limit button to lock the volume limit, your iPod touch displays four squares for entering a code number. Tap the calculator-style number pad to type numbers for your code and be sure to make up a code that you can remember! (If you don't want to enter a code, tap the Cancel button in the upper-left corner.)

Tweaking the Sound

Maybe you want more bone-rattling bass or treble highs that are as clear as a bell. The equalizer allows you to fine-tune sound spectrum frequencies in a more precise way than with the typical bass and treble controls you find on home stereos and powered speakers.

Or maybe some of your songs are just too loud. I don't mean too loud stylistically, as in thrash metal with screeching guitars; I mean too loud for your ears when you're wearing headphones or so loud that the music sounds distorted in your speakers. And some songs are just too soft; you have to increase the volume to hear them and then lower the volume to listen to louder songs. To remedy instances like these, you can set the volume in advance in iTunes.

With songs, audio books, podcast episodes, and videos that you already know are too loud (or too soft), consider setting the volume for those items in advance so that they always play with the desired volume adjustment. You can even set the volume for entire albums or podcasts.

To adjust the overall volume of a particular item in advance so that it always plays at that setting, perform the following steps in iTunes:

1. **Select one or more items in your iTunes library.**

   You can select multiple songs in List view or in the list pane below Cover Flow view, or select an entire album in the column browser or in Album List or Grid views (see Chapter 4 for browsing details). To set the volume for a whole podcast, select the podcast title instead of individual episodes.

2. **Choose File⇨Get Info.**

   The information dialog appears.

3. **Click the Options tab.**

4. **Drag the Volume Adjustment slider left or right to adjust the volume lower or higher, as shown in Figure 7-9.**

   You can do this while playing the file.

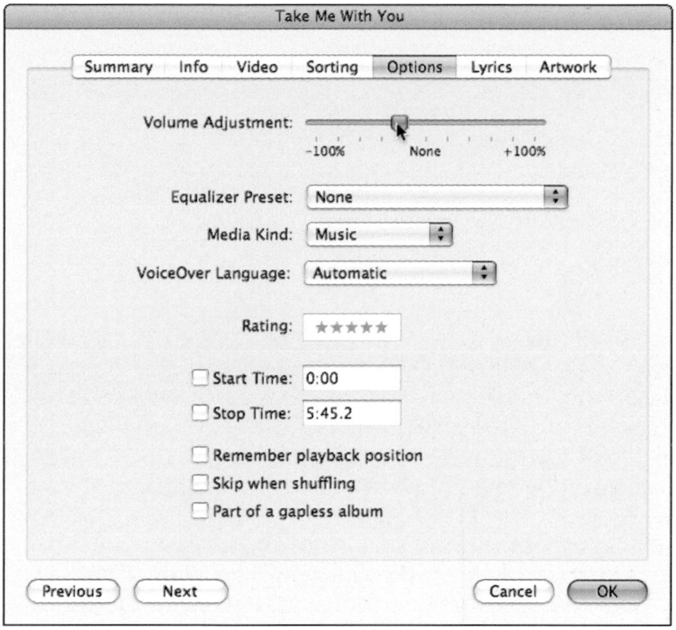

Figure 7-9: Adjust the volume setting in advance for a song.

Peaking with the Sound Check

You can standardize the volume level of all the songs in your iTunes library with the Sound Check option in iTunes. This option has the added benefit of applying the same volume adjustment when you play the songs back on your iPod touch.

Sound Check scans the audio files, finds each track's peak volume level, and then uses this peak volume information to level the playing volume of tracks so that they have the same peak volume (this is called *normalization* in audio terms). The sound quality isn't affected, nor is the audio information changed: The volume is simply adjusted at the start of the track to be in line with other tracks. If you mix early '60s music with today's much louder music, like I do, all the songs play at relatively the same volume (so I don't have to adjust the volume) without any loss in quality.

To enable Sound Check to work in your iPod touch, first follow these steps in iTunes:

1. **Drag the iTunes volume slider to set the overall volume for iTunes.**

   The volume slider is located in the top-left corner of the iTunes window, to the right of the play button.

2. **Choose iTunes⇨Preferences (Mac) or Edit⇨Preferences (Windows).**

3. **In the iTunes Preferences dialog that appears, click the Playback tab.**

   The Playback preferences appear.

4. **Select the Sound Check box.**

   iTunes sets the volume level for all songs according to the level of the iTunes volume slider.

5. **Click OK.**

   The Sound Check option sets a volume adjustment based on the volume slider on all the songs so that they play at approximately the same volume.

The operation runs in the background while you do other things. If you quit iTunes and then restart it, the operation continues where it left off when you quit. You can switch Sound Check on or off at any time.

To take advantage of volume leveling already set up in your iTunes library, you need to turn on Sound Check in your iPod touch. Choose Settings⇨Music from the Home screen to show the Music settings screen, and tap the Off button next to Sound Check to turn it on. Tap On to turn it back off.

All things being equal (ized)

You can use the iPod touch's built-in equalizer to improve or enhance the sound coming through a particular stereo system and speakers. With the equalizer settings, you can customize playback for different musical genres, listening environments, or speakers.

The iPod touch equalizer uses a bit more battery power when it's on, so you might have less playing time.

The quality of the sound is no better than the speakers you play it on. When you adjust the sound coming from your iPod touch, use your everyday listening environment as a guide. If you tweak the sound specifically for your computer speakers or for your home stereo and speakers, though, remember that with an iPod touch you have other potential listening environments — different headphones, car stereo systems, portable boom boxes, and so on.

To set the equalizer setting, choose Settings⇨Music from the Home screen and tap EQ to display a list of presets. You can scroll the list of presets and tap a preset to select it — a check mark appears next to it after you select it. The equalizer is set to Off until you select one of the presets.

Each equalizer preset offers a different balance of frequencies designed to enhance the sound in certain ways. For example, Bass Booster increases the volume of the low (bass) frequencies; Treble Booster does the same to the high (treble) frequencies.

To see what a preset actually does to the frequencies, choose Window⟶ Equalizer in iTunes to open the iTunes equalizer; then select the same preset by namc. Thc fadcrs in thc cqualizcr show you cxactly what thc preset does.

Find out how to assign standard iTunes presets or your own custom presets to specific songs, audio books, podcast episodes, and videos — and use those presets when playing these items back on your iPod touch — by visiting the tips section of my Web site (www.tonybove.com).

8

Tapping Videos, Books, and Podcasts

In This Chapter

▶ Playing movies and TV shows
▶ Playing YouTube videos
▶ Playing podcasts and audio books

*T*he iPod touch is a terrific video player, with crisp, clear picture quality. Video appears horizontally on the screen (in what's known as *landscape mode*), and if you rotate the iPod touch 180 degrees to the opposite horizontal position, the video adjusts accordingly. All the controls you expect in a DVD player are right on the screen at the touch of a finger.

You can also play audio books and podcasts on this multimedia machine. The iTunes Store offers an amazing selection of TV shows, movies, audio books, and podcasts. (See Chapter 4.) This chapter shows you how to control video playback, skip forward or backward, and scale the picture to fit your screen. It also shows you how to watch videos on YouTube, the free video-sharing Web site started in 2005 that has since exploded with video clips from all corners of the globe.

Everything's Coming Up Videos

Movies, TV shows, and music videos are easy to locate and play. Videos you purchase from the iTunes Store are ready to use, but videos you bring in from other sources may have to be converted first for use on your iPod touch. You can tell if a video needs to be converted by selecting the video in iTunes and checking the Advanced menu: The Create iPod or iPhone version option is grayed out.

To convert a video using iTunes, select the video and choose Advanced⇨ Create iPod or iPhone Version.

You can use a variety of applications to convert your video, such as Handbrake (`http://handbrake.fr`) for Mac or Windows, which converts formats not supported by iTunes and can even convert video from a DVD.

To find out more about why videos need to be converted and how to prepare your own videos and convert imported videos for use with an iPod touch, visit the tips section of my Web site (`www.tonybove.com`).

To locate and play a video on your iPod touch, follow these steps:

1. **Tap the Videos icon on the iPod touch Home screen.**

2. **Scroll the Videos screen to see the sections for Movies, TV Shows, Music Videos, and Podcasts (video podcasts only).**

   The video titles are listed in alphabetical order within these sections.

3. **Tap the title of an item to play it.**

Playback under your thumb

Tap the screen to show video controls (as shown in Figure 8-1). You can tap again to hide them.

Tap the play/pause button while a video is playing to pause the playback. To raise or lower the volume, drag the volume slider along the bottom of the screen. (See Figure 8-1.)

You can fast-forward through a video by touching and holding down the next/fast-forward button, and you can rewind a video by touching and holding down the previous/rewind button.

To skip to any point in a video, drag the playhead along the scrubber bar. To start a video over from the

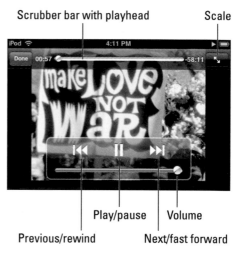

Figure 8-1: Tap the screen to use playback controls.

beginning, drag the playhead on the scrubber bar all the way to the left or tap the Previous/Rewind button (if the video doesn't contain chapters).

If the video contains chapters, you can skip to the previous or next chapter by tapping the previous/rewind or next/fast-forward button. To start playing at a specific chapter, tap the bullet-list button that appears in the top-right corner — but remember, this trick works only if the original video was set up to contain chapters.

To stop watching a video before it finishes playing, tap the Done button in the upper-left corner of the display or press the Home button on the device.

If a video offers an alternative audio language or subtitles, a Subtitles button appears. Tap the Subtitles button and then choose a language from the Audio list, or a language from the Subtitles list, or tap On to turn off subtitles.

Videos are automatically set to remember the playback position when you pause. This feature lets you pause a video or TV episode in iTunes while you synchronize your iPod touch. After syncing, you can continue playing the video or episode on your iPod touch from where you paused. This feature also works in reverse: If you start playing a video on your iPod touch and then pause, and then you sync it with iTunes, the video retains the playback position so that you can continue playing it in iTunes from where you paused.

You can delete a video directly from your iPod touch by flicking left or right across the video selection in the Videos menu and then tapping the Delete button that appears. If your video is still in your iTunes library, you can sync the video with the iPod touch again or copy the video back to it manually (as I explain in Chapter 5). If you delete a *rented* movie from the iPod touch, it's deleted permanently.

Scaling the picture

Videos are displayed in landscape mode in widescreen format. You can also scale the video picture to fill the screen or to fit entirely within the screen. Tap the scale button in the upper right corner of the screen (refer to Figure 8-1) or double-tap the video picture itself to switch from one to the other. The scale button shows two arrows facing away from each other (as in Figure 8-1) when the picture fits entirely within the screen. The two arrows face toward each other when the picture fills the screen edge-to-edge.

Filling the screen may crop the sides or the top and bottom of the picture to give you a larger view of the center of the picture. Fitting entirely within the screen assures that the entire picture is shown, but you may see black bars on the sides or top and bottom.

YouTube in Your Hand

The newest and most popular videos in YouTube are right in your hand. All you need to do is connect by Wi-Fi. (See Chapter 4 to set up Wi-Fi.) You can search for and play videos, bookmark favorites for later playback, and share videos with others by e-mail.

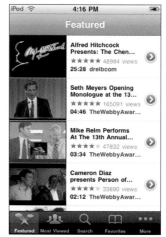

Tap YouTube on the Home screen to run the YouTube app. If this is your first visit to the YouTube app, the Featured screen appears, as shown in Figure 8-2. Otherwise, the screen you were viewing when you last used the app appears.

Figure 8-2: Featured videos in YouTube.

You can tap icons along the bottom of the display to get to other screens, such as Most Viewed, as shown in Figure 8-3, which offers buttons at the top for today's most-viewed videos, the faves for this week, and all of the most-viewed videos.

After you've saved your favorites as bookmarks (see the "Bookmarking and sharing" section later in this chapter), you can go right to your favorite videos by tapping the Favorites icon. Tap the More icon to see even more screens, including Top Rated (the most popular), Most Recent (the most recent videos added), and History (all the videos you've played so far). You can also tap the Sign In button in the upper left corner of the Favorites screen to sign into your YouTube account and access the My Videos section of your account.

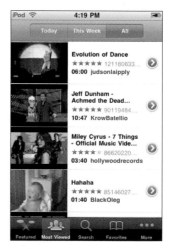

TIP

The History screen offers a Clear button so that you can clear your history at any time.

Figure 8-3: Most viewed videos in YouTube for today, this week, and for all time.

Running down a stream: Playback control

Tap a selection to play the video. YouTube *streams* the video to your iPod touch — sending it bit by bit — so that you can start playing it immediately.

Tap the video picture to see the controls (see Figure 8-4), which are exactly like the video controls described in the previous section. The progress of the downloaded video stream appears in the scrubber bar. Even though you can play the video as it streams, you might want to pause it for a few seconds so that more of the stream is downloaded. You can then play the video without any hiccups.

Bookmarking and sharing

YouTube offers a couple of handy buttons on its videos (see Figure 8-4 for both buttons):

- **Bookmark button (a book icon):** This button appears to the left of the previous/rewind button, and you can use it to bookmark the video so that you can easily find it on the Favorites screen.

- **Share button (an envelope icon):** This button is located to the right of the next/fast-forward button. Tap it to bring up the e-mail sending screen to share the video with others via e-mail — see Chapter 11 for details on how to fill out the e-mail message.

Tap the bookmark button to save a bookmark for the video — the video selection appears in the Favorites screen, which you can access later by tapping the Favorites icon in the bottom row. (The bookmark button is gray rather than white if the video is already bookmarked.)

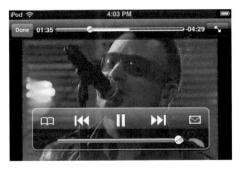

Figure 8-4: YouTube controls for video playback, bookmarking, and sharing.

You can also bookmark or share the video without playing it, and you can even view information about the video as well as related video selections. Tap the right-arrow button on the right side of each selection (refer to Figure 8-3) to see information about the video and to use the bookmark or share buttons.

All you have to do is stream

If you're a stream lover (like I am), YouTube isn't nearly enough. You can find streaming Web radio stations and video streams on the Web using apps such as Pandora (radio stations), CBS Sports (live games), and Truveo (TV stations). Your iPod touch needs to be connected to Wi-Fi and the Internet to stream video — see Chapter 4 to get set up.

Pandora lets you type the name of an artist, song, or composer, and Pandora creates a custom station that streams to your iPod touch the music you chose — and more music like it. You can tap the thumbs-up or -down buttons to let Pandora know your musical tastes.

CBS Sports NCAA March Madness on Demand streams live video of every game from the NCAA Division I Men's Basketball Championship.

And with Truveo, it's easy to search for streaming video across sites that include NBC, CNN, The Disney Channel, HBO, Discovery Channel, Comedy Central, PBS, MTV, The Wall Street Journal, YouTube, and Dailymotion, and browse featured videos, top searches, channels, or categories. My favorite feature of Truveo is that it lets me look up the most Twittered videos of the day.

To delete entries from your Favorites screen, tap the Favorites icon at the bottom of the display to show your bookmarked favorites, and then tap the Edit button in the top-right corner of the screen. The Favorites screen changes to include circled minus (–) signs next to the video selections. To delete a bookmarked video selection, tap the circled minus sign, which then rotates and displays a Delete button over the selection — tap the Delete button. To cancel deletion, tap the rotated circled minus sign again. Tap the Done button in the top-right corner of the Favorites screen to finish editing.

Searching for videos

To search for videos on YouTube, tap the Search icon in the bottom row of icons. Then tap the Search Entry field that appears at the top of the screen. The onscreen keyboard pops up, ready for your search term. (For instructions on using the onscreen keyboard, see Chapter 2.)

If the entry field already has a search term, tap the circled X in the right corner of the field to clear its contents. Then tap out the letters of the search term using the onscreen keyboard and tap the Search key on the keyboard. Immediately after tapping Search, video selections from YouTube appear below, as shown in Figure 8-5 (in which I type just **u2** to get the latest U2 music videos).

You can scroll this list by dragging up and down. If a video selection appears that satisfies your search, tap it to play it without further ado.

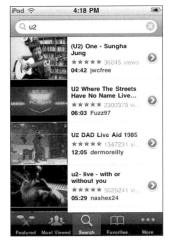

Figure 8-5: YouTube finds videos based on the search term.

One Chapter at a Time: Audio Books and Podcasts

Audio books are, naturally, organized into chapters or parts. Podcasts are also organized into parts, called *episodes,* and both play the same way. The audio book title or podcast name and episode appear on your iPod touch display along with its cover — similar to a book or album cover.

After syncing your audio books and podcast episodes along with the rest of your content (as I describe in glorious detail in Chapter 5), you can find them in the Music screen: Tap the Music icon on the Home screen and then tap the More icon at the bottom-right corner of the Music screen to see the More screen.

Tap Audiobooks on the More screen and then scroll the Audiobooks screen to select an audio book. Tap an audio book on the Audiobooks screen that appears and then tap a chapter or part to play it, starting from that point. The audio book chapters or parts are listed in proper order for each book.

Tap Podcasts on the More screen and then scroll the Podcasts screen to select a podcast. Podcasts are organized by podcast title (which is like an album name), and podcast episodes are listed within each podcast in the order that they were released (by date). A blue dot appears next to any podcast title that has unplayed episodes, and next to any unplayed episodes.

You control the playback of an audio book or podcast episode exactly the same way as a song (see Chapter 7) — you can pause playback by tapping the play/pause button, and so on. You can control video podcasts the same way you control videos. (See the "Everything's Coming Up Videos" section, earlier in this chapter.)

Audio books and podcasts are automatically set to remember the playback position when you pause. If you pause playback on your iPod touch and then sync with iTunes, you can resume playback at that position on either the iPod touch or in iTunes.

Pocketing Your Pictures

*T*he world is awash in pictures, from photos and video stills to cartoons, images, and famous paintings. In this chapter, I refer to everything you can *see* as a picture — whether it be a photo, graphic image, or a video clip (a moving picture). If you like to send and receive pictures by e-mail, you're going to love the fact that you can now use your iPod touch to display and share thousands of pictures synced from your computer, and take pictures as well. This chapter shows you how.

Syncing with Photo Albums and Folders

After importing pictures taken with a camera or your iPod touch into your computer, you can organize them into albums or collections that sync through iTunes. On a Mac, you can sync photos and images with iPhoto (version 4.0.3 or newer) or Aperture, and photos, images, and videos with iPhoto 5 or later. Newer versions of iPhoto let you organize pictures by events, places, and faces as well as in albums — you can assign pictures to an event, assign locations to pictures, and assign faces to pictures, and then browse by events, places, or faces. On a Windows PC, you can sync photos with Adobe Photoshop Elements (version 3.0 or newer).

You can then set up your iPod touch to sync with your entire photo library or with specific photo albums in your library (also known as *collections* in Adobe Photoshop Elements Organizer) so that any changes you make to the library or to those photo albums or collections are copied to the iPod touch. Additionally, any pictures you collect from e-mails on your iPod touch are synced to the photo library on your computer.

You don't have to use these applications— you can use any other photo-editing or photo-organizing software and store your photos in their own folder on your hard drive (such as the Pictures folder in your user folder on a Mac, or the My Pictures folder in your My Documents folder in Windows). You can then use iTunes to sync pictures from this folder, treating the folder as a single photo album.

If you want pictures in a folder to appear in multiple photo albums on your iPod touch, use the Finder (on a Mac) or Windows Explorer (in Windows) to create subfolders inside the folder and organize your picture files inside these subfolders. iTunes syncs the subfolder assignments as if they were album assignments. This technique is useful for Adobe Photoshop users who set up Adobe Bridge to organize images.

To find out more about organizing photos into albums, visit the tips section of my Web site (www.tonybove.com).

Putting pictures on the iPod touch

You can take pictures with the iPod touch (as I show in "Shooting Photos and Videos" in this chapter), but most of us already have pictures organized on our computers. To copy the pictures from your computer to your iPod touch using iTunes, follow these steps:

1. **Connect your iPod touch to your computer and then select the iPod touch name in the Devices section of the iTunes source pane.**

   iTunes displays the Summary page (under the Summary tab of the sync pages) to the right of the source pane. (See Chapter 5 for details.)

2. **Click the Photos tab of the sync pages.**

   The Photos sync options appear, as shown in Figure 9-1 (on a Mac, with Sync Photos from iPhoto selected).

3. **Select the Sync Photos From check box and then pick the source of your photos from the pop-up menu: a photo application, the Pictures (Mac) or My Pictures (Windows) folder, or the Choose Folder option.**

Figure 9-1: Sync your iPod touch with photos.

Pick your photo application (such as iPhoto on a Mac, or Adobe Photoshop Elements in Windows) from the pop-up menu. If you don't use these applications, pick the Pictures folder on a Mac or the My Pictures folder on a Windows PC. If you don't use those folders for your pictures, pick Choose Folder to use browse your hard drive or other storage media for the folder containing your pictures. After selecting the folder, click Choose (Mac) or OK (Windows).

4. **Select all pictures, or choose pictures organized in folders or photo albums or by events or faces.**

   If you are syncing photos from the Pictures (Mac) or My Pictures (Windows) folder, choose the All Photos option to copy all the pictures in the folder; or choose Selected Folders and then choose subfolders in the Pictures or My Pictures folder, which are treated as photo albums by the Photos app on your iPod touch.

   If you are syncing photos with an Adobe Photoshop Elements library, Aperture, or a version of iPhoto older than version 8, choose the All Photos (or All Photos and Albums) option to copy all the pictures in the library; or choose Selected Albums and then choose photo collections in the library, which are treated as photo albums by the Photos app on your iPod touch.

If you are syncing with iPhoto version 8 or newer, which organizes pictures by album, collection, events, or faces, select one of the following options below the Sync Photos From check box:

- *All Photos, Albums, Events, and Faces:* Select this option to copy all pictures from the library and retain album and face assignments.

- *Selected Albums, Events, and Faces, and Automatically Include:* Select this option to be more specific about which albums, events, and/or faces to sync, and to include recent events automatically. You can choose how many recent events (or events from the last month or several months) from the pop-up menu, or choose All Events or No Events. After selecting this option, you can then make selections in the Albums, Events, and Faces columns.

- *Albums column:* Click the check box next to each photo album you want to sync. (In Figure 9-1, I chose "Tony and Band" and "Tony and Special Guests" from my iPhoto library.)

- *Events column:* Click the check box next to each name or date of an event to sync the event's pictures.

- *Faces column:* Click the check box next to each face's name to sync all photos for that face. (Near the bottom of Figure 9-1, I selected Jimi Bove to include all the photos with Jimi's face in my iPhoto library.)

5. **(Optional) Select the Include Videos option.**

   Select the Include Videos option to sync video clips from your iPhoto library or from your Picture or My Picture folder (iTunes doesn't sync video clips from Adobe Photoshop Elements).

6. **Click the Apply button to apply changes and click the Sync button if synchronization hasn't already started automatically.**

   iTunes copies the pictures you selected to your iPod touch. In the process, it also deletes all other pictures from the iPod touch except those saved in Camera Roll, which I describe in the next section.

Syncing recently saved pictures

The Photos app on the iPod touch stores all recently saved pictures — the pictures (photos and video clips) you take with your iPod touch, pictures that you receive via e-mail on your iPod touch, images that you tap on Web pages in Safari to save, images you save from other apps, and screen images of the iPod touch screen — in a special photo album on your iPod touch called Camera Roll. (I describe how to take pictures, save the pictures you receive by e-mail, and take screen images later in this chapter.)

To synchronize these new pictures with your computer, connect your iPod touch to your computer as you normally would to sync it.

On a Mac, iPhoto pops up automatically (unless you set some other application to pop up for cameras in the Image Capture application's preferences) — click the Import All button, or select the pictures you want and click the Import Selected button. After importing the pictures into the iPhoto library, iPhoto asks whether you want to delete the original pictures from the iPod touch. Click Delete Originals to delete them from the iPod touch (they're safe in the photo library on your computer now) or click Keep Originals to save them on your iPod touch — in case you want to sync them with another computer, e-mail them, or upload them to social networks from your iPod touch. (If you use Aperture rather than iPhoto, you can select the project or folder you want to put the pictures in before syncing.)

On a Windows PC, follow the instructions that came with your photo application to import the pictures from a digital camera, or use the Microsoft Scanner and Camera Wizard, which saves the pictures to a folder of your choice. (The iPod touch can trick your PC into thinking it's a digital camera.) Most applications also provide an option to delete the pictures from the camera (the iPod touch) after importing.

Viewing Pictures

To view pictures on your iPod touch, follow these steps:

1. **Tap the Photos icon on the Home screen.**

   The Photos app displays the last screen you viewed when you used the app before — Albums, Events, Faces, or Places. If this is the first time, the Albums screen appears, as shown in Figure 9-2 (left side), with a list of photo albums — including Camera Roll if you've already taken pictures or saved pictures from apps on your iPod touch.

2. **Browse Albums, Faces, or Places, and tap an album name, face, or place as follows:**

   • *Albums:* You can tap a photo album's name (or the arrow to the right of the name) or tap Photo Library to see all pictures. Thumbnail images appear, as shown in Figure 9-2 (right side). Photo Library displays thumbnails of *all* the pictures in your iPod touch. Selecting an album displays thumbnails of only the pictures assigned to that album.

- *Events:* Shows a list of event titles or dates with thumbnails of the first picture of each event (based on the date of pictures in iPhoto). Tap a thumbnail or the event title or date to display thumbnails of pictures from that event.

- *Faces:* Shows a list of names with thumbnails of faces — if you've assigned faces to pictures in iPhoto. Tap a face or the name to display thumbnails of pictures with that face.

- *Places:* Shows a world map with pins of locations associated with pictures. Tap a map pin to see a label showing how many pictures were taken at that location, and tap the label to see thumbnails of those pictures.

3. **Flick your finger to scroll the thumbnails and tap a thumbnail to select a picture.**

   You might have several screens of thumbnails. Flick your finger to scroll the thumbnails and tap one to select it and view it.

To view a picture in landscape orientation, rotate the iPod touch sideways. The picture automatically changes to fit the new orientation, and expands to fit the screen if the picture is in landscape orientation. To move to the next picture in the album or collection, flick horizontally across the picture with your finger. You can flick across to go backward or forward through the album or the entire library.

Options

Figure 9-2: Tap a photo album, Photo Library, or Camera Roll (left), and then tap a thumbnail (right).

In this chapter, I use the word *picture* for any kind of photo, still image, or video clip.

Photos and images are usually higher in *resolution* (meaning that they have more pixels) than a video clip. To zoom into a photo or image to see more detail, double-tap the area you want to zoom into. Double-tap again to zoom out. You can also zoom into a photo or image by unpinching with two fingers, and zoom out by pinching. To pan around a photo or image, drag it with your finger.

Tap a photo or image to show or hide the navigation controls, as shown in Figure 9-3 (left side). You can go to the next or previous picture in the album or library by tapping the next or previous buttons at the bottom of the picture.

If the picture is a video clip, it appears with a circled play button in the center of the picture; tap the circled play button to view the clip. While playing the clip, you can tap the picture to see the previous and next buttons at the bottom of the picture, along with a frame viewer at the top that shows thumbnails of frames in the video clip and a scrubber bar, as shown in Figure 9-3 (right side). You can drag the scrubber with your finger(or tap a tiny thumbnail) to go to another position in the video clip.

Figure 9-3: Navigation controls for a photo (left) and video clip (right).

On with the Slideshow

Slideshows are an especially entertaining way of showing pictures because you can include music as well as transitions between pictures. You can display your slideshow on the iPod touch or on a television by connecting your iPod touch to the TV using the Universal Dock, Component AV Cable, or Composite AV Cable from Apple (available in the Apple Store).

Setting up a slideshow

To set up a slideshow, follow these steps:

1. **Choose Settings⇨Photos from the Home screen.**

   The Photos Slideshow Settings screen appears, as shown in Figure 9-4.

2. **Tap the Play Each Slide For option to set the duration of each slide.**

   You can select ranges from 2 to 20 seconds.

3. **Tap the Transition option to pick a transition to use between pictures in the slideshow.**

   The Wipe Across transition is my favorite, but you can select Cube, Dissolve, Ripple, or Wipe Down. Tap the Photos button to return to the Photos Slideshow Settings screen.

4. **Select other preferences as appropriate for your slideshow:**

   • *Repeat:* Repeats the slideshow.

   • *Shuffle:* Shuffles pictures in the slideshow in a random order.

5. **Tap the Settings button to return to the Settings screen or press the Home button on the device to return to the Home screen.**

iPod 🔋	4:17 PM	
Settings	**Photos**	
Slideshow		
Play Each Slide For	3 Seconds	>
Transition	Wipe Across	>
Repeat		OFF
Shuffle		OFF

Figure 9-4: The Photos Slideshow Settings screen.

 To set your iPod touch to display properly on a television, choose Settings⇨ Video. You can then turn Widescreen format on or off (depending on your television) and change your TV signal to PAL (Phase Alternating Line) for European and other countries that use PAL as their video standard. NTSC (National TV Standards Committee) is the U.S. standard and set by default.

Playing a slideshow

To play a slideshow, follow these steps:

1. Tap the Photos icon on the Home screen.

2. Choose a collection type (such as Albums, Events, Faces, or Places) as described previously, select a collection, choose a picture, and then tap the picture to show the navigation controls and buttons.

3. To start the show, tap the play button at the bottom of the picture. (Refer to Figure 9-3, left side.)

4. Use the navigation buttons to move back and forth in your slideshow.

   Tap any picture to see the navigation controls (refer to Figure 9-3) to move to the next or previous picture.

5. Tap a picture or press the Home button to stop the slideshow.

   The Home button returns you to the Home screen. You can also stop a slideshow while remaining in the Photos app by tapping the picture.

To hear music along with the slideshow, tap the Music icon on the Home screen and select a song (see Chapter 7 for details). Then double-tap the Home button to show the four most recently used apps in the bottom row of the screen, and tap Photos again to go back to your slideshow (assuming that it was recently set up in the steps above — you may have to flick left-to-right to see more recently used apps, or repeat Step 1). For more details on multitasking your apps, see Chapter 2.

Shooting Photos and Videos

The main photo and video camera is on the back of the iPod touch. The lens is on the back so that you can see the picture you are about to take on the display. The back camera can record HD (720p) video at 30 frames per second with audio, and shoot photos at 960 x 720 pixel resolution. The back camera offers 5x digital zoom and the ability to tap the picture to adjust the exposure for lighting conditions.

The iPod touch also has a front camera that can record VGA-quality photos and video at up to 30 frames per second as well as show FaceTime video calls.

You can use the Camera app to shoot photos and video clips in portrait or landscape orientation with either back or front cameras. You can record video clips that are suitable for sharing on YouTube, and you can copy them to your computer for further editing, or edit them with Apple's iMovie app.

To take a picture, choose Camera from the Home screen. If you've turned Location Services off (see Chapter 3 for details), the Camera app asks if you want to turn Location Services on if it is not already on, and if you would like Camera to use your current location. You don't have to turn Location Services on to take pictures. But if you *do* turn it on, and give Camera permission by tapping OK, Camera can then tag photos and videos with location information — which is useful for posting photos and videos on Web sites, or just for tracking the locations of your shots and clips. Camera photos are tagged with location data that includes your current geographical coordinates provided by the built-in compass.

After choosing Camera, the view through the lens appears in the iPod touch display, with the Photo/Video switch in the bottom-right corner. The switch cameras button (circular arrow) in the top-right corner lets you switch from the back camera to the front camera. When you tap the picture on the back camera, the view through the lens includes the area for automatic exposure adjustment (a blue rectangle), and the 5x digital zoom slider along the bottom, as shown in Figure 9-5 (left side).

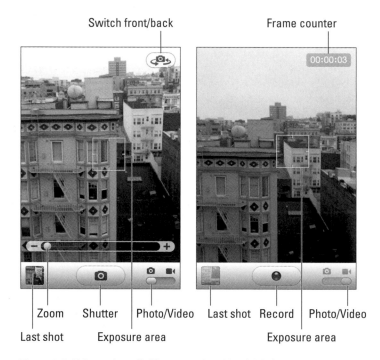

Switch front/back   Frame counter

00:00:03

Zoom   Shutter   Photo/Video   Last shot   Record   Photo/Video

Last shot   Exposure area   Exposure area

Figure 9-5: Take a photo (left) or record a video (right).

You can hold the iPod touch vertically (for portrait mode) or horizontally (for landscape mode) to snap a photo. Make sure the Photo/Video switch is set to Photo, as shown in Figure 9-5 (left side); if not, tap or slide the switch to set it to Photo.

You can tap an area of the photo if you want to change the exposure adjustment. The blue rectangle on the photo (refer to Figure 9-5, left side) shows the area where Camera is sensing the lighting conditions for adjusting the exposure. Change the area by tapping the photo in the spot where you want to focus. The Camera app automatically adjusts the exposure of the shot based on the lighting conditions for that area of the photo. Tapping the picture also displays the digital zoom slider at the bottom of the screen (camera mode only). You can zoom in or out by dragging the slider.

Tap the shutter button to take the photo. An image of a shutter closing appears on the display to indicate a photo was taken. The iPod touch makes a shutter sound unless you set the Ringer and Alerts volume all the way down by choosing Settings➪Sounds (see Chapter 3 for details on sound effects).

The photo is stored in the Camera Roll of the Photos app at high resolution. A thumbnail of your last shot appears in the lower-left corner of the Camera screen.

To shoot video, hold the iPod touch vertically (for portrait mode) or horizontally (for landscape mode), and tap or slide the Photo/Video switch to set it to Video, as shown in Figure 9-5 (right side). The shutter button turns into a red record button. Tap the record button to start recording — it blinks while recording. Tap the blinking record button again to stop recording. You can also tap an area of the video picture if you want to change the exposure adjustment, just as I describe above with photos.

You can get better results when shooting pictures if you learn more about photography and video recording, and a great place to start is *iPhone Photography & Video For Dummies,* by Angelo Micheletti.

Viewing or deleting the last shot

To see the pictures (photos and video clips) you've taken, tap the last shot button in the lower-left corner (refer to Figure 9-5) to see the last picture taken. You can then delete that picture if you don't want to include it with the pictures to be synced to your computer. To delete the picture, tap the trash icon in the lower-right corner, and then tap the Delete Photo or Delete Video button (or Cancel to cancel).

If you're not in Camera, or you want to see more of your pictures, you can also choose Photos from the Home screen. The Photos app displays the Camera Roll choice at the top, followed by Photo Library and a list of photo albums (refer to Figure 9-2, left side). After choosing Camera Roll, thumbnail images appear for all the pictures in your Camera Roll.

Trimming a video clip

To trim the video clip you just shot, tap the last shot button in the lower-left corner (refer to Figure 9-5, right side). To trim one of several video clips you've shot, choose Photos from the Home screen, tap Camera Roll, and then tap a video clip's thumbnail to select the clip.

The video clip appears with a circled play button in the middle. Tap the circled play button to play the video. You can also tap anywhere in the picture to show or hide the navigation controls shown in Figure 9-6 (left side). The frame viewer appears above the video clip.

To view the clip in landscape orientation, rotate the iPod touch sideways. The video clip automatically changes to fit the new orientation, and expands to fit the screen.

To trim the beginning or ending of the clip, touch and hold either the beginning or the end of the frame viewer so that the Trim button appears in the upper-left corner. You can then drag the beginning or end of the frame viewer to a new position. For example, you can drag the right end of the frame viewer (the end of the clip) to the left, and the left end of the frame viewer (the beginning of the clip) to the right, to trim both the beginning and end of the clip — as I do in Figure 9-6 (right side).

Tap the play button to view the temporarily trimmed video clip. You can adjust the ends of the frame viewer to trim more precisely, drag either end to its original position, or tap Cancel in the upper-left corner (to restore the full clip without trimming).

To save the trimmed version, tap the Trim button in the upper-right corner. You can then choose Trim Original, Save as New Clip, or Cancel. Tap Save as New Clip to create a second trimmed version of the clip, which is saved in the Camera Roll album along with the original. Tap Trim Original to trim the original clip.

After you tap Trim Original, the video clip is trimmed for good — you can't restore it to its original length.

Frame viewer

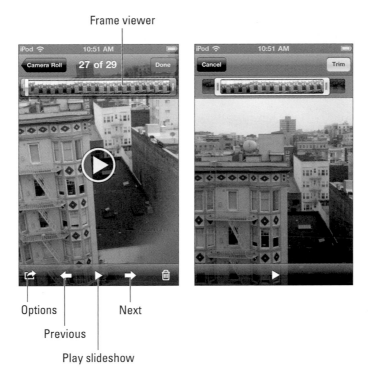

Options

Previous

Play slideshow

Next

Figure 9-6: Tap the video picture to see the controls (left); drag the ends of the frame viewer to trim the clip.

The iPod touch displays the Trimming Video message at the bottom of the screen with a progress bar. When finished, the video clip is trimmed. After trimming, you can tap Done to return to Camera (if that's where you came from), or tap Camera Roll to return to the Camera Roll thumbnails.

To learn more about shooting and managing photos and video clips, visit the free tips section of my Web site (www.tonybove.com).

Sharing Photos and Videos

What good is it to take pictures — photos and video clips — without sharing them with other people? You can share pictures stored in your iPod touch by attaching them to e-mail messages, uploading them to social networks, and sharing them over the Web using MobileMe.

Sending a picture by e-mail

To send a photo or video clip in an e-mail, tap the Photos icon on the Home screen, tap Camera Roll, Photo Library, or a photo album (refer to Figure 9-2, left side), and tap a thumbnail (refer to Figure 9-2, right side). The picture appears; tap it to see the navigation controls (refer to Figure 9-3, left side, for a photo, and right side for a video clip). Tap the options button in the lower-left corner of the screen to see the Options menu, which I show in Figure 9-7 (left side for a photo, right side for a video clip), and then tap Email Photo or Email Video to e-mail the picture.

Figure 9-7: Share a photo (left) or video clip (right).

The New Message screen appears with the photo or video clip embedded in the message. You can tap in the message field to enter text. Then fill in the To and Subject fields as described in Chapter 11.

You can also use the Options menu to assign the photo to a contact in your Contacts list (see Chapter 13 for details) or use the photo as the iPod touch wallpaper (see Chapter 3).

Sharing pictures with MobileMe and YouTube

If you've set up a gallery on MobileMe to share with others, you can include photos and video clips from your iPod touch in this gallery so that others can immediately see them. And if you have an account on YouTube, you can upload a video clip to the account. Tap the options button as described in the previous section, and then tap the Send to MobileMe button or the Send to YouTube button. You can then sign into your MobileMe account or YouTube account (if you're not already signed in), edit the video clip's description, set it to Standard Definition or HD format, select a specific MobileMe gallery or YouTube category and tags, and tap the Publish button in the top-right corner to publish it.

You can also share photos using services such as Facebook and MySpace — both offer iPod touch apps that let you upload photos from your iPod touch. See Chapter 13 for a sociable description.

Selecting and copying multiple pictures

To select more than one photo or video clip to copy and paste into another app or to share by e-mail, tap the Photos icon on the Home screen, tap Camera Roll, Photo Library, or a photo album (refer to Figure 9-2, left side), and then tap the options button in the top-right corner of the thumbnail images (refer to Figure 9-2, right side). The Select Items screen appears with thumbnails for both photos and video clips; otherwise the screen's title is Select Photos (for thumbnails of only photos) or Select Videos (for thumbnails of only video clips). Tap each thumbnail in the Select Items, Select Photos, or Select Videos screen, as shown in Figure 9-8 (left side), to select it for copying. When you tap each thumbnail, a check mark appears in the thumbnail to indicate that it is part of the selection, and the Share and Copy buttons appear at the bottom of the screen.

To e-mail selected photos, tap the Share button, and then tap Email (the Share button is disabled if video clips are selected — *copy* them instead, as I describe next). The Mail app launches and starts a new e-mail message that includes all of the selected photos (see Chapter 11 for details on sending e-mails). Note that if you select too many photos, the Share button is automatically disabled because the e-mail attachment would be too large. If you still want to share them by e-mail, you should *copy* them.

To copy the selected photos and video clips and paste them in an existing e-mail message or into another app, tap the Copy button. You can paste the photos into any app that accepts pasted images — such as a saved e-mail draft message in Mail. Touch and hold to mark an insertion point in the e-mail message (which brings up the keyboard), so that the Select/Select All/Paste bubble appears, as shown in Figure 9-8 (right side). Tap Paste to paste the images into the message.

Figure 9-8: Select images for copying or sharing (left) and paste them into a draft e-mail message (right).

Saving Pictures Attached to Messages

You probably receive photos and short video clips from others by e-mail. Now that you can get your e-mail on your iPod touch (see Chapter 11 for details on how to check your e-mail), you may also want to save the pictures you receive directly on your iPod touch so that you can view them with the Photos app or include them in a slideshow.

A down-arrow button appears within a message that contains an attached picture, as shown in Figure 9-9 (left side). Tap the down-arrow button to download the picture to your iPod touch. After the download completes, tap the picture itself in the e-mail message, and the Save Image and Cancel buttons appear, as shown in Figure 9-9 (right side). Tap the Save Image button to save the picture for the Photos app (in Camera Roll) or tap Cancel to cancel. If the message has more than one picture (such as three), you can tap a button to save them all (such as the Save 3 Images button in Figure 9-9, right side).

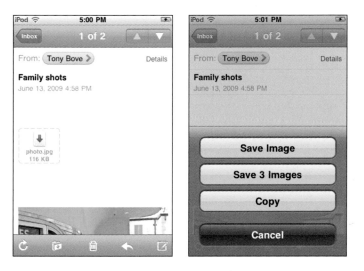

Figure 9-9: An e-mail with an image attached (left); saving images in your iPod touch (right).

Capturing a Screen Image

You too can capture images of the iPod touch screen and display them in a book or Web site, just as I have. No matter what application you're running, touch and hold down the Home button and quickly press the sleep/wake button, and release both buttons at the same time. The iPod touch screen flashes (and if your volume is up, you can hear a shutter click). This indicates that the screen was saved in Camera Roll — choose Camera Roll in the Photos app to see the image. You can capture as many screen images as you like. The next time you sync your iPod touch to your computer, your photo application (such as iPhoto) launches to receive these new images.

Part IV
Touching the Online World

The 5th Wave — By Rich Tennant

"Hold on Barbara. Let me launch Safari and see if I can find a forum on this."

In this part . . .

*T*he iPod was always in a class by itself as a media player. But the iPod touch takes the concept of playing media to an entirely new level by providing access to the world of online content. Now you can visit Web sites around the world, download songs, play YouTube videos, check your e-mail, and even monitor your stock portfolio.

Chapter 10 spins the Web and shows you how to surf Web pages with Safari. You discover how to search with Google, Bing, or Yahoo! and interact with Web services to do everything from checking live news feeds to making travel reservations.

Next, in Chapter 11, you find out how to turn your iPod touch into a lean, clean, e-mail machine. You can check e-mails from multiple e-mail accounts, send messages, and manage your e-mail settings.

Then, in Chapter 12, the weather becomes more predictable, your stocks proudly show their charts, and the Earth itself reveals its secrets in satellite and map views — all on your iPod touch.

10

Surfin' Safari

In This Chapter

▶ Browsing the Web with your iPod touch

▶ Saving and using Web page bookmarks

▶ Navigating, scrolling, and zooming into Web pages

▶ Saving Web site icons to your Home screen

*T*he World Wide Web makes the world go 'round a whole lot faster than ever before. I browse the Web for many different kinds of content and services. It's gotten to the point where I now make travel, restaurant, and entertainment reservations, and I purchase everything on the Web, from music, videos, books, and clothing to electronics equipment, garden supplies, groceries, and furniture. I get to track my shipments and purchases, review the latest news, check up on the blogs of my friends and associates, read novels, view slide shows and movies posted on the Internet, and even scan text messages from cell phones — all thanks to the Internet.

You can do all this on your iPod touch, using the Safari app after connecting to the Internet, as I describe in Chapter 4. You can also search using Google, Bing, or Yahoo! — all three services are built into Safari, and you can always browse any other search site.

Safari offers privacy settings for secure browsing, including a fraud warning, the ability to block pop-ups, control cookies, and clear your browsing history, cookies, and cache. To change your privacy settings, tap Settings⇨Safari. To learn about these settings (such as why you don't need cache for cookies!), see Chapter 15.

Take a Walk on the Web Side with Safari

Safari on the iPod touch not only lets you browse through Web sites but also lets you add bookmarks and icons to your Home screen for convenient access. (You can also synchronize those bookmarks with your computer's Web browser, as I describe in Chapter 6.)

Go URL own way

It's a snap to browse any Web site. Just tap out the site's address on the onscreen keyboard. (For instructions on using the onscreen keyboard, see Chapter 2.)

The Web site address is known as a URL (Uniform Resource Locator) and usually begins with `http://www.` followed by the name of the Web site or other characters (such as `http://www.apple.com` or `http://www.tonybove.com`). However, you can leave off the `http://www.` part and just go with the rest of the characters of the URL (`apple.com` or `tonybove.com`).

For the blow-by-blow account, check out the following steps:

1. **Tap the Safari icon on the Home screen.**

   The iPod touch displays the last Web page you visited or a blank page, with the rectangular URL entry field at the top-left corner and an oval search entry field in the top-right corner, as shown in Figure 10-1. (If you don't see these two entry fields side by side, tap the status bar at the top of the screen to jump to the top of the Web page.)

2. **Tap the URL field.**

   The onscreen keyboard appears. Above that is an entry field for typing the URL.

3. **If the entry field already has a URL, tap the circled X in the right corner of the field to clear its contents.**

4. **Tap out the URL for the Web page using the onscreen keyboard.**

   Immediately as you start typing the characters of the URL, you see a list of suggested Web sites that match the characters you typed so far (as shown in Figure 10-2). You can scroll the suggested list by dragging

Add   Pages

Navigation bar   Bookmarks

Figure 10-1: Safari's URL and search fields and navigation bar.

up and down. If the Web site you want appears, tap it to go directly to the site without further ado. Otherwise, keep typing the URL, including the extension — the keyboard includes a .com button, next to the Go button, and if you touch and hold the .com button, you can drag upward slightly to select .net, .edu, .org, or .us.

5. **Tap the Go button on the keyboard (or tap Cancel to cancel).**

   When you tap the Go button, your iPod touch closes the keyboard, displays Loading in the status bar, and loads the Web page from the Internet, if the page exists. If you mistyped the URL or the page doesn't exist, you get the message Safari Can't Open the Page because It Can't Find the Server. Tap OK and start again from Step 2.

Figure 10-2: Start entering the URL and suggestions appear.

To cancel entering a URL, tap the Cancel button in the top-right corner of the screen (refer to Figure 10-2).

> To stop a Web page from loading if you change your mind, tap the *x* on the right side of the URL entry field. This *x* turns into a circular arrow after the page is loaded. To reload an already loaded Web page to refresh its contents, tap the circular arrow.

Bookmarking As You Go

The best way to keep track of Web pages you've visited and want to visit again is to create bookmarks for the pages. You can then quickly go back to that page by selecting the bookmark. The bookmarks you create in your iPod touch synchronize with your Safari bookmarks on your Mac, or with your Safari or Internet Explorer bookmarks on your PC, as I describe in Chapter 6.

Follow these steps to save a bookmark:

1. **Browse to the Web page you want.**

2. **Tap the add (+) button in the middle of the navigation bar (refer to Figure 10-1).**

   The Add options menu appears, as shown in Figure 10-3 (left side), with the Add Bookmark, Add to Home Screen, Mail Link to This Page, and Cancel buttons.

3. Tap the Add Bookmark button to add a bookmark.

The name of the Web site appears in the title field, ready for editing, along with the onscreen keyboard, as shown in Figure 10-3 (right side). Below that is the actual URL for the Web page, and below that, the Bookmarks folder.

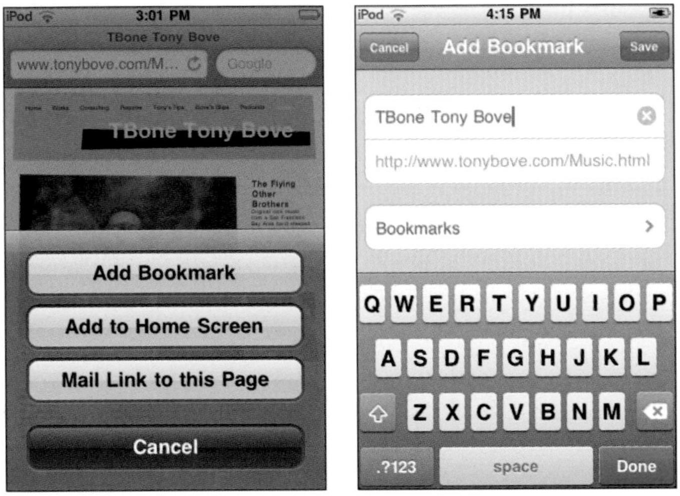

Figure 10-3: Tap Add Bookmark (left) and choose a bookmark folder (right).

4. (Optional) Edit the bookmark's title.

Before saving a bookmark, you can edit its title with the onscreen keyboard. Tap the circled X on the right side of the title field to clear its contents, or use the delete key on the keyboard to erase backward from the end of the title, and type the new title.

5. (Optional) Choose a bookmark folder.

Before saving a bookmark, you can choose a bookmark folder for saving it; otherwise, Safari saves the bookmark in the topmost level of bookmarks. Tap Bookmarks to see the list of bookmark folders — you can flick to scroll the list quickly, or drag it slowly. Select a bookmark folder by tapping it.

6. Tap the Save button to save the bookmark or tap Cancel to cancel.

The Save button appears in the upper-right corner of the display (refer to Figure 10-3, right side), and the Cancel button appears in the upper-left corner.

You can also add bookmarks to your iPod touch by syncing bookmarks from your computer's Web browser, as described in Chapter 6.

After saving or adding bookmarks, you can go directly to a bookmarked page on the Web by selecting the bookmark. Follow these steps:

1. **Tap the Safari icon on the Home screen (if it is not already running).**

   Your iPod touch displays the last Web page you visited or a blank page. A navigation bar that includes the Bookmarks button appears along the bottom, as shown in Figure 10-1.

2. **Tap the Bookmarks button — the one that looks like an open book.**

   The Bookmarks menu appears with a scrollable list of folders including the special History folder that records your page visits, and other Bookmark-related folders (such as Bookmarks Bar and Bookmarks Menu, provided with the Safari application on Macs and PCs). You can scroll this list by dragging up and down.

3. **Tap a bookmark folder to access its bookmarks.**

   For example, tapping Bookmarks Menu opens the folders and bookmarks from the Bookmarks Menu section of Safari on your Mac or PC. Tapping Bookmarks Bar opens the folders and bookmarks in the Bookmarks Bar section. Tapping History opens the history of the Web pages you've visited.

4. **Tap a bookmark to load the Web page.**

   Folders have a folder icon to the left of their names, and actual bookmarks have an open-page icon next to their Web page names. Tap a folder to reveal its contents and tap a bookmark to load a Web page.

You can edit your bookmarks and bookmark folders. Tap the Bookmarks button in the navigation bar as I describe above, and choose the folder to edit or the folder that has the bookmark you want to edit. Then tap the Edit button in the lower-left corner of the Bookmarks menu. The Edit Bookmarks display appears, with circled minus (–) signs next to the bookmark folders.

You can then do any of the following:

   ✔ To make a new folder within the selected folder, tap the New Folder button. If you want to create a new folder at the topmost level, tap the Bookmarks button in the upper-left corner to go back to the topmost Bookmarks list, tap the Edit button, and then tap New Folder.

✔ To delete a bookmark or folder, tap the circled minus (–) sign next to the bookmark or folder and then tap Delete.

✔ To reposition a bookmark or folder, drag the move icon on the right side of each bookmark or folder to a new position in the list.

✔ To edit the name of a bookmark or folder, tap the bookmark or folder and use the onscreen keyboard to type the new title. (Tap the circled X in the title field to clear its contents first, if you want.)

✔ To change where a bookmark or folder is stored, tap the Bookmark Folder field for the selected bookmark or folder and then tap a new folder to hold the bookmark or folder chosen for editing.

Tap the Done button in the bottom-left corner of the Edit Bookmarks display to finish editing.

Sending a Web link by e-mail

As I describe in Chapter 11, your iPod touch can send e-mail as well as receive it, as long as it's connected to a Wi-Fi network that's connected to the Internet. And if you want to share a Web page you just found with your friend, the steps are simple:

1. **Browse to the Web page and then tap the add (+) button in the middle of the navigation bar at the bottom of the screen. (Refer to Figure 10-1.)**

   The Add options menu magically pops up from the bottom (refer to Figure 10-3, left side), with the Add Bookmark, Add to Home Screen, and Mail Link to This Page buttons, along with a Cancel button.

2. **Tap the Mail Link to This Page button.**

   Keep in mind that you must have already set up an e-mail account on your iPod touch, as I describe in Chapter 6.

   An e-mail message appears, ready for you to finish composing. The Subject field is already filled in with the Web page name, and the link itself is already inserted in the body of the message. The To and Cc fields are left blank — ready for you to fill in.

3. **Tap the circled addition symbol (+) on the right side of the To field to select a name from your Contacts list, or use the onscreen keyboard to enter the e-mail address.**

   See Chapter 11 for details on sending an e-mail.

4. **Tap Send at the top-right corner of the display to send the message.**

Pearl diving with Google, Yahoo!, or Bing

If you've done any Web surfing at all, you already know all there is to know about search engines. They're simply *the* tool for finding Web sites. The three most popular search engines out there — Google, Yahoo!, and Bing — are built in to Safari on your iPod touch.

Google is set up to be your default Web search engine, but you can quickly change that. To choose Yahoo! or Bing (or to go back to Google), tap Settings⇨Safari⇨Search Engine, and tap Yahoo!, Bing, or Google. Turning on one search engine turns off whichever search engine was active before.

Follow these steps to search from within Safari:

1. **Tap the Safari icon on the Home screen.**

   The iPod touch displays the last Web page you visited or a blank page. You can find the URL entry field in the top-left corner and the oval search entry field, with Google, Yahoo!, or Bing in gray, in the top-right corner (you can see it in Figure 10-1). (If you don't see these two entry fields side by side, tap the status bar at the top of the screen to jump to the top of the Web page.)

2. **Tap the oval search entry field.**

   The onscreen keyboard appears. Above that is the search entry field (with a magnifying glass icon).

3. **Tap inside the search entry field.**

4. **Tap out the letters of the search term using the keyboard.**

   Immediately as you start typing characters, you see a list of suggested bookmarks in your bookmarks folder or history list. You can scroll this list by dragging up and down.

5. **If a bookmark appears that satisfies your search, tap it to go directly to the Web page without further ado. Otherwise, keep typing the search term.**

6. **Tap the Search button on the keyboard.**

   Doing so closes the keyboard and displays the search results. (***Note:*** The Search button replaces the Go button on the keyboard when searching.)

Let Your Fingers Do the Surfing

After you've found the Web page you want, you can use your fingers to navigate its links and play any media it has to offer. You can also bounce around from previous to next pages in your browsing session, open multiple pages, zoom into pages to see them clearly, and scroll around the page to see all of its sections while zooming.

Scrolling and zooming

To zoom into a Web page in Safari, spread two fingers apart on the screen (unpinch). To zoom back out, bring your fingers together (pinch).

Double-tap the display to zoom into any part of the page. You can also double-tap a column to automatically zoom in so that the column fills the iPod touch display. Double-tap again to zoom back out.

To scroll around the page, touch and drag the page. (If you happen to touch a link, drag the link so that you don't follow the link.) You can drag up, down, or sideways to see the entire Web page; or flick your finger up or down to quickly scroll the page. Use two fingers to scroll within the frame on a Web page or one finger to scroll the entire page.

To jump to the top of a Web page, tap the status bar at the top of the iPod touch screen.

All of these gestures work the same way in either portrait or landscape orientation. To view a Web page in landscape orientation, rotate the iPod touch sideways. Safari automatically reorients and expands the page. To set it back to portrait, rotate the iPod touch again.

It's all touch and go

To follow a link on a Web page, tap the link. Text links are usually underlined (sometimes in blue). Many images are also links you can tap to navigate to another page or use to play media content.

If a link leads to a sound or movie file supported by the iPod touch, Safari plays the sound or movie; if the link points to YouTube, the YouTube app launches to play the video. (See Chapter 7 for sounds and Chapter 8 for videos.) Tap an e-mail link and your iPod touch launches Mail.

You can see the link's destination — without following it — by touching and holding down on the link until the destination address appears (next to your finger). You can touch and hold an image to see whether it has a link.

To move to the previous page in your browsing sequence, tap the left-arrow button in the left side of the navigation bar at the bottom of the screen. (Refer to Figure 10-1.) Safari replaces the current page with the previous one. If you've just started browsing and this is the first page you've opened, the left-arrow button is grayed out.

To move to the next page, tap the right-arrow button (to the right of the left-arrow button) in the navigation bar at the bottom of the screen. (Refer to Figure 10-1.) Safari replaces the current page with the next one in the browsing sequence. This button is grayed out unless you've navigated backward to some previous page.

You can always go back to any of the pages you visited by tapping the Bookmarks button in the navigation bar and then tapping History. To clear your History list on your iPod touch, tap Clear.

Surfing multiple pages

Although you can open Web pages one at a time and switch back and forth between them, you can also open several pages and start a new browsing sequence with each page, just like opening separate browser windows or tabs.

Some links automatically open a new page instead of replacing the current one, leaving you with multiple pages open. Safari displays the number of open pages inside the Pages icon in the right corner of the navigation bar at the bottom of the screen. If there's no number on the icon, it means only the currently viewed page is open.

To open a separate page, tap the Pages icon on the right side of the navigation bar at the bottom of the screen; then tap the New Page button in the bottom left corner of the screen. Safari brushes aside the existing page to display a new one. You can then use your bookmarks, enter a Web page URL, or search for a Web page. (If you change your mind and don't want to open a new page, tap the Done button to cancel.)

To close a separate page, tap the Pages icon on the right side of the navigation bar to display the page thumbnail images and then tap the red circled X in the top-left corner of the Web page thumbnail for the page you want to close. The page disappears.

To switch among open pages, tap the Pages icon to display the page thumbnail images, as shown in Figure 10-4, and flick left or right to scroll the images. When you get to the thumbnail image of the page you want, tap it!

Interacting with pages

Many Web pages have pop-up menus for making choices. For example, Craigslist (www. craigslist.org) offers a pop-up menu for searching through its classified listings. To make choices for a pop-up menu, tap the menu. Safari displays a list of possible choices for that pop-up menu (for example, Craigslist offers the "search craigslist" pop-up with choices for Housing, Jobs, Personals, Services, For Sale, and so on). Choose one by tapping it; you can also flick to scroll the list of choices, or start typing to scroll directly to the first match.

Figure 10-4: Switch among open Web pages.

After choosing an option, tap the Done button to finish with that pop-up menu. You can also tap the Previous or Next buttons to move to the previous or next pop-up menu.

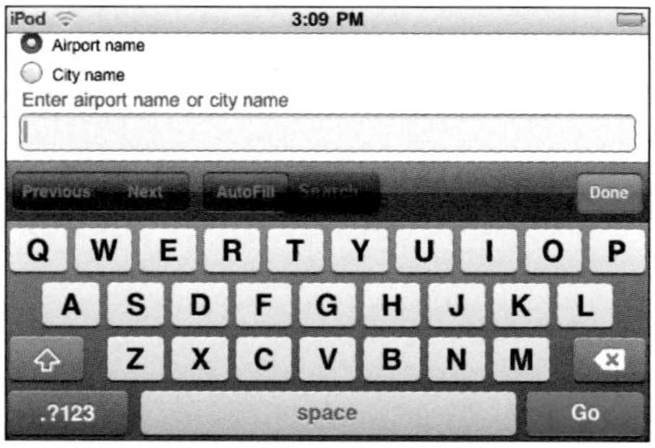

Entering text into a Web site — such as reservation information, passwords, credit card numbers, search terms, and so on — is as easy as tapping inside the text field. Safari brings up the keyboard, as shown in Figure 10-5, and you can type the text. You may want to rotate the iPod touch sideways to view Web pages in landscape (horizontal) orientation, so that the keyboard is wider and easier to use.

Figure 10-5: Entering text for a field on a Web page.

You can move to the next or previous text field by tapping the Next or Previous buttons or by tapping inside another text field. To finish typing with the keyboard, tap the Done button. If you don't like what you typed, use the delete key to delete it before tapping Done.

After you finish filling out all the required text fields on the page, tap Go on the keyboard (or tap Search, which some pages use rather than Go). If the Web page is a form, tapping Go automatically submits the form. Some Web pages offer a link for submitting the form, which you must tap in order to finish entering information.

The AutoFill button (refer to Figure 10-5) can help you fill out Web forms. To activate AutoFill, choose Settings⇨Safari and tap the AutoFill button. To use information from the Contacts app for autofilling (such as your name, phone number, e-mail, and address), turn on the Use Contact Info option, tap My Info, and then select the contact. Safari uses information from this contact to fill in fields on Web forms. To use information from names and passwords, turn on the Names & Passwords option so that Safari remembers names and passwords of Web sites you visit and automatically fills in the information when you revisit them. To remove all AutoFill information, tap Clear All.

Copying text

You may want to copy one or more paragraphs of text from a Web page to paste into another app (such as Notes) or into an e-mail. Although you can e-mail a link to a Web page (as I show you in the "Sending a Web link by e-mail" section in this chapter), you may want to copy a section of text and then paste the section into the message.

To copy a section of text from a Web page, touch and hold somewhere within the section (also known as a *long tap*). Safari automatically highlights the section with selection handles on either end, and it displays the Copy bubble (see Figure 10-6). Tap Copy to copy the selection.

Figure 10-6: Copy a selected section of text on a Web page.

If you zoomed into the Web page and the long tap selects only a single word, try zooming out first (pinching) and then trying the long tap (touch and hold) again. You can also make a more precise selection by dragging one of the handles. A rectangular magnifier appears for dragging the handle precisely. After you remove your finger to stop dragging, the Copy bubble appears.

For details on pasting the selected text into apps such as Notes or into an e-mail, see Chapter 2.

Bringing It All Back Home

Got some favorite Web site pages? You can add Web thumbnail icons for them to the Home screen so that you can access each page with one touch. Web icons appear on the Home screen along with the icons of other apps. (Discover how to rearrange the icons and add multiple screens to the Home screen in Chapter 2.)

Follow these steps to add a Web page to your Home screen:

1. **Browse to the Web page you want.**

2. **Tap the add (+) button in the middle of the navigation bar.**

   The Add options menu appears, with Add Bookmark, Add to Home Screen, Mail Link to This Page, and Cancel buttons (refer to Figure 10-3, left side).

3. **Tap the Add to Home Screen button.**

   The name of the Web page appears in the title field, ready for editing, along with the keyboard. The icon to be added to the Home screen — a thumbnail image of the site, or a graphic image defined by the site for this purpose (usually a logo) — appears to the left of the title field.

4. **(Optional) Edit the Web icon's title.**

   Before saving a Web icon to the Home screen, you can edit its title with the keyboard. Tap the circled X on the right side of the title field to clear its contents, or you can use the delete key on the keyboard to erase backward from the end of the title and then type the new title.

5. **Tap the Add button to add the Web site icon, or tap Cancel to cancel.**

   The Add button appears in the upper-right corner of the display, and the Cancel button appears in the upper-left corner.

The Postman Always Beeps Once

In This Chapter

▶ Checking and sending e-mail with an iPod touch

▶ Changing message settings and sending options

▶ Setting the Push and Fetch features for optimal e-mail retrieval

*Y*our e-mail is just a touch away. The Mail app on your iPod touch can display richly formatted messages, and you can send as well as receive photos and graphics, which are displayed in your message along with the text. You can even receive Portable Document Format (PDF) files, Microsoft Word documents, and Microsoft Excel spreadsheets as attachments and view them on your iPod touch.

The Mail app on your iPod touch can work in the background to retrieve your e-mail when you're online (see Chapter 4 for instructions about getting online). If you signed up for Apple's MobileMe service (formerly the .Mac service, now www.me.com), as I describe in illustrious detail in Chapter 6, your iPod touch can receive e-mail the instant it arrives in the mailbox on the MobileMe service. Services such as MobileMe, Microsoft Exchange, and Yahoo! Mail *push* e-mail messages to your iPod touch so that they arrive immediately, automatically. You get a single beep when your mail has arrived (unless you turned off the New Mail sound, as I describe in Chapter 3).

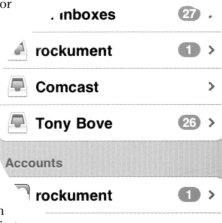

Other types of e-mail account services let you *fetch* e-mail from the server — when you select the account in Mail on your iPod touch, Mail automatically starts fetching the e-mail, and you can browse your e-mail accounts or even use other apps while Mail fetches messages. You can tell Mail to fetch more messages by tapping the Fetch (circular arrow) icon on the lower-left corner of the Mail, Mailboxes, or message screens. You can also balance pushing and fetching to save battery power, as I describe in this chapter.

You need to set up your e-mail accounts on your iPod touch in order to use Mail with them. See Chapter 6 for details on syncing, setting up, deleting, and changing settings for e-mail accounts.

Checking E-Mail

You know that you have unread e-mail if the Mail icon on the iPod touch Home screen shows a number — this is the number of unread messages in your inboxes. As e-mail is pushed (or fetched) to your iPod touch, this number increases until you read the messages. Tap the Mail icon to start the Mail app.

Mail starts out by displaying the Mailboxes screen, which gives you quick access to all your inboxes and access to your account mailboxes. If you've set up a single e-mail account, a list of its mailboxes appears, as shown in Figure 11-1 (left side). If you've set up more than one e-mail account, the Mailboxes screen lists all your inboxes, followed by the e-mail accounts you synced with your iPod touch (see Figure 11-1, right).

Tap an inbox for an e-mail account to see its message headers, or tap All Inboxes to see incoming message headers for all your accounts. A list of incoming message headers appears with the sender's name, subject, and the first sentence or two of each message, along with a blue dot if the message hasn't been read yet.

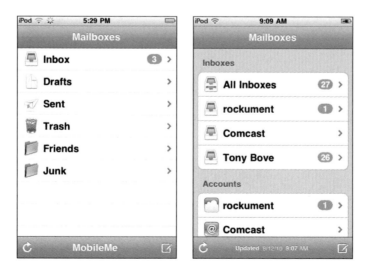

Figure 11-1: Mailboxes for a single account (left), and for multiple e-mail accounts (right).

The message is the medium

After you tap a message header to read the message, you can scroll the message by flicking or dragging your finger, and zoom into and out of the message by unpinching and pinching with your fingers. You can also zoom directly into a column in the message by double-tapping the message, and zoom out by double-tapping it again.

If you keep messages organized by thread (I show you how to change that setting in the "What you see is what you got" section, later in this chapter), related messages appear as a single entry in the mailbox. Message threads have a number next to the right arrow, showing the number of messages in the thread — as in the "4" in the header for the message from Carolyn Schmidt in Figure 11-2 (left side). The message header displayed is for the oldest unread message, or the most recent message if all the messages are read. A blue dot appears for any message in the thread you haven't read.

To see the messages in a thread, tap the thread in the mailbox. The messages in the thread appear, as shown in Figure 11-2 (right side). To read a message in a thread, tap the message. Within a message, tap the up or down arrows to see the next or previous message in the thread.

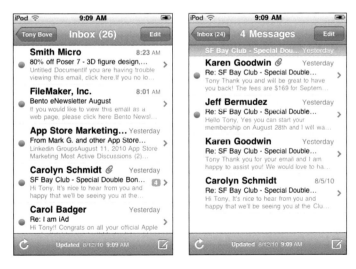

Figure 11-2: Tap a message header thread (left) to see its message headers (right).

If the e-mail includes an attachment, a button appears within the message showing the icon of an attached file and a right arrow, as shown in Figure 11-3 (left side) — to view the attachment, just tap the right arrow. If the format of the attached file is one of the supported formats (which include files that have the extensions .doc, .docx, .htm, .html, .pdf, .txt, .xls, or .xlsx), Mail downloads and opens the attachment as shown in Figure 11-3 (right side); if not, Mail displays a document icon with the name of the file — but you can't open it.

You can see all the recipients of a message (except Bcc, or *blind carbon copy,* recipients) by opening the message and tapping the blue word Details in the top-right corner of the message. Tap a name or e-mail address that appears to see the recipient's contact information. Tap Hide to hide the recipients.

You can add the sender or recipient to your Contacts list on your iPod touch by tapping the name or e-mail address. A menu appears with the contact's e-mail address and the Create New Contact and Add to Existing Contact buttons. Tap Create New Contact to create a new contact (or tap Add to Existing Contact if you want to add the information to an existing contact). Tap the e-mail address to send an e-mail to that recipient's address. (See the "Sending E-Mail" section, later in this chapter.)

Links appear in a message underlined in blue, and images embedded in the message may also have links. Tapping a link can take you to a Web page in Safari, open a map in Maps, or open a new pre-addressed e-mail message in Mail. To return to your e-mail, press the Home button on your device and tap the Mail icon.

You can mark a message as unread so that it stays in your Inbox: Open the message, tap the blue Details text in the top-right corner (refer to Figure 11-3, left side), and tap the blue Mark as Unread text next to the blue dot inside the message. The message is marked as unread — a blue dot appears next to the message header in the mailbox list until you open it again.

Deleting a message

To delete an open message, tap the Trash icon at the bottom center of the message display. Mail deletes the message from your iPod touch (but *not* from your computer or mail server unless it's set up that way — see Chapter 6) and displays the next message in sequence. You can also move to the previous or next message by tapping the up and down arrows in the top-right corner.

Previous   Next

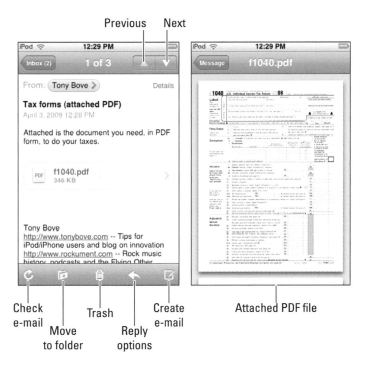

Check
e-mail
Move
to folder
Trash
Reply
options
Create
e-mail
Attached PDF file

Figure 11-3: The e-mail message appears with an attachment (left side); tap the right arrow to view the attachment (a PDF file).

You can also delete a message without opening it. In the list of message headers, drag your finger across a message header and tap the Delete button that appears.

To delete a list of messages quickly, choose the mailbox (such as Inbox) and tap the Edit button in the top-right corner of the screen. The messages appear with empty circles next to them. Tap each message so that a check mark appears in the empty circle. After checking off the messages to delete, tap the Delete button in the bottom-left corner.

Sending E-Mail

You can use the Mail app to reply to any message instantly and send e-mail to any e-mail address in the world. You can even send a message to a group of people without having to select each person's e-mail address.

To send an e-mail, follow these steps:

1. **Tap the Mail icon on the Home screen.**

   The Mailboxes screen appears. If you've set up more than one e-mail account, you should look at Step 2; otherwise, skip to Step 3.

2. **(Optional) Scroll to see your accounts and then choose an e-mail account from the Mailboxes screen for sending the e-mail.**

   You can skip this step if you synced only one e-mail account. If you have several e-mail accounts on your iPod touch, you can select one of them, or you can use the default account for sending e-mail. (See the section "Message Settings and Sending Options," later in this chapter, to set the default account.) You can also defer this decision until Step 6.

3. **Tap the pencil-document icon in the lower-right corner of the Mail screen.**

   The New Message screen appears, as shown in Figure 11-4, along with the onscreen keyboard. If you have multiple accounts set up on your iPod touch, the default account for sending e-mail appears in the Cc/Bcc, From field.

Figure 11-4: The New Message screen.

4. **Enter the recipient's e-mail address in the To field.**

   If your recipient is listed in your Contacts on your iPod touch, tap the circled addition symbol (+) on the right side of the To field (see Figure 11-4) and choose a contact to add the contact's e-mail address to the To field. You can repeat this process to add multiple e-mail addresses to the To field from your contacts.

   If your recipient isn't listed in your Contacts or if you don't know whether the recipient is listed, tap the To field entry and use the keyboard to type one or more e-mail addresses (and use a comma to separate each address). As you type an e-mail address, e-mail addresses that match from your Contacts list appear below. Tap one to add it to the To field.

5. **(Optional) Add more addresses to the Cc or Bcc fields.**

   You can add e-mail addresses to the Cc (carbon copy) and Bcc (blind carbon copy) fields to copy others. While Cc addresses appear on messages received by recipients indicating that they were copied on the message, Bcc addresses don't appear on messages received by recipients — they're like stealth readers. Tap the Cc/Bcc letters to expand the message to include the Cc and Bcc fields; then enter addresses the same way you do in Step 4.

6. **(Optional) Change the From address.**

   You can change the e-mail address for the sender to one of your e-mail accounts. The default e-mail account for sending e-mail is already selected; tap the From letters to display a pop-up menu of e-mail accounts and then tap an e-mail account to use as the sender's account.

7. **Enter the e-mail subject.**

   Tap the Subject entry field (refer to Figure 11-4) to type a subject with the keyboard; then tap underneath the Subject field to type a message. Press Return on the keyboard when you're finished.

8. **Tap Send in the upper-right corner of the display (refer to Figure 11-4) to send the message.**

You can also forward and reply to any message you receive. Open the message and tap the reply options button — the curled left-arrow that appears in the bottom-left side of the message display. Then tap Reply to reply to the sender of the message, Reply All to reply to all of the recipients as well as the sender (if there are other recipients), or Forward to forward the message to someone else (or Cancel to go back to the message). The New Message screen appears with the onscreen keyboard so that you can type your reply or add a message to the one you're forwarding. Tap Send to send the reply or forwarded message.

When you reply to a message, files or images attached to the initial message aren't sent with the reply. When you tap Forward to forward a message, a pop-up menu with the Include or Don't Include buttons appears for a message with an attachment. Tap Include to include the attachment in the forwarded message, or Don't Include to forward the message without the attachment.

To save a message as a draft so you can work on it later, start typing the message as described in the preceding steps, but before tapping Send, tap Cancel in the upper-left corner of the display (refer to Figure 11-4). Then, from the menu that appears, tap Save to save the message in your Drafts mailbox or tap Don't Save to discard the message (or Cancel to go back to typing the message). You can find the saved message in the Drafts mailbox of the same e-mail account. Tap the message to add to it or change it and then send it.

To send a photo in a message, tap the Photos icon on the Home screen and choose a photo for viewing, as described in Chapter 9.

Message Settings and Sending Options

To change your e-mail message settings and sending options, choose Settings⇨Mail, Contacts, Calendars from the Home screen. In the Mail, Contacts, Calendars settings screen that appears, use your finger to scroll down to the Mail section to change your e-mail message settings and sending options, as shown in Figure 11-5 (the upper part on the left side, and the lower part on the right).

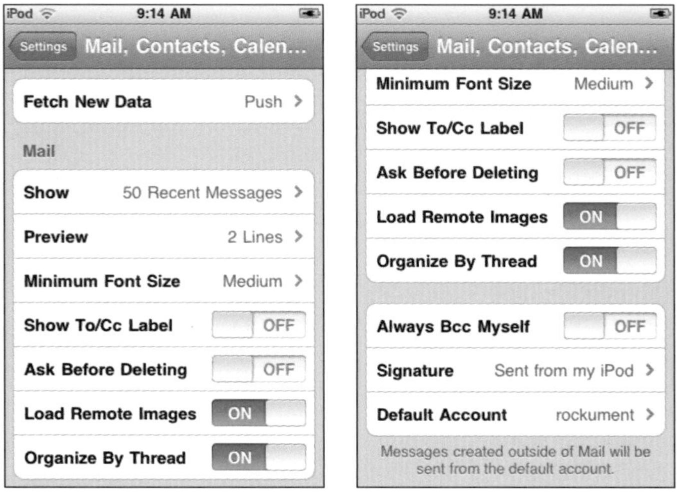
iPod
9:14 AM
Settings
Mail, Contacts, Calen...
Fetch New Data
Push
Mail
Show
50 Recent Messages
Preview
2 Lines
Minimum Font Size
Medium
Show To/Cc Label
OFF
Ask Before Deleting
OFF
Load Remote Images
ON
Organize By Thread
ON
iPod
9:14 AM
Settings
Mail, Contacts, Calen...
Minimum Font Size
Medium
Show To/Cc Label
OFF
Ask Before Deleting
OFF
Load Remote Images
ON
Organize By Thread
ON
Always Bcc Myself
OFF
Signature
Sent from my iPod
Default Account
rockument
Messages created outside of Mail will be sent from the default account.

Figure 11-5: The upper (left) and lower (right) parts of the Mail section of Mail, Contacts, and Calendars settings.

In the Mail section, you can change global settings for messages in all accounts. To set the number of messages you can see at once in a mailbox, tap Show and then choose a setting. You can choose to see the most recent 25, 50, 75, 100, or 200 messages. (To download additional messages when you're in Mail, scroll to the bottom of your Inbox and tap Download More.)

TIP

If you think you have shaky fingers and might delete a message by mistake, you can set Mail to confirm that you want to delete a message first before deleting. Tap the Off button to turn on the Ask Before Deleting option. (Tap it again to turn it off.) If Ask Before Deleting is on, Mail warns you first when you delete a message, and you have to tap Delete to confirm the deletion.

What you see is what you got

You can also set how many lines of each message are previewed in the message list headers. Choose Preview (refer to Figure 11-5, left side) and then choose to see any amount from zero to five lines of each message. To set a minimum font size for messages, tap Minimum Font Size and then choose Small, Medium, Large, Extra Large, or Giant.

If you want to see the Internet images linked to your e-mails, turn on the Load Remote Images option. However, images downloaded from the Internet can also be used by spammers to collect information, or even harbor malicious code. If you leave it off, your messages appear faster, but you have to touch each image icon to download and see it.

If you care about whether a message was sent directly to you or whether you were sent it as a Cc copy (which still might make it important, but at least you know), you can set whether Mail shows the To and Cc labels in message lists. Tap the Off button for the Show To/Cc Label option to turn it on. (Tap On to turn it off.) If Show To/Cc Label is on, you see To or Cc in the list next to each message.

If you don't want messages to be organized into threads, turn off the Organize By Thread option (tap On to turn it off). All messages appear as single messages without threads.

Return to sender, address unknown

For those who are obsessive about making sure e-mails are sent — and you know who you are — Mail can send you a copy of every message you send. Tap the Off button to turn on the Always Bcc Myself option (refer to Figure 11-5, right side). Tap On to turn it off. The Bcc refers to *blind carbon copy,* and it means that your message is sent and copied back to you without your e-mail address appearing in the recipient's list.

You can add a *signature* to your messages that can include any text — not your real, handwritten scrawl but rather a listing of your name, title, phone number, favorite quote, or all of these — to personalize your e-mails. Tap Signature (refer to Figure 11-5, right side) and then type a signature with the onscreen keyboard. The signature remains in effect for all future e-mails sent from your iPod touch.

To set the default e-mail account for sending messages, tap Default Account (refer to Figure 11-5, right side) and then choose an e-mail account. Your iPod touch will use this account whenever you start the process of sending a message from another application, such as sending a photo from Photos or tapping the e-mail address of a business in Maps.

For details on synchronizing e-mail accounts automatically from iTunes or MobileMe, as well as for setting up an account, changing account settings, and deleting accounts manually on your iPod touch, see Chapter 6.

If Not Push, Then Fetch

The Push and Fetch options control how your iPod touch receives e-mail. You can set these options for each account and for all accounts.

MobileMe, Microsoft Exchange, and Yahoo! Mail e-mail accounts can *push* messages *to* your iPod touch so that they arrive immediately after arriving at the account's e-mail server. Other types of accounts *fetch* messages *from* the account's e-mail server — either on a time schedule or manually. (If manually, you select the account before your iPod touch retrieves the email.) Push accounts (such as MobileMe e-mail) can be set to either push or fetch.

You can turn the Push feature on or off as you please. Keeping it on uses more battery power because the iPod touch receives messages immediately — whenever it's connected to Wi-Fi. When you turn the Push feature off, push accounts fetch the e-mail instead, and you can set the timetable for fetching, or set fetching to manual.

For optimal battery life, turn Push off and set Fetch to Manually so that fetching occurs only when you tap the e-mail account to read or send e-mail. Pushing e-mail as it arrives, or fetching e-mail often, uses up a considerable amount of battery power; doing both drains the battery even more quickly.

To turn Push on or off, choose Settings⇨Mail, Contacts, Calendars from the Home screen, scroll to the Mail section (refer to Figure 11-5, left side), and tap Fetch New Data. The Fetch New Data screen appears, as shown in Figure 11-6 (left side). Tap the On button for Push to turn it off (and vice versa).

Don't fret over whether you will remember to check your e-mail. You can set a timetable for fetching e-mail automatically. Choose a time interval in the Fetch New Data screen — pick Every 15 Minutes, Every 30 Minutes, or Hourly. You can also pick Manually so that the iPod touch fetches only when you tap the e-mail account to read or send e-mail.

You can also set Push or Fetch settings for individual accounts. Scroll the Fetch New Data screen to the bottom and touch Advanced. The Advanced screen appears, as shown in Figure 11-6 (right side). Each account in the list shows Push or Fetch, depending on whether the account offers push e-mail or not. Tap the account to change its settings separately.

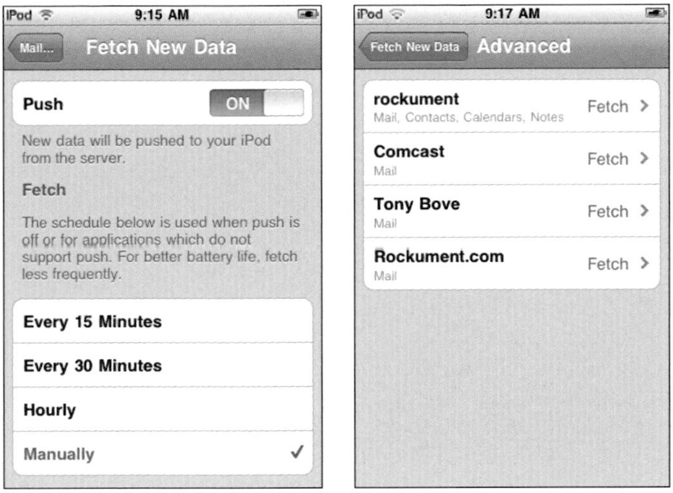

Figure 11-6: Push and Fetch settings for all accounts (left) and individual accounts (right).

Setting Push to Off or setting Fetch to Manually in the Fetch New Data screen overrides the individual account settings.

Earth, Wind, and Finance

In This Chapter

▶ Using the Maps app to find locations

▶ Getting step-by-step directions to locations

▶ Checking the weather in various cities

▶ Keeping track of your stock portfolio

*Y*our iPod touch can find almost anything on Earth, even itself, and show the location on a map or satellite picture. And although you can't harness the forces of nature, or even the influences that drive Wall Street, you can use your iPod touch to make better guesses about the weather and the stock market.

This chapter describes how to use the Maps app to find any location on Earth and obtain driving directions — without having to ask someone out on the street. Your iPod touch offers Location Services to nail down the unit's physical location, and it offers that information to the Maps app and any other app that needs it, so that you can instantly find out where you are in the world.

I also describe how to use the Weather and Stocks apps. Your iPod touch can go online (as I describe in Chapter 4) and then get real-time information about the weather and the stock market. You can personalize the Stocks app to reflect your exact portfolio, and you can add cities to the Weather app to check conditions before you travel to them.

Tapping Your Maps

I once had to find my way to a meeting on a university campus that I was already late for, and, after driving endlessly around the campus looking for the proper entranceway, I tapped the Maps icon on my iPod touch and was able to immediately look up the location, see a map of it, and get directions. The Maps app is that good — most paper maps aren't even accurate for city streets, let alone campus driveways. (And yes, I pulled over to the curb first for safety.)

The Maps app provides street maps, satellite photos, and hybrid street-satellite views of locations all over the world. It also offers detailed driving (or walking, or public transportation) directions from any location to just about any other location — unless you can't get there from here.

Where are you?

To use Maps, tap the Maps icon on the Home screen. The Maps app appears, as shown in Figure 12-1 (left side), ready for zooming, scrolling, or searching specific locations. The blue dot shows your (actually my) location.

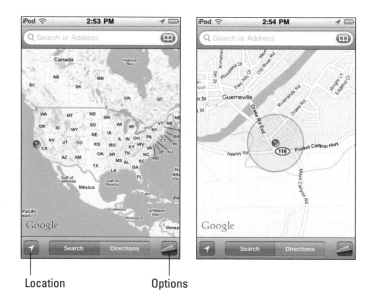

Location   Options

Figure 12-1: Tap the location button (left) to show your location closely (right).

How does Maps already know where I am? I tapped the location button in the lower-left corner of the map screen. When you do this, a dialog appears, asking whether Maps can use your current location; tap OK to use it. The map then changes to show your general location with a pulsating circle emanating from a blue dot representing your approximate physical location, as shown in Figure 12-1 (right side). This circle continues to shrink as Maps retrieves more accurate information.

You can zoom in to the map by double-tapping the map with one finger or unpinching with your fingers. To zoom out, pinch with your fingers or double-tap with two fingers. You can also drag the map to pan around it and see more areas.

Searching locations

To find a location and see a map, tap the Maps icon on the Home screen and then tap the Search field at the top of the Maps screen that appears. The onscreen keyboard appears so that you can enter information.

You can find any location by its address or closest landmark, or you can find the physical address of a friend: Type the name of someone in your contacts list, or an address, an intersection, the name of a landmark or of a general area, or a zip code.

For example, to search for a friend, start typing the person's name. If the letters you type match any names with street addresses in your Contacts list, Maps offers them up as suggestions. Tap a suggested name to look up that person's home or business address.

You can also use the Contacts app to view your contacts list and then tap a contact's address to see that person's address in Maps.

To search for a landmark, an intersection, a zip code, or a type of business, enter as much as you know into the Search field — such as *94111 pizza* for a pizza shop in the 94111 zip code. If the landmark is well known (such as Elvis Presley's Graceland in Memphis, TN), start typing its name. Then tap a suggestion that appears, or finish typing its name, as I do in Figure 12-2 (left side), and tap the Search key on the onscreen keyboard. A red pin appears to mark the location you've searched for on the map, with a label showing the name of the location or the address (see Figure 12-2, right side, for Graceland).

To clear the entry from the Search field quickly, tap the *x* on the right side of the field. You can then type a new search term.

Figure 12-2: Type a search term and tap a suggestion or the Search button (left) to see the location (right).

If you search for the name of a business or type of business *after* searching for your own location, as I do in Figure 12-3 (left side) for the nearest Starbucks, Maps is smart enough to locate the closest ones. Multiple red pins appear on the map, showing the location of each business, as shown in Figure 12-3 (right side).

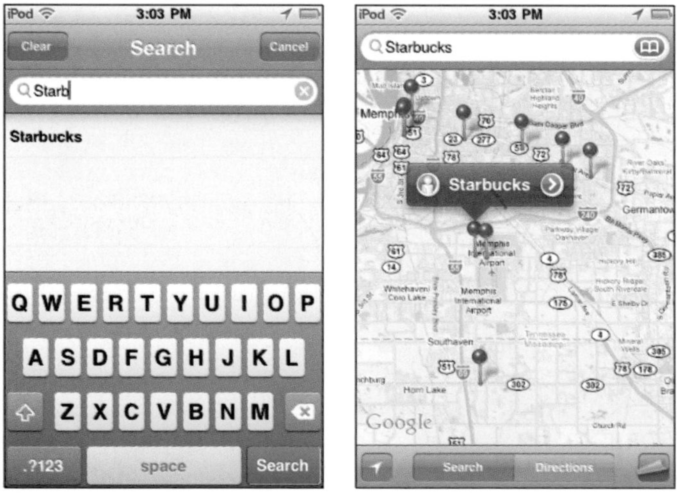

Figure 12-3: Type the name of a popular business (left) to see its nearest locations (right).

Pinpointing the spot

Red pins mark the locations you've searched for on the map (refer to Figure 12-2 and Figure 12-3, right side), and each has a label (such as Graceland and Starbucks). You can also drop your own pin on the map to pinpoint an exact spot so that you can bookmark it. The pin you drop is purple until you bookmark it and give it a name. (See the "Bookmarking the spot" section, later in this chapter.)

To drop your own pin, follow these steps:

1. **Drag the map to pan around and see more areas and zoom in to the location you want to pinpoint by double-tapping the map with one finger or unpinching with your fingers.**

2. **After finding the right location, tap the options button — the curled page icon in the bottom-right corner (refer to Figure 12-1, left side).**

   You see a menu underneath the map, as shown in Figure 12-4 (left side).

3. **Tap the Drop Pin button in the menu.**

   A purple pin appears on the map with the label Dropped Pin (see Figure 12-4, center).

4. **Touch the pin and drag it on the map to put it where you want it.**

   You can unpinch the map to zoom in further; drag the pin to a precise point, such as an intersection; pinch to zoom out; and drag to pan the map to see other areas, as shown in Figure 12-4 (right side).

Figure 12-4: Tap options (left) to drop a pin (center) and then pinpoint its location (right).

To remove the pin, tap the circled right arrow on the right side of the pin's label to see the Info screen, and then tap Remove Pin.

To see a list of all pinpointed places on your map, tap the options button and tap List. You can then tap any location in the list to select that specific pin and its label.

Bookmarking the spot

Do you want to save these locations? You can add as many pins as you want to your map and save them as bookmarks. It makes sense to bookmark your home, your zip code (to make it easy to find businesses in your area), your office, and any other locations you visit often. After you've saved bookmarks, you can go back to any location by tapping the bookmarks icon in the search field (refer to Figure 12-1, left side) to bring up a list of bookmarked locations and then tapping a location.

To bookmark a location after searching for it or dropping a pin, tap the circled right arrow on the right side of the pin's label to see the Info screen, as shown in Figure 12-5 (left side). You can then mark the spot with a bookmark that includes a name and description or do other things such as get directions. (See the "Getting directions" section, later in this chapter.)

Scroll the Info screen to find and tap the Add to Bookmarks button, which brings up the onscreen keyboard so that you can type a name for the location, as shown in Figure 12-5 (right side). Tap Save in the upper-right corner of the Add Bookmark screen to save the bookmark (or Cancel to cancel the bookmark). Tap Map in the upper-left corner of the Info screen to go back to the map. After adding a pin to your bookmarks, it changes from purple to red.

You can also touch the pin or its label and then tap Directions To Here or Directions From Here (refer to Figure 12-5, left side) to get directions. (See the later section, "Getting directions.")

To go directly to a bookmarked location, tap the bookmarks icon in the search field (refer to Figure 12-1, left side) and then tap a location, or tap the Done button in the upper-right corner to return to the map.

The bookmarks icon in the search field also offers a list of the recently searched locations as well as access to your Contacts list. Tap the bookmarks icon and then tap the Recents button at the bottom of the screen to see a list of recent locations found on the map. Tap the Contacts button next to Recents to view your Contacts and select one to see that person's address on the map. Tap the Done button in the upper-right corner to return to the map.

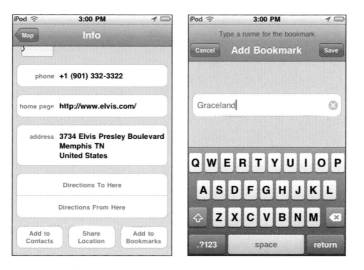

Figure 12-5: The Info screen for the location (left) for saving a bookmark (right).

A bird's-eye view

Do you want to see what the location looks like? You can change the view of the location to show a satellite image (if available), a hybrid of street view and satellite, or a list of bookmarked locations. Tap the options button — the curled page icon in the bottom-right corner (refer to Figure 12-1, left side) — to see the options menu underneath the map. Then tap Satellite to view a satellite image of the site, as shown in Figure 12-6 (center). You can zoom in to the image the same way you zoom in to the map.

You can also view a hybrid of satellite image and street map, as shown in Figure 12-6 (right side) — tap Hybrid in the menu underneath the map.

Getting directions

To get driving directions from one location to another, tap a pin on a map to see the Info screen for one of the locations (refer to Figure 12-5, left side), and then tap Directions To Here or Directions From Here to get directions. The Directions screen appears, with the first location selected as either the Start or End. For example, after tapping the Graceland pin to show the Info screen in Figure 12-5 (left side), I tapped Directions To Here, which automatically placed the location in the End field, as shown in Figure 12-7 (left side).

Figure 12-6: The options menu (left); after tapping Satellite (center) and Hybrid (right).

You can also search for or pinpoint a location, as described in the previous section, and then tap Directions at the bottom of the map screen. For example, if you want to get directions from your current location to a bookmarked location, first find your physical location on the map by tapping the location button in the lower-left corner of the map screen (refer to Figure 12-1, left side). Then tap Directions, and in the Directions screen that appears, your current location already occupies the Start field. Tap the bookmarks icon in the End field and select a bookmarked location for the End field.

You can also type entries or select bookmarks for both the Start and End fields by tapping those fields and using the onscreen keyboard.

Are you taking a round trip? You can switch the entry for Start to End (or vice versa) by tapping the looped arrow button to the left of the Start and End fields (refer to Figure 12-7. left side). Using this button, you can get directions one way; then tap the button to reverse the Start and End fields to get directions for the way back.

After setting your Start and End locations, tap Route in the bottom-right corner of the onscreen keyboard (refer to Figure 12-7, left side) to mark the route on the Directions map, as shown in Figure 12-7, right side. Alternatively, you can tap Clear in the upper-left corner to reenter your Start and End fields, or Cancel in the upper-right corner to cancel getting directions.

Figure 12-7: Set the Start and End fields and tap Route (left) to see the route on the Directions map (right).

As shown in Figure 12-7 (right side), the route on the Directions map is purple, with pins marking the start and end locations. Tap the car icon at the top of the Directions map to see driving directions and the approximate driving time. If traffic data is available, the driving time is adjusted accordingly, but don't expect miracles — the information depends on data collected and services provided by third parties, not by Apple, and traffic patterns change. You can also tap the bus icon to see public transit directions, or tap the walking man icon to see walking directions.

To view directions one step at a time on the map, tap Start in the upper-right corner of the Directions map (refer to Figure 12-7, right side) to see the first leg of the journey. Then tap the right-arrow button in the upper-right corner of the first leg's screen (see Figure 12-8, left side) to see the next stretch, and keep tapping all the way to the end (see Figure 12-8, right side). You can also tap the left-arrow button in any of the step-by-step directions to go back a step. The Maps application graciously walks you through your entire journey.

To view all the legs of your journey in a list, tap the options button in the lower-right corner of the display, and tap List. Then tap any location in the list to see a map showing that leg of the trip.

Figure 12-8: Move step by step through the directions from beginning (left) to end (right).

To see your most recent set of directions, tap the bookmarks icon in the search field and tap Recents at the bottom of the Bookmarks screen to change it to the Recents screen. If you close Maps and return to it later, your directions appear automatically. Tap the Done button in the upper-right corner to return to the map.

You can also get travel directions in advance (using Google Maps on your computer) and then transfer them to your iPod touch by e-mail. You can then open the e-mail on your iPod touch and tap the Google Maps embedded link — Maps opens automatically to show you the directions. As you open more e-mails and tap more links, your directions are remembered in Maps on your iPod touch in the Recents screen.

Digging into Google Earth

Find the source of the Nile River and follow it all the way to the great pyramids in Egypt (which you can see in the fourth figure). Or just take a peek in your neighbor's backyard or the streets where I live (the second figure with blue dot). Google Earth, available for free for desktop computers, lets you fly anywhere on Earth to view satellite imagery, maps, terrain, 3D buildings, from galaxies in outer space to the canyons and mystery spots of the ocean.

The Google Earth app for the iPod touch displays the same imagery and offers the same navigational capabilities as the desktop version, and it includes layers with geo-located Wikipedia articles and Panoramio photos with details (as shown in the third figure), as well as map labels and borders. With the Search Near Me function, query results are not only geo-located within Google Earth, but also are automatically relevant to your location — search for *pizza* while in San Francisco, and it shows a collection of San Francisco pizza restaurants. The Auto tilt feature uses the iPod touch built-in accelerometer to change your view in Google Earth when you tilt the iPod touch — you can tilt at an angle to see a skyline view of a location or tilt it all the way to see the sky itself. You can even track your movements on the planet: Tap the Location button to see a blue dot corresponding to your location (see the second figure with blue dot), and as your location changes, the dot and your view in Google Earth are updated accordingly.

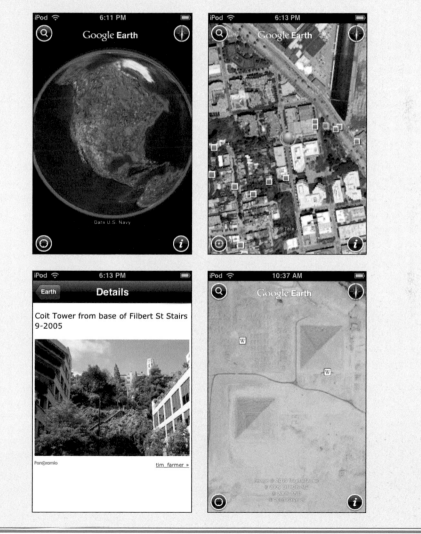

Riding on the Storm

The Weather app provided with your iPod touch looks up the current temperature and weather conditions, and it provides a six-day forecast for any city of your choice. (Of course, your iPod touch needs to be connected to the Internet for the Weather app to work — see Chapter 4 for details on getting online.) Weather (which uses Yahoo! for its data) isn't the only app that does this — you can try other apps such as The Weather Channel, WeatherBug, or WeatherHD.

To use Weather, tap the Weather icon on the Home screen. In daytime, the weather screen is light blue, and at night it's dark purple. What makes Weather useful is your ability to add your own cities — as many as you need — so that you can look up the weather in multiple locations instantly.

To add a city, follow these steps:

1. **Tap the *i* button in the lower-right corner of the weather display for your city, as shown in Figure 12-9 (left side).**

2. **Tap the add (+) button in the upper-left corner of the Weather screen (Figure 12-9, center).**

   A location field appears with the onscreen keyboard (Figure 12-9, right side).

Figure 12-9: Tap the *i* button in Weather (left) to view the list of cities (center) and to add another city (right).

3. **Enter the city's name or zip code — as you type, suggestions appear below in a list.**

4. **Choose one of the suggestions or continue typing the city name or zip code and then tap Search.**

   The city you chose appears in the list of cities in the Weather screen, with a circled minus (–) sign next to it on the left and three horizontal gray bars on the right, as shown in Figure 12-10 (left side).

   At this point, you can add more cities by tapping the add (+) button in the upper-left corner again. You can also reorder the list of cities by dragging the three gray bars next to a city to a new place in the list, as shown in Figure 12-10 (right side).

Figure 12-10: Reorder the list of cities in Weather (left) by dragging the three gray horizontal bars for the city (right).

To delete a city, tap the circled minus sign next to the city name to show the Delete button and then tap the Delete button (or tap the circled minus sign again to leave it alone).

Tap the Done button in the top-right corner of the Weather screen to finish adding cities and see the weather display for your city.

To switch from one city to the next, flick your finger over the city weather display horizontally or tap the tiny white buttons at the bottom of the city weather display (refer to Figure 12-9, left side).

Tapping Your Moneymaker

You can check your financial stocks, funds, and indexes with your iPod touch as long as it's connected to the Internet (see Chapter 4 for details on getting online). (Whether the news is good or bad, you can quickly e-mail your broker — see Chapter 11.)

Tap the Stocks icon on the Home screen. The Stocks app displays a few stocks and indexes you may be interested in (such as Apple, of course), and it shows updated quotes if the iPod touch is connected to the Internet (although quotes may be delayed by up to 20 minutes). Scroll the Stocks list by dragging or flicking it with your finger.

Swipe the lower section of the Stocks screen to see a summary, a graph (as shown in Figure 12-11, left side), or the latest news. To see a current graph of the stock, swipe the lower section to the center and then tap the 1d (one day), 1w (one week), 1m (one month), 3m (three months), 6m (six months), 1y (one year), or 2y (two years) buttons above the graph in the stock reader. Tap the change number next to each stock to switch to show the percentage change, the market cap, or the change in price.

Figure 12-11: Touch the *i* button in Stocks (left) to view the list (center) and to add another stock, fund, or index (right).

Of course, you'll want to add your portfolio to Stocks. To add a stock, index, or fund to watch, here's what you do:

1. **Tap the *i* button in the lower-right corner of the stock reader, as shown in Figure 12-11 (left side).**

2. **Tap the add (+) button in the upper-left corner of the Stocks screen (Figure 12-11, center).**

   The Add Stock field appears with the onscreen keyboard (Figure 12-11, right side).

3. **Enter the stock symbol or company name (or index or fund name).**

   As you type, suggestions appear below in a list.

4. **Choose one of the suggestions or continue typing the symbol or name and then touch Search.**

The stock, fund, or index you chose appears in the list in the Stocks screen, with a circled minus (–) sign next to it on the left, and three horizontal gray bars on the right (refer to Figure 12-11, center).

At this point, if you want to add more stocks, funds, or indexes, tap the add (+) button in the upper-left corner again. To reorder a list of stocks, drag the three gray bars next to a stock to a new place in the list, in the same way that you can reorder cities in the Weather app (refer to Figure 12-10).

To delete a stock, tap the circled minus sign next to the stock name to show the Delete button and then tap the Delete button (or tap the circled minus sign again to leave it alone).

Tap the Done button in the top-right corner of the Stocks screen to finish adding stocks and see the stock reader.

Part V
Staying in Touch and Up-to-Date

The 5th Wave   By Rich Tennant

"You ever notice how much more streaming media there is than there used to be?"

In this part . . .

By now you should be accustomed to using your iPod touch like a small computer — and that's just what it is, a computer in your pocket that runs apps from the App Store. Some of these apps are just as powerful as the ones on your computer, especially ones that connect you to your social world.

Chapter 13 puts you in contact with your contacts, helps you manage your calendar, and connects you not only to your contacts with FaceTime video calls, but also with the most popular social networks on the planet — Facebook, MySpace, and Twitter.

I saved the unfun stuff for Chapter 14: how to keep your iPod touch software up-to-date, how to reset the software and your settings, and how to restore your iPod touch to pristine factory condition.

13

A Day in the Social Life

A s John Lennon once sang, "Life is what happens to you when you're busy making other plans." And while life happens to you in real time, you can consult your iPod touch Calendar app to view your appointments, change them, and make new ones. One of the major benefits of using an iPod touch is the onscreen keyboard, which you can use to enter text, such as calendar entries, as I describe in this chapter.

In this chapter, I also demonstrate how to look up contact names, addresses, and phone numbers with your iPod touch, change contact information, and add new contacts. Any changes you make to calendars and contacts are synchronized with your desktop applications (as I describe in Chapter 6).

5:10 PM
Recording 00:02

To socialize and stay in contact with friends, relatives, and associates, you can use social networks, such as Facebook and MySpace, to share photos, thoughts, links, and profile information. The App Store offers social networking apps that link you directly to these networks and to messaging sites such as Twitter. Even better, you can make FaceTime video calls with people you know who are using either a fourth-generation iPod touch or iPhone 4.

You'll find all this and more in this chapter on your social life with iPod touch.

Checking Your Calendar

The Calendar app isn't just for looking up dates (though it's quite good at that). If you see a blank calendar, it means you need to synchronize your iPod touch with your calendar files from iCal (Mac) or Outlook (Windows), as I describe in Chapter 6. If you opened Calendar before, the app shows the calendar and view opened previously, such as the Month view shown in Figure 13-1 (right side).

If you've synced multiple calendars to your iPod touch (see Chapter 6 for details), they are merged into one calendar. You can select individual calendars by tapping the Calendars button in the upper-left corner to see the list of calendars, shown in Figure 13-1 (left side). Tap All at the top to view all calendars merged into one or tap a specific calendar to see only that calendar. You can also tap the Hide All Calendars button to hide all events, or tap the e-mail for your MobileMe account to show the calendar synced with MobileMe.

Tap any day to see the events on that day, which are displayed below the calendar view in a list; tap the event to see the event's information.

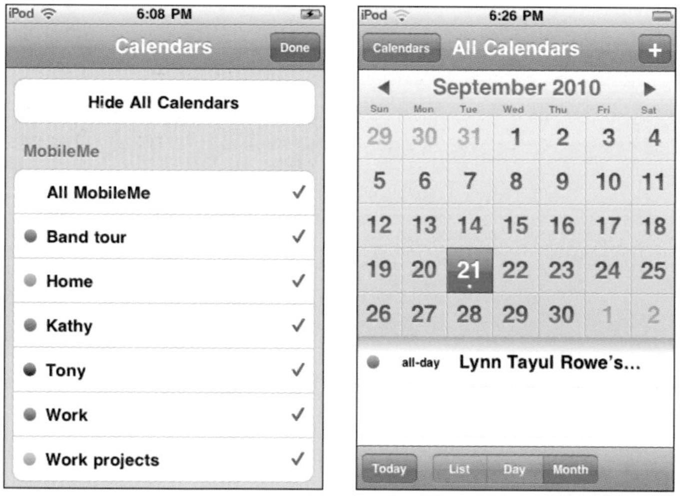

Figure 13-1: The Calendar app's list of calendars (left) and monthly view (right).

Tap the List, Day, or Month buttons to change the calendar view to a list of events, a full day of scheduled events, or a month view, respectively. In Day or Month view, tap the left or right arrows at the top of the calendar to switch days or months. If you roam around from day to day or month to month, tap the Today button in the lower-left corner of the display to see the calendar for today.

A change is gonna come

Change happens, and you'll want to change your schedule or even add new events as you learn about them. Although you can enter appointments and events on your computer and sync them with your iPod touch, as I show you in Chapter 6, you can also enter and change appointments and events directly in your iPod touch and keep changes and additions synced with your computer and with other devices using MobileMe.

To add an event, follow these steps:

1. **Open the Calendar app as described earlier.**

   The Calendar app opens (refer to Figure 13-1) — either the Calendar view appears, or if you have multiple calendars, the list of calendars appears — in which case you need to tap a calendar to use for the new event.

2. **Tap the add (+) button in the upper-right corner of the Calendar screen.**

   The Add Event screen appears, as shown in Figure 13-2 (left side).

3. **Tap the Title/Location button and enter the event's title and location using the onscreen keyboard, as shown in Figure 13-2 (right side).**

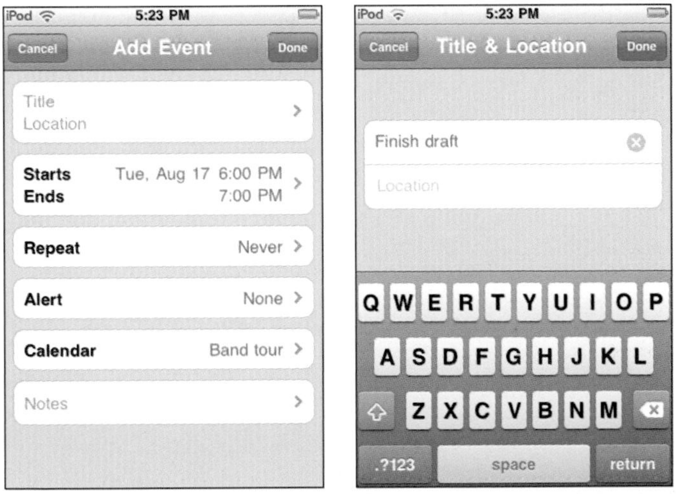

Figure 13-2: Add an event in Calendar (left) and give it a title and location (right).

4. **Tap Done in the upper-right corner to save the entry (or Cancel in the upper-left corner to cancel the entry).**

   The Add Event screen appears again for selecting more options, as shown in Figure 13-3 (left side).

5. **Tap the Starts/Ends button to enter the starting and ending times and dates.**

   The Start & End screen appears, as shown in Figure 13-3 (right side), with a slot-machine-style number wheel to select the date and time.

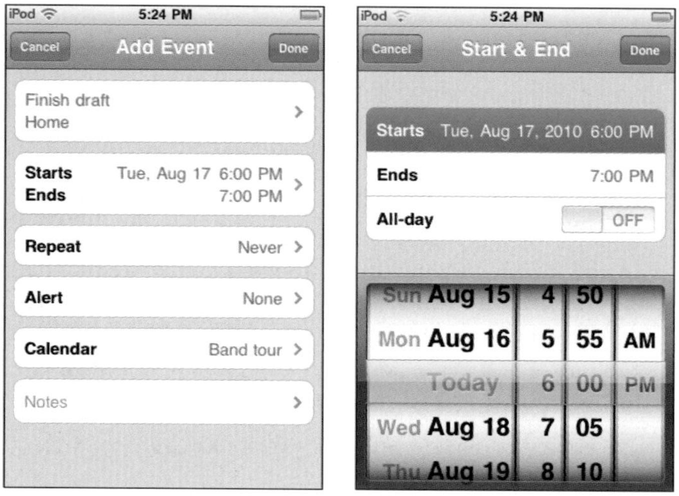

Figure 13-3: Tap Starts Ends (left) and enter starting and ending dates and times (right).

6. **Tap the Starts button and select the date and time or tap the Off button for All-Day to turn on the All-Day option.**

   Slide your finger up and down the slot-machine-style number wheel to select the date and time. If you turn on the All-Day option, the number wheel changes to show only dates; select a date for the all-day event and skip the next step.

7. **Tap the Ends button and select the date and time as you did in Step 6.**

8. **Tap Done in the upper-right corner to save the entry (or Cancel in the upper-left corner to cancel the entry).**

The Add Event screen appears again for selecting more options (refer to Figure 13-3, left side).

9. **(Optional) Set the event to repeat by tapping Repeat and selecting a repeat time; then tap Done (or Cancel).**

   You can set the event to repeat every day, every week, every two weeks, every month, or every year (or none, to not repeat). After you tap Done (or Cancel), the Add Event screen appears again for selecting more options.

10. **(Optional) Set an alert for a time before the event by tapping Alert and choosing an alert time; then tap Done (or Cancel).**

    You can set the alert to occur from five minutes to two days before the event. You can also set a second alert time in case you miss the first one. Tap Done (or Cancel) to finish, and the Add Event screen appears again for selecting more options.

11. **(Optional) If you have multiple calendars synced with your iPod touch, you can change the calendar for the event by tapping Calendar and choosing a calendar.**

    The Calendars screen appears with a list of your calendars. Tap a calendar's name to choose it. After you tap Done (or Cancel), the Add Event screen appears again.

12. **(Optional) Enter notes about the event by tapping Notes and using the onscreen keyboard to type notes.**

    The Notes field appears along with the keyboard so that you can type your notes. Tap Done (or Cancel).

13. **Finally, tap Done in the upper-right corner of the Add Event screen to save the event (or Cancel in the upper-left corner to cancel the event).**

    The new event now appears in your calendar in the lower portion of the Calendar screen when you select the day, as shown in Figure 13-4 (left side).

To edit an event, tap the event in the lower portion of the Calendar screen, and then tap Edit in the upper-right corner of the Event screen. The event information appears and is ready for editing or deleting, as shown in Figure 13-4 (right side). To edit the event information, follow Steps 3–13 in this section.

The Delete Event button appears only when you're editing an event. After tapping Delete Event, a warning appears to confirm the deletion — tap Delete Event again or tap Cancel. The Calendar screen appears.

Figure 13-4: Tap the event title (left) to edit or delete the event (right).

Yesterday's settings (and today's)

You can set alerts for meeting invitations and choose how many weeks of events to sync back to (to clear out old events). Choose Settings⇨Mail, Contacts, Calendars from the Home screen and then scroll the Mail, Contacts, Calendars settings screen to the Calendars section, as shown in Figure 13-5 (left side).

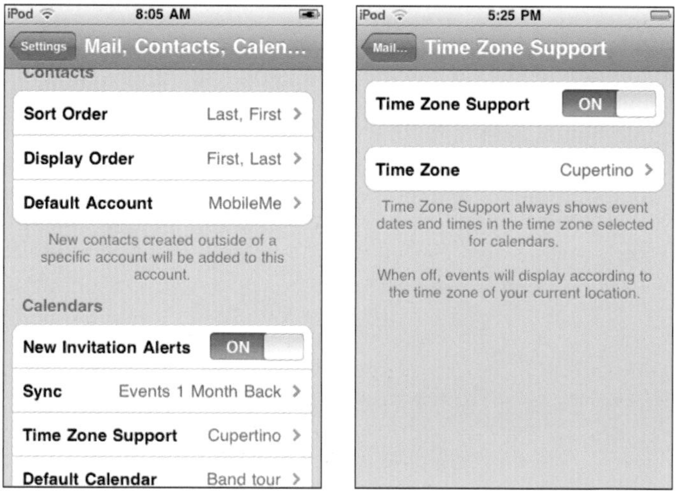

Figure 13-5: The Contacts and Calendars sections for settings (left) and the Time Zone setting (right).

To set the option for how far back in time to sync your calendar events, tap Sync and choose a period of time (such as Events 2 Weeks Back).

If you have a Microsoft Exchange account set up with Calendars enabled, you can receive and respond to meeting invitations from others in your organization that also use Exchange. To set a sound as an alert for receiving a meeting invitation, tap the Off button for New Invitation Alerts to turn it on.

You can also turn time zone support on or off. When time zone support is on, event dates and times are displayed in the time zone of the city you selected. When time zone support is off, events are displayed in the time zone of your current location as determined by the network time. You might want to turn it on and select your home city so that dates and times are displayed as if you were in your home city, rather than where you actually are. For example, if you live in San Francisco and you're visiting New York, turning on Time Zone Support and selecting San Francisco keeps the dates and times in your calendars on San Francisco time. Otherwise, they would switch to New York time.

To turn on time zone support, tap Time Zone Support, and on the Time Zone Support screen (refer to Figure 13-5, right side), tap Off to turn on Time Zone Support (or tap On to turn it off). Then tap Time Zone and enter the name of a major city. As you type, city names are suggested based on what you've typed. Select the city to return to the Time Zone Support screen and then tap the Mail button in the upper-left corner to return to the settings screen — or, if you're finished making changes, press the Home button to leave settings altogether and return to the Home screen.

You can set your iPod touch to play a beeping sound for your calendar alert. Choose Settings➪General➪Sounds and tap the Off button for Calendar Alerts to turn it on. (Tap it again to turn it off.)

Using Your Contacts

The bits of information that you're most likely to need on the road are people's names, addresses, and phone numbers. You can use the Contacts app on your iPod touch to store this information and keep it all in sync with your computer. (For sync info, see Chapter 6.)

To view contacts on an iPod touch, tap the Contacts icon on the Home screen. The All Contacts screen appears. If you've organized contacts into groups, you can tap the Groups button in the upper-left corner of the screen to show the Groups screen, and then tap a group to see just that group, or tap All Contacts to return to the All Contacts screen.

The contact list is sorted at first in alphabetical order by last name (in bold) but displayed so that the first name comes first, as shown in Figure 13-6 (you can change contact sorting and displaying, as I show in the next section). Scroll the list of contacts with your finger or tap a letter of the alphabet along the right side to go directly to names that begin with that letter. Then tap a contact to see that person's info screen.

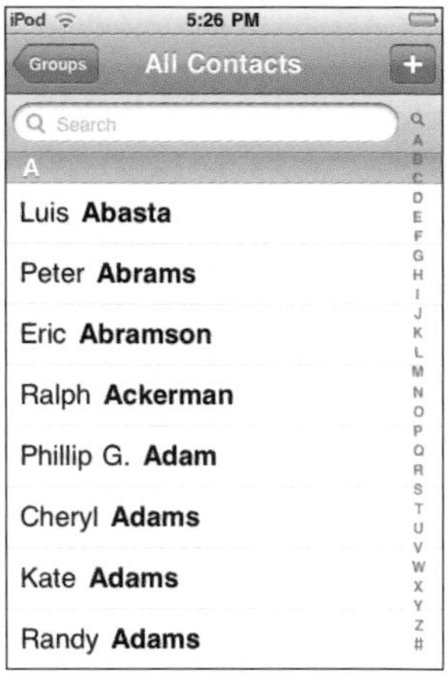

The contact's info screen shows all the information about reaching that contact. Tap an e-mail address to bring up the Mail app and send an e-mail to that contact. Tap a Web site address to load that page into Safari. Tap a physical address (with a street address) to bring up the Maps app and locate the contact on the map.

Figure 13-6: Scroll the alphabetical list or tap a letter along the right side.

Orders to sort and display

You can change which way the contacts sort so that you can look up people by their first names (which can be time-consuming with so many friends named Elvis). Choose Settings⇨Mail, Contacts, Calendars and then scroll the Mail, Contacts, Calendars settings screen to the Contacts section (refer to Figure 13-5, left side). Tap Sort Order and then tap one of these options:

- ✔ **First, Last:** Sorts the contact list by first name, followed by the last name, so that *Brian Jones* sorts under the letter *B* for *Brian* (after *Brian Auger* but before *Brian Wilson*).

- ✔ **Last, First:** Sorts the contacts by last name, followed by the first name, so that *Brian Jones* sorts under the letter *J* for *Jones*. (*Jones, Brian* appears after *Jones, Alice* but before *Jones, Norah*.)

You can also display contacts with their first names followed by their last names, or last names followed by first names, regardless of how you sort them. Choose Settings⇨Mail, Contacts, Calendars and then scroll the Mail, Contacts, Calendars settings screen to the Contacts section. Tap Display Order and then tap one of these options:

- ✔ **First Last:** Displays the contacts list by first name and then last name, as in *Paul McCartney*.

- ✔ **Last, First:** Displays the contacts list by last name followed by a comma and the first name, as in *McCartney, Paul*.

Soul searchin'

Can't remember the person's full name or last name? You can search for any part of a person's name in Contacts by tapping the Search entry field at the very top of the list of contacts. The Search entry field appears with the onscreen keyboard, as shown in Figure 13-7, and suggestions appear as you type.

Tap a suggested name to open the Contacts record for that person. You can then edit or delete the contact information.

Adding, editing, and deleting contacts

Figure 13-7: Search for a contact by typing part of a name.

You meet people all the time, so why not enter their information immediately? You can enter new contacts, edit existing contacts, and even delete contacts directly on your iPod touch, and keep your contacts in sync with your computer. (For sync info, see Chapter 6.)

To add a contact, follow these steps:

1. **Tap the Contacts icon on the Home screen.**

2. **Tap the add (+) button in the upper-right corner of the Contacts display.**

   The New Contact screen appears, as shown in Figure 13-8 (left side).

3. **Tap the First/Last/Company button and enter the contact's first and last name, as well as the company name, into each field using the onscreen keyboard.**

   The First, Last, and Company fields are ready for you to enter text (see Figure 13-8, right side) with the keyboard. (If you tap the field to set an insertion point, the Paste bubble appears so that you can paste text you recently cut or copied — see Chapter 2 to find out how to copy or cut and paste text.)

4. **Scroll the screen and tap the Phone button next to the Mobile label to enter a phone number.**

   After tapping Phone, as shown in Figure 13-9 (left side), the numeric keyboard pops up for typing the number. (After typing a number, another Phone button appears below it, so that you can type more numbers.)

Figure 13-8: Add a new contact (left) and enter the contact's name (right).

5. **(Optional) tap the Mobile label to change the phone number's label.**

Tap the number's label to select a different label for the type of phone (mobile, home, work, main, home fax, and so on), as shown in Figure 13-9 (right side).

To enter a pause in a phone number (sometimes required for extensions or code numbers), tap the +*# button and tap Pause, which inserts a comma representing the pause. Each pause lasts two seconds; you can enter as many as you need.

6. **(Optional) Scroll down and tap the next Phone button to add more phone numbers, following the instructions in Steps 4 and 5 for each phone number.**

After typing a number, another Phone button appears below it, so that you can type more numbers — scroll the screen to see it.

7. **Tap the Email button to add an e-mail address using the onscreen keyboard and tap the Home label to change the label for the type of e-mail address.**

After tapping Email, the onscreen keyboard appears under the field to enter the e-mail address. Tap the Home label to change the label describing the e-mail address. After typing an e-mail address, another Email button appears below it, so that you can type more e-mail addresses — scroll the screen to see it.

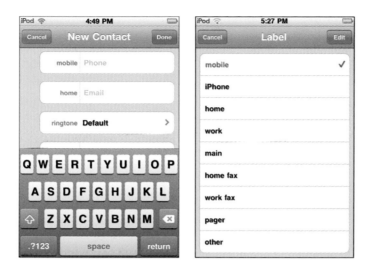

Figure 13-9: Enter the contact's phone number (left) and change the number's label (right).

8. **(Optional) Scroll down and tap the next Email button to add more e-mail addresses, following the instructions in Step 7 for each e-mail address.**

9. **(Optional, fourth-generation iPod touch only) Tap Ringtone to set a unique ringtone for this contact to use in FaceTime.**

   The ringtone you choose will play whenever that contact makes a FaceTime call to you. See the later section, "Communicating with FaceTime," for details on making and receiving FaceTime video calls.

10. **(Optional) Tap the URL button to add a Web page URL for the contact, and tap the Home Page label to change the label for the type of Web page.**

   After typing a Web page URL, another URL button appears below it, so that you can type more Web page URLs — scroll the screen to see it.

11. **Tap Add New Address on the New Contact screen (refer to Figure 13-8, left side), and add the address information; then tap the Home label to change the label for the type of address.**

   The keyboard appears with two entry fields for Street and one each for City, State, and ZIP. Tap the country button to set the country, and the label button (set to Home) for the type of address. After typing the address, another Add New Address button appears below it, so that you can type more addresses — scroll the screen to see it.

12. **(Optional) Tap Add Field to add more fields to the contact.**

    You can add a prefix, middle name, suffix, phonetic first and last names, nickname, job title, department, birthday, date, or note. As you tap each field, the New Contact screen appears with the keyboard to type in the information.

13. **(Optional) Add a photo.**

    To add a photo, tap Add Photo in the upper-left corner of the New Contact screen (see Figure 13-8, left side). A pop-up menu appears with Take Photo, Choose Photo, or Cancel. The Take Photo option takes you to the Take Picture screen, where you can tap the camera shutter button to take a picture (or tap Cancel to cancel). The Choose Photo option takes you to the Photos app, where you can tap a photo album and then tap a photo. Finally, tap Set Photo (or Cancel).

14. **Tap Done in the upper-right corner of the New Contact screen to save the contact information (or Cancel in the upper-left corner to cancel the contact information).**

To edit a contact, tap the contact to see the contact's Info screen and then tap Edit in the upper-right corner of the Info screen to show the circled minus (–) sign and add (+) button.

You can edit or delete any information for a contact while leaving the rest of the information intact. Tap any field to edit the information in that field. Tap the circled minus (–) sign next to the information to reveal a Delete button; tap the Delete button to delete the information, or tap the circled minus sign again to leave it alone.

To change a photo, tap the existing photo in the upper-left corner of the Info screen. A pop-up menu appears for you to tap Take Photo, Choose Photo, Edit Photo, Delete Photo, or Cancel. Tap Take Photo or Choose Photo as described in Step 13 earlier. To move or scale the photo, tap Edit Photo to show the Move and Scale screen. Then pinch the image with your fingers to zoom out or unpinch to zoom in, and drag the image with your finger to show only a portion of it. Tap the Set Photo button in the bottom-right corner of the Move and Scale screen to save the edited image (or tap Cancel). You return again to the Info screen.

Tap Done in the upper-right corner of the Info screen to finish editing and return to the contact information.

To delete a contact entirely, tap Edit, scroll down to the bottom and then tap Delete Contact. Remember, if you do this, the contact will also be deleted from your contact list on your computer when you sync your iPod touch.

Instant voice and text messaging

The iPhone gets all the glory for its communicating abilities with its phone and SMS text messaging services provided by the service carrier (AT&T in the U.S.), but the iPod touch is no slouch in this department — in fact, the iPod touch can make you carrier-free. All you need to do is go online with a Wi-Fi connection that accesses the Internet (see Chapter 4). Not only can you use FaceTime to make video calls to other FaceTime users, but you can use other apps to make Internet phone calls or send instant messages.

Skype is a service that lets you make phone calls over the Internet. Calls to other Skype users are free, but calls to other landlines and mobile phones require some money on your part. The Skype for iPhone app (free) works on the iPod touch to give you phone service and instant text messages to anyone else on Skype. For voice calls, all you need is a Wi-Fi connection. For an older iPod touch, you also need a microphone — you can use the Apple In-Ear Headphones with Remote and Mic (available in the Apple Store) or products from other companies, such as V-MODA Vibe II with Microphone Headphone/Headset for iPhone/iPod, or TouchMic Handsfree Lapel Microphone and Adapter, which adds a microphone and volume control to any regular headset.

If all you need is instant messaging, try the AOL Instant Messenger (AIM) app, which is popular in the U.S. You can send and receive instant messages on your iPod touch, view your buddy list, and rearrange the entries in groups or separate them as favorites. If you're using a lot of different chat clients, the IM+ Lite app may be a better choice — it supports AIM, Yahoo! Messenger, MSN, Google Talk, Jabber, ICQ, and MySpace. Palringo is another excellent multifunctional instant messaging app that supports MSN, Yahoo! Messenger, AIM, Gadu-Gadu, ICQ, Jabber, Google Talk, and iChat.

Yahoo! Messenger folks are just a chat away (with the free Yahoo! Messenger app), and apps are available for chatting with Facebook, MySpace, and Twitter (see "Socializing on Networks" in this chapter) as well as Bebo, Flickr, and other social networks. There are even a few social networks set up specifically for iPhone and iPod touch users — for example, WhosHere (see figure) is a social proximity application that connects you with people who are nearby or anywhere in the world. You can send unlimited, free text and image messages to other WhosHere participants.

Recording Voice Memos

The Voice Memos app lets you record audio through the internal iPod touch microphone or an external microphone (such as the Apple In-Ear Headphones with Remote and Mic). You can then send recordings to others by e-mail, or sync them back to your computer's iTunes library. After syncing with iTunes (as I describe in Chapter 5), the recordings appear in the music portion of your iTunes library in the Voice Memos playlist (created for you if you don't already have one).

To start recording, tap the Voice Memos app on the Home screen and then tap the red dot button on the left side of the VU meter on the microphone recording screen. (You can also press the center button on the control capsule of the Apple In-Ear Headphones to start recording.) The red dot changes to a Pause button, as shown in Figure 13-10 (left side), and the list button on the right side of the VU meter changes to a Stop button. Tap the Pause or Stop button to stop recording.

Tap the list button on the right side of the VU meter to see the Voice Memos screen with your list of recordings, as shown in Figure 13-10 (center). Select a recording, and you can then tap Share to send it by e-mail, or tap Delete to delete it. After tapping Share, tap Email Voice Memo to open a new e-mail with the recording (or tap Cancel). See Chapter 11 for details on sending an e-mail.

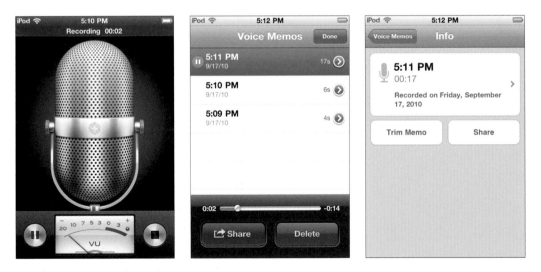

Figure 13-10: Record your voice (left), select a saved recording (center), and open the Info screen (right).

You can also tap the Play button on the left of the recording to play it, and tap the right arrow on the far right side of the recording to open the Info screen for that recording, as shown in Figure 13-10 (right side).

How can you specify what the recording is about, besides its date and time? You can assign a label to the recording by tapping the recording's information in the Info screen. A list of labels appears, including Interview, Lecture, and Memo, as well as Custom for setting your own label. Tap a label to assign the label and then tap Info in the top-left corner to return to the Info screen.

The Info screen also lets you trim the recording to be shorter — tap Trim Memo to view the playback timeline, as shown in Figure 13-11, and tap along the timeline to set a stop time. Then tap Trim Voice Memo (or Cancel to cancel).

Tap Voice Memos in the top-left corner of the Info screen to return to the Voice Memos screen, and tap Done in the top-right corner to return to the microphone recording screen.

Figure 13-11: Trim your voice recording before sharing it.

Socializing on Networks

Connecting socially by computer isn't new, but connecting on a digital network anytime and from anywhere makes social networking more instant and gratifying. You can use your iPod touch to stay in touch with your connections on the leading social networks, including Facebook, MySpace, and Twitter — viewing and typing messages, chatting, uploading and sharing photos, joining groups, and so on.

You've got a Facebook friend

Facebook is the fastest-growing free-access social networking site as of this writing, with more than 400 million active users worldwide. If you're one of them (as I am), you already know that you can add friends, send them messages, and update your personal profile with photos, videos, links, and all sorts of Facebook widgets that extend the service's functions. Although you can do all this using a browser on your computer and using Safari on your iPod touch, the site itself is far too cumbersome for easy access that way.

You can instead use the Facebook app, which lets you check your friends' status updates and photos, start a conversation in Facebook Chat, and upload images from your iPod touch.

After downloading the Facebook app (see Chapter 4 for details on downloading apps), tap the Facebook icon on the Home screen. If this is your first time using the app, a dialog appears asking whether you would like Facebook to push notifications, such as alerts, sounds, and numeric icon badges, whenever your Facebook account receives messages and notifications. (See Chapter 3 for details on setting app notifications.) Tap OK to allow notifications, or tap Don't Allow to stop them from happening. (You may want to disallow them to save battery power.)

You can then log in to your Facebook account, as shown in Figure 13-12 (left side). Tap the Email field and the keyboard appears; type your e-mail address for signing in, and then tap the Password field and type your password. Figure 13-12 (center image) shows your news feed set to Photos — scroll the slot machine selector to choose Live Feed, Status Updates, Pages, and so on. Tap the multiple-squares button in the upper left to see icons for all the app's features (Figure 13-12, right). If you have messages in your Inbox, a number appears on the Inbox icon; if you have notifications, they appear below the icons (you can see that I have seven messages in my Inbox, and two notifications at the bottom; Figure 13-12, right).

After logging in, the Facebook app remembers your username and password so that you don't have to type them to log in again. (Of course, that means if anyone grabs your iPod touch they'll have access to your Facebook account — use a passcode to lock up your iPod touch, as I describe in Chapter 3, so that no one can use it without the passcode.) If you don't want the Facebook app to remember your login info, tap the Logout button in the upper-left corner of Facebook's icons screen (refer to Figure 13-12, right side).

The Facebook icons screen (see Figure 13-12, right) includes the Profile icon for showing your profile, the Friends icon to access a list of your Facebook friends, and the Inbox icon to check your messages. You can also tap Chat to chat directly with any of your friends who are online.

The Facebook app even lets you upload and share photos: Tap the Photos icon and then tap the add (+) button to add a new album — you can then type its name and description. You can tap the camera icon and choose Take Photo to snap a photo, or tap Choose From Library to pick a photo from your iPod touch photo albums.

Figure 13-12: Log in (left) to see status updates, photos, and other choices (center) and access other Facebook features (right).

MySpace odyssey

So you want to be a MySpace cowboy or cowgirl? MySpace, owned by Fox Interactive Media, was the most popular mainstream social networking site until Facebook came along. Today, it's the number-two service, and it's still an awesomely huge network. MySpace focuses on music, movies, and TV shows — just about every band in the universe has a MySpace page, and it's easy to add music to your profile.

You can use Safari on your iPod touch to access MySpace, but like most social networks, the home page you see is far too cumbersome for easy access on your iPod touch. The MySpace Mobile for iPhone app is much easier to use and works fine on your iPod touch. It lets you send and receive messages, check status updates and photos, stay up-to-date on bulletins, and upload images from your iPod touch.

After downloading the MySpace app (see Chapter 4 for app downloading details), tap the MySpace icon on the Home screen, and the log-in screen appears as shown in Figure 13-13 (left side). To log into your MySpace account, tap the blank field under E-Mail and the keyboard appears; type your e-mail address for signing in, and then tap the field under Password and type your password. As you log in, you can turn on the Remember Me option so that after logging in, the MySpace app remembers your username and password so that you don't have to log in again.

After you log in, your MySpace Home screen appears, as shown in Figure 13-13 (right side), with menu selections for viewing and editing your profile, checking the status and mood messages from your friends, checking friend updates, adding comments, reading bulletins, reading blogs, and changing your settings.

Figure 13-13: Log in to your MySpace account (left) to see your Home screen (right).

Along the bottom of the MySpace screen are the Home icon for returning to the Home screen, the Mail icon to check your messages (with the "+" badge if you have messages waiting), the Requests icon to view and respond to requests, the Friends icon for a list of your MySpace friends, and the Photos icon to upload photos to your MySpace page. To add photos, tap the Photos icon to see the photos already on your MySpace page and then tap the Add Photos button. You can then choose Camera to snap a photo or Photo Library to pick a photo from your iPod touch photo albums.

Dedicated follower of Twitter

The most talked-about newcomer to the social network scene is Twitter, a free social messaging utility for staying connected with people in real time. With Twitter, you can post and receive messages that are 140 characters or less — called *tweets*. All public tweets are available to read on the public timeline, or you can read just the ones posted by the Twitter members you follow. You can post a tweet that can be read by all of your followers and by anyone reading the public tweets.

Members use Twitter to organize impromptu gatherings, carry on a group conversation, or just send a quick update to let people know what's going on. Companies use Twitter to announce products and carry on conversations with their customers. You can use Safari on your iPod touch to access Twitter, but there are alternatives that offer a better Twitter experience on your iPod touch.

For example, you can use the Twitter app with your iPod touch to easily flip through all your messages with the flick of a finger. Tap the Twitter app icon on your Home screen and then tap the Login button in the upper-right corner to log into your Twitter account or tap the Sign Up button to sign up for a Twitter account, as shown in Figure 13-14 (left side). After logging in or signing in, you can see recent tweets, search the Twitter timeline, post new tweets, send direct messages and replies to others on Twitter, and add new friends (called *followers*), as shown in Figure 13-14 (right side).

Figure 13-14: Log in or sign up for a Twitter account (left), and see tweets (right).

There are several iPod touch–compatible apps in the App Store for accessing Twitter, but my favorites as of this writing are Twitterific and TweetDeck (both free). They do all the basic stuff you'd expect a Twitter-compatible app to do: You can read messages from people you follow, post messages of your own, and get alerted to private direct messages and public replies.

And wherever you go, "tweetness follows." The Twitter, Twitterific, and TweetDeck apps use the iPod touch's built-in location services so that, with your permission, it can let your followers know where you are and let you know when your followers are posting from a nearby location. Tweet dreams!

Communicating with FaceTime

I saved the best for last: making and receiving video calls with Apple's truly innovative FaceTime technology. No matter how we communicate, it helps sometimes to have a little face time. Apple has engineered a solution that lets you make video calls over Wi-Fi, without any need for a special account or screen name. You can use either the front or back camera with FaceTime — the front camera has just the right field of view and focal length to focus on your face at arm's length, but you can switch to the back camera to show what's happening around you. And FaceTime can the use the cameras in either portrait or landscape orientation.

FaceTime calls are not any more intrusive than phone calls — your iPod touch rings (you can sync ringtones to your iPod touch, as I show in Chapter 5), and an invitation pops up on your screen asking if you want to accept the call. Tap Accept, and the video call begins.

To use FaceTime, you need a fourth-generation iPod touch and to be connected to the Internet over Wi-Fi, as I describe in Chapter 4. The person you're calling also needs to be connected to the Internet over Wi-Fi and using a fourth-generation iPod touch or iPhone 4.

You also need to sign into FaceTime using the FaceTime app and an Apple ID. If you already have an iTunes Store account, MobileMe account, or other Apple account, you can use that Apple ID with FaceTime (see Chapter 4 about getting an iTunes Store account). Once you've signed in, you don't need to do it again for every call.

Setting up your calling address

To sign in, tap the FaceTime icon on the Home screen, tap the Get Started button, enter your Apple ID and password, and then tap Sign In. If you don't already have an Apple account, tap Create New Account to set one up. You can then enter your account information on the New Account screen (see Chapter 4 for details on setting up an account).

On the Location screen, choose your current region and tap Next. You can then enter your e-mail address, which is the address that others use to call you in FaceTime, and then tap Next. If this is the first time for using this address for FaceTime, you need to check for new e-mail in that account and reply to the confirmation message from Apple — tap Verify Now in the confirmation message, and sign into your account to verify it. (If you've already added the account to Mail on your iPod touch, verification is automatic.) The e-mail address doesn't need to be the same as the address you entered for your account ID, but it must be a working e-mail address.

If you use more than one e-mail address, you can add the others to FaceTime so that people can use them to call you. Choose Settings⇨FaceTime, then tap Add Another Email. FaceTime verifies the e-mail address as I described previously. Now others can call you using any of the e-mail addresses you provided.

Making a video call

You can make a FaceTime video call using the FaceTime app, or by selecting a contact in the Contacts app. To use the FaceTime app, tap the FaceTime icon on the Home screen, and then tap the Favorites, Recents, or Contacts icons along the bottom of the FaceTime screen. For example, I tapped the Contacts icon, and then chose a contact to display the contact's information, shown in Figure 13-15 (left side).

 If you want to build a list of favorites that appear when you tap the Favorites icon at the bottom of the FaceTime app screen, tap the Add to Favorites button in the contact information for each contact you want to designate as a favorite.

Figure 13-15: Choose a contact and tap FaceTime (left), and then choose an e-mail address or phone number (right).

Tap the FaceTime button in the lower-left corner of the contact information screen to start the call. A menu pops up, as shown in Figure 13-15 (right side), with the contact's e-mail addresses and phone numbers. Choose an e-mail address or phone number to establish the video call.

FaceTime places the call, and sends an invitation to the contact. If your contact taps the Accept button in this invitation, you then see the screen shown in Figure 13-16, with your contact's face on the other end (or in this case, his fingers, as he hadn't truly woken up yet).

What you can do while calling

While communicating with your contact in FaceTime (refer to Figure 13-16), a picture-in-picture window shows the image from your iPod touch that the other person sees. You can drag the picture-in-picture window to any corner. You can use FaceTime in portrait or landscape orientation — when you rotate the iPod touch, the image your contact sees changes to match.

Switch camera

Figure 13-16: A FaceTime call in progress.

To avoid unwanted orientation changes as you move the camera around, lock the iPod touch in portrait orientation as I describe in Chapter 2.

To switch from the front camera to the back camera, tap the switch camera button once; tap it again to switch back to the front camera. You can also tap the mute button to mute your iPod touch microphone so that your contact can't hear you, although your contact can still see you, and you can still see and hear your contact. To end the video call, tap the End button.

Don't be shy about using another app during a FaceTime call, if you want to. Just press the Home button, and choose any app. You can still talk with your contact over FaceTime, but you can't see each other. To return to the video portion of the call from another app, tap the green bar that appears at the top of the app's screen.

If you had a previous FaceTime video call with someone, you can make another video call with that person by tapping the Recents icon at the bottom of the FaceTime app screen (refer to Figure 13-15, left side), and then tapping an entry in the Recents list that appears.

It's easy to spot the contacts you've called before. A videocam icon appears on the FaceTime button in the contact if you've previously had a FaceTime call with that contact.

You can turn FaceTime off if you don't want to receive any calls — choose Settings⇨FaceTime, and tap On at the top of the FaceTime settings screen to turn FaceTime off. You can also sign in to your FaceTime account, or create a new account, from the settings screen by tapping Account or Create New Account. To view your account information, tap Account, sign in if you haven't already, and then tap View Account. Tap Add Another Email to add another e-mail address that people can use to call you, or tap an existing e-mail address and then tap Remove This Email to remove an address from your FaceTime account.

RARY
♫ Music   📺 TV Shows   ⑫   📖 Books
🎬 Movies   🎙 Podcasts   ⑱   📲 Apps

14

STORE   LIBRARY
📀 iTunes Store   ♫ Music   📺 TV Sh
⭐ Purchased   🎬 Movies   🎙 Podc

Resetting, Updating, and Restoring

In This Chapter

▶ Resetting your iPod touch system

▶ Updating iPod touch software with the newest version

▶ Restoring your iPod touch settings

▶ Restoring an iPod touch to its factory condition

his no-nonsense chapter may not be fun, but it's necessary. Humans aren't perfect, and neither are the machines they make. If your iPod touch stops working as it should, or an app causes it to freeze up, you can turn to this chapter. You also find out how to reset your network settings and the keyboard dictionary.

This chapter also covers updating the firmware and software on your iPod touch. (*Firmware* is software encoded in hardware.) All software devices need to be updated now and then — it's a good thing, because new versions fix known bugs and add improvements.

Finally, I describe how to restore your iPod touch to its factory default condition. Restoring to factory condition is a drastic measure that erases any music or information on the iPod touch, but it usually solves a software glitch when nothing else does.

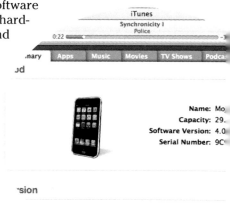

Powering Down and Resetting

Sometimes problems arise with electronics and software that can prevent an iPod touch from returning from an app or from turning on properly with all its content and playlists. If your iPod touch freezes while running an app, touch and hold the Home button below the screen for at least six seconds, until the app quits.

If that doesn't work, press and hold the sleep/wake button on the top for a few seconds until a red slider that says `Slide to power off` appears on the screen. Slide the slider with your finger to turn off the iPod touch. Then press the sleep/wake button. The iPod touch starts up again.

Resetting your iPod touch system

You probably won't be too surprised to discover that, on the off chance your iPod touch gets confused or refuses to turn on, you can fix it by resetting it and restarting the system — just like computers and other iPods. Resetting does *not* restore the iPod touch to its original factory condition, nor does it erase anything — your content and settings remain intact.

To reset the iPod touch, press and hold the sleep/wake button and the Home button at the same time for at least fifteen seconds, ignoring the red Slide to Power Off slider, until the Apple logo appears.

After resetting, everything should be back to normal, including your music and data files.

Resetting your settings

You can reset all or part of your iPod touch settings while leaving your content and personal information intact. To see your resetting options, choose Settings➪General➪Reset from the Home screen. The Reset screen appears, as shown in Figure 14-1.

You have several options for resetting:

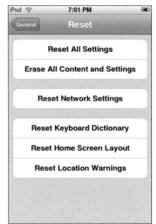

Figure 14-1: Options for resetting your iPod touch settings and clearing all content.

- ✔ **Reset All Settings:** To return your iPod touch to its original condition with no preferences or settings while still keeping your content or your personal information (including contacts, calendars, and e-mail accounts) intact, tap Reset All Settings.

- ✔ **Erase All Content and Settings:** To erase *everything,* first connect the iPod touch to your computer or a power adapter and then tap Erase All Content and Settings. This operation can take hours! You can't use the iPod touch until it finishes. It may be easier and faster to do a full restore from iTunes, as I describe later in this chapter, in the section "Restoring your iPod touch."

✔ **Reset Network Settings:** You can reset your network settings so that your previously used networks are removed from the Wi-Fi list. This type of reset is useful if you can't find any other way to stop a Wi-Fi network from connecting automatically to your iPod touch — just tap Reset Network Settings, and you're automatically disconnected from any Wi-Fi network. (Wi-Fi is turned off and then back on.) For more details about choosing Wi-Fi networks, see Chapter 4.

✔ **Reset Keyboard Dictionary:** To reset the keyboard dictionary, tap Reset Keyboard Dictionary. This erases all words that have been added to the dictionary. (Words are added when you reject words suggested by the onscreen keyboard and type the word — see Chapter 2 for details.)

✔ **Reset Home Screen Layout:** If you rearranged the icons on your Home screen (as I describe in Chapter 2), you may want to set them back to their original positions. To reset your Home screen to the default arrangement, tap Reset Home Screen Layout.

✔ **Reset Location Warnings:** Location warnings are requests by apps to use the Location Services. The iPod touch stops displaying these warnings the second time you tap OK. If you want the iPod touch to start displaying the warnings again, tap Reset Location Warnings.

Updating Your iPod touch

You should always keep your iPod touch updated with new versions of the software that controls the device. iTunes automatically checks for updates of this software and lets you update your iPod touch without affecting the music or data stored on it.

Make sure that you use the newest version of iTunes. To check for the availability of an updated version for Windows, choose Help➪Check for iTunes Updates.

If you use a Mac and you enabled the Software Update option in your System Preferences, Apple automatically informs you of updates to your Apple software for the Mac, including iTunes, Safari, iCal, and Address Book. All you need to do is select which updates to download and then click the Install button to download them. iTunes includes updates for all generations of iPods and can detect which iPod model you have.

Checking the software version

To determine which version of iPod software is installed on your iPod touch, choose Settings⇨General⇨About. Next to the word Version is information that describes the software version installed.

You can also determine the software version on your iPod touch by using iTunes. Connect the iPod touch to your computer and select it in the iTunes source pane (in the Devices section). The iPod touch summary page appears to the right of the source pane, and the software version appears next to Software Version in the iPod section at the top of the page (see Figure 14-2).

Updating with newer software

iTunes tells you whether your iPod touch has the newest software installed. Connect the iPod touch to your computer and select it in the iTunes source pane (in the Devices section). The iPod touch Summary page appears to the right of the source pane, as shown in Figure 14-2, and the Version section of the page tells you whether your iPod touch software is up-to-date and when iTunes will check for new software.

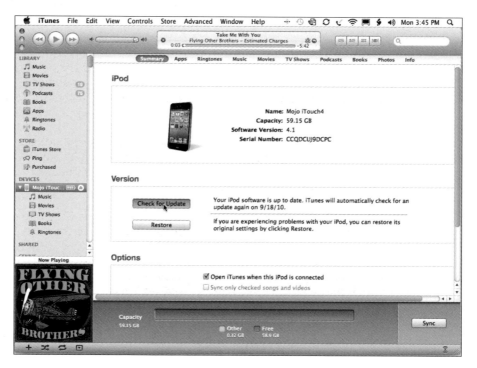

Figure 14-2: Use iTunes to update or restore your iPod touch.

If an update is available, a dialog appears to ask permission to download it. Go ahead and click OK to update the iPod touch software; you'll be happy you did. After updating the software, iTunes continues syncing with the iPod touch until it is finished.

You can also check for new software at any time by clicking the Check for Update button on the Summary page.

Restoring Your iPod touch

You can restore your iPod touch to its original factory condition. This operation erases its storage and returns the iPod touch to its original settings. If you intend to change the computer you're using for syncing your iPod touch, you have to restore the device, especially if you're switching from a Mac to a PC as your sync computer.

The restore operation wipes out your content and apps. If you don't restore from previous settings (see the next section), you need to replace the content and apps that were erased by the restore operation by syncing your iPod touch from your computer's iTunes library, as I describe in Chapter 5.

Restoring previous settings

iTunes provides protection and backs up your iPod touch settings so that you can restore them. This backup comes in handy if you want to apply the settings to a new iPod touch or to an iPod touch that you had to restore to its factory conditions.

Whenever you synchronize your iPod touch, iTunes automatically copies all the settings you use to customize your iPod touch and its apps, including Wi-Fi network settings, the keyboard dictionary, and settings for contacts, calendars, and e-mail accounts.

To restore your settings, connect your new or restored iPod touch to the same computer and copy of iTunes you used before, so that iTunes remembers the backup settings. iTunes should open automatically. (If it doesn't, open iTunes manually.) Then follow the step-by-step instructions in Chapter 1 for connecting your iPod touch to iTunes and setting it up. As you continue through the setup screens, iTunes provides the option to restore the settings from a previously backed-up iPod touch or to set up the iPod touch as new. Choose the option to restore the settings and then click Continue to finish setting up your iPod touch. iTunes uses the previous settings for syncing the iPod touch.

To delete the backed-up settings for your iPod touch, open iTunes and choose iTunes⇨Preferences (on a Mac) or Edit⇨Preferences (on a Windows PC). Click the Devices tab, select the iPod touch in the Device Backups list, and then click Remove Backup. You don't need to connect your iPod touch to do this.

Restoring to factory conditions

Restoring an iPod touch erases its storage and sets all settings to their original default values. It's the last resort for fixing problems, and it's the only choice if you want to switch computers for syncing.

To restore an iPod touch, follow these steps for both the Mac and Windows versions of iTunes:

1. **Connect the iPod touch to your computer.**

   iTunes opens automatically.

2. **Select the iPod touch in the Devices section of the source pane and click the Summary tab if it isn't already selected.**

   The iPod touch Summary pane appears to the right of the source pane.

3. **Click the Restore button.**

   An alert dialog appears to confirm that you want to restore the iPod touch.

4. **Click the Restore button again to confirm the restore operation.**

   A progress bar appears, indicating the progress of the restore operation. iTunes notifies you when the restore is finished.

5. **Sync your iPod touch with content from your iTunes library, or manually manage your content, as I describe in Chapter 5.**

6. **Sync your iPod touch with personal information, as I describe in Chapter 6.**

7. **When you finish syncing, eject the iPod touch by clicking the eject button next to its name in the source pane.**

Now, with your iPod touch restored, refreshed, and re-synced, you're ready to rock!

Part VI
The Part of Tens

The 5th Wave   By Rich Tennant

"Other than this little glitch with the landscape view, I really love my iPod touch."

In this part . . .

*Y*ou've reached the last part, the part you've come to expect in every *For Dummies* book that neatly encapsulates just about all the interesting aspects of this book's topic. Like the compilers of other important lists — David Letterman's Top Ten, the FBI's Ten Most Wanted, the Seven Steps to Heaven, the 12 Gates to the City, the 12 Steps to Recovery, The 13 Question Method, and the Billboard Hot 100 — I take seriously this ritual of putting together the *For Dummies* Part of Tens.

And so, I offer in Chapter 15 the top ten tips not found elsewhere in the book, including keeping your battery juiced and your screen clean, rating your songs, deleting apps, videos, and podcasts from your iPod touch, changing Safari privacy settings, and using international keyboards for different languages.

In Chapter 16, the last chapter of this book, I've compiled the top ten apps for the iPod touch that shook the iPod world and changed it forever. These consist of the apps not mentioned elsewhere in this book that you can obtain from the App Store — many of them for free.

Ten Tangible Tips

In This Chapter

▶ Keeping your battery juiced and your screen clean

▶ Rating your songs

▶ Deleting apps, videos, and podcasts from your iPod touch

▶ Using international keyboards for different languages

This book is filled with tips, but I've put in this chapter ten truly handy ones that didn't fit in elsewhere but which can help make your iPod touch experience a completely satisfying one.

Saving the Life of Your Battery

Follow these simple rules:

6:30 AM
1100 si
Today   Aug 2
1100 si |

✔ Don't keep an iPod touch in a snug carrying case when charging — that snug case can cause overheating.

✔ Top it off with power whenever it's convenient.

✔ Set your iPod touch to automatically go to sleep by choosing Settings➪General➪Auto-Lock from the Home screen.

Everything else you need to know is in Chapter 1.

Keeping Your Screen Clean

If the iPod touch display has excessive moisture on it from humidity or wet fingers, wipe it with a soft, dry cloth. If it's dirty, use a soft, slightly damp, lint-free cloth — an inexpensive eyeglass cleaning cloth sold in vision care stores or pharmacies is a good choice.

Do not use window cleaners, household cleaners, aerosol sprays, solvents, alcohol, ammonia, or abrasives to clean the iPod touch display — they can scratch or otherwise damage the display. Also, try not to get any moisture in any of the openings, as it could short out the device.

Getting Healthy with Nike

Use your iPod touch as a workout companion with Nike+ running shoes and a Nike+ iPod Sport Kit. Its sensor fits inside your Nike+ shoe under the insole. The second- and third-generation iPod touch models include a receiver, but the first-generation iPod touch requires a separate receiver.

When you have the kit and the shoes, activate the app on your iPod touch — choose Settings⊳Nike + iPod and tap Off for the Nike + iPod option to turn it on. You can track your pace, time, and distance from one workout to the next, and you can pick songs and playlists to match. You can even sync your workout data with nikeplus.com, see all your runs, and share motivation with runners across the world.

Rating Your Songs

Ratings are useful — the iTunes DJ and Genius features are influenced by ratings, and you can define smart playlists with ratings to select only rated songs so you can avoid the clunkers and spinal tappers. In fact, when you try to put a music library on your iPod touch that's larger than the device's capacity, iTunes decides which songs to synchronize based on — you guessed it, *ratings*.

iTunes lets you rate your songs, but so does your iPod touch. You can rate any song on your iPod touch while you listen to it. Ratings you assign on your iPod touch are automatically resynchronized back to your iTunes library when you connect your iPod touch again.

To assign a rating to a song on your iPod touch, follow these steps:

1. **Start playing a song (see Chapter 7 for details).**

    The Now Playing screen appears.

2. **Tap the list button to display a list of the album or playlist contents.**

   The list button is in the upper-right corner.

3. **Tap the title of any song in the track listing or leave selected the song that's playing.**

4. **Drag across the ratings bar at the top of the track listing to give the song zero to five stars.**

   The upper limit is five stars (for the best).

Deleting Apps from Your iPod touch

You can turn off the synchronization of certain apps in your iTunes library before syncing your iPod touch to iTunes (see Chapter 5) so that the apps disappear from your iPod touch. But you can also delete apps directly from your iPod touch — except, of course, the bundled apps from Apple.

Touch and hold any icon on the Home screen until all the icons begin to wiggle (as if you're about to rearrange them or add Home screens). To delete an app, tap the circled X that appears inside the app's icon while it wiggles. Your iPod touch displays a warning that deleting the app also deletes all its data; tap Delete to go ahead and delete the app and its data or tap Cancel to cancel.

To stop the icons from wiggling the Watusi, press the Home button, which saves any changes you made to your Home screens.

Deleting Videos and Podcasts from Your iPod touch

Need more room on your iPod touch? You can delete a video or podcast episode directly from your iPod touch. Scroll the Videos screen to see your videos, or select a podcast in the Podcasts screen to see its episodes (as I describe in Chapter 8). Flick left or right across the video or podcast episode selection, and then tap the Delete button that appears, as shown in Figure 15-1.

Your video or podcast episode is deleted from your iPod touch only. When you sync your iPod touch with iTunes, the video or podcast episode is copied back to your iPod touch. If you want to prevent the video or podcast episode from appearing on your iPod touch after syncing, deselect it first before syncing your iPod touch, or switch to manually managing music and videos, as I describe in Chapter 5. *Note:* If you delete a rented movie from an iPod touch, it's gone forever (or until you rent it again).

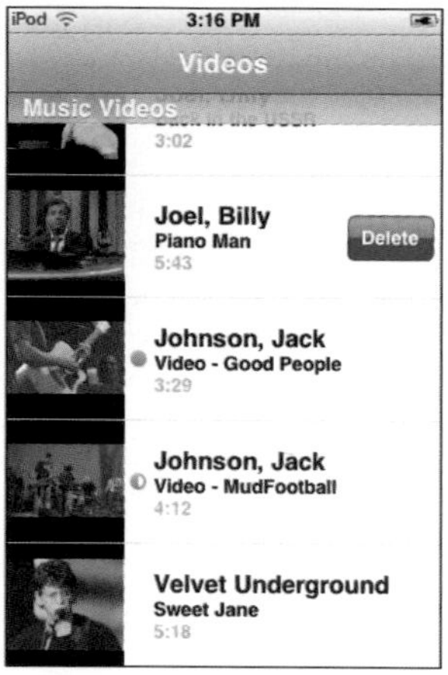

Figure 15-1: Flick left or right across the selection to see the Delete button.

Measuring Traffic in Maps

The Maps app not only shows you the route to take, but in some areas it can also show you traffic patterns so you can avoid the jams. The traffic data is constantly updated and aggregated from a variety of Internet sources by Google. It is available for more than 30 major U.S. cities, including New York, Los Angeles, San Francisco, and Washington.

To use Maps, tap the Maps icon on the Home screen. The Maps app appears (refer to Chapter 12). You can obtain directions first, as I describe in Chapter 12, or just display any location on the map that has highways. To show traffic information, tap the options button (the curled page icon in the bottom-right corner) to see a menu underneath the map, and then tap Show Traffic.

When the map shows traffic, highways are color-coded according to the flow of traffic:

- Green for highways moving faster than 50 miles per hour (mph)
- Yellow for 25–50 mph
- Red for less than 25 mph

If you don't see color-coded highways, you may need to zoom out to see highways and major roads.

To stop showing the traffic, tap the option button and then tap Hide Traffic.

Adding International Keyboards and Changing Layouts

You can change the layout and language settings for the onscreen keyboard by choosing Settings⇨General⇨Keyboard and tapping International Keyboards. The Keyboards screen appears with a language button for the currently selected keyboard language (which is English on my iPod touch). Tap the language button to see layout options for the keyboard, as shown in Figure 15-2 (left side).

The Software Keyboard Layout section offers options for the onscreen (Software) keyboard. These include the AZERTY key arrangement rather than the typical QWERTY arrangement for English. The Hardware Keyboard Layout section offers the virtual layout options for an Apple Wireless Keyboard.

Tap the Keyboards button in the upper-left corner to return to the Keyboards screen.

From the Keyboards screen (choose Settings⇨General⇨Keyboard if you need to start again), you can add keyboards for different languages and use them simultaneously. Tap International Keyboards and then tap Add New Keyboard to add another keyboard. A list of languages appears, as shown in Figure 15-2 (right side) — scroll the list to find the language you want and then tap the language. After tapping a language, the Keyboards screen appears with buttons for the languages you've chosen. You can add as many keyboards as you need, or tap a language to change its keyboard layout how I describe above.

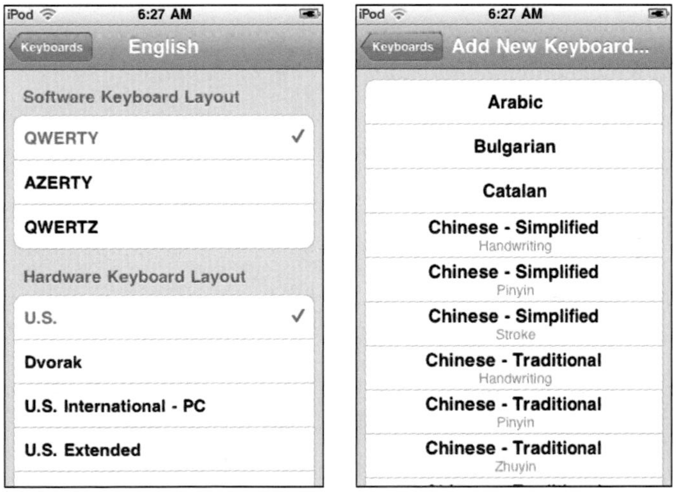

iPod 🔋 6:27 AM 🔋	iPod 🔋 6:27 AM 🔋
‹ Keyboards English	**‹ Keyboards Add New Keyboard...**
Software Keyboard Layout	**Arabic**
QWERTY ✓	**Bulgarian**
AZERTY	**Catalan**
QWERTZ	**Chinese - Simplified** Handwriting
Hardware Keyboard Layout	**Chinese - Simplified** Pinyin
U.S. ✓	**Chinese - Simplified** Stroke
Dvorak	**Chinese - Traditional** Handwriting
U.S. International - PC	**Chinese - Traditional** Pinyin
U.S. Extended	**Chinese - Traditional** Zhuyin

Figure 15-2: Change the keyboard layout (left) or add a language (right).

You can then switch keyboards while typing information by tapping the globe icon, as shown in Figure 15-3, that appears to the right of the .?123 key when more than one international keyboard is turned on. The language of the newly active keyboard appears briefly in the spacebar.

Each time you tap the globe icon, the keyboard layout switches to the next language you've turned on, in the order that they appear in the international keyboards list.

For example, if you turned on English, French, German, and Japanese Romaji (for a total of 4 keyboards), tapping the globe icon switches from English to French. Tapping it again switches to German, and tapping it again switches to Japanese Romaji. Tapping the globe icon one more time switches back to English.

Figure 15-3: Tap the globe icon to switch to another language.

Changing Safari Privacy and Browser Settings

You can change Safari's privacy and browser settings on your iPod touch by choosing Settings⇨Safari from the Home screen.

To speed up text entry into Web pages, turn on AutoFill to automatically fill out Web forms using your contact information, and automatically fill in the names and passwords you previously entered. Choose Settings⇨Safari⇨ AutoFill, and then turn on the Use Contact Info option. You can then tap My Info and select the contact you want to use for autofilling. To autofill your names and passwords, turn Names & Passwords on, so that Safari automatically fills them in when you revisit the Web site. To remove all AutoFill information, tap Clear All.

Fraud Warning is usually turned on. It warns you of a potentially fraudulent site and doesn't load the page. You can turn it off if you are sure that the site you are visiting is not fraudulent, but be careful!

To browse faster, you can sacrifice JavaScript: choose Settings⇨Safari and turn off JavaScript. Although you need JavaScript for most Web apps and services, you can browse pages faster by limiting the browser to HTML and CSS. You can also turn off the Plug-Ins option to speed up browsing. Plug-ins enable Safari to play some types of audio and video files and to display Microsoft Word files and Microsoft Excel documents.

To block or allow pop-ups, turn Block Pop-ups on or off. Blocking pop-ups stops only those pop-ups that appear when you close a Web page or open one by typing its address. Sorry, the option doesn't block pop-ups that can appear when you tap a link.

You usually leave a "cookie" trail when you visit Web sites. Web sites use *cookies* to personalize your experience with the site (such as remembering your username and password). Some pages won't load correctly unless you turn on the Accept Cookies option. You have a choice of accepting cookies from sites you visited (tap From Visited, which is what I do), or from all sites (tap Always), or Never. To clear cookies from Safari, tap Clear Cookies.

If you need to clear the history of pages you visited, tap Clear History. If a Web page you open doesn't show updated content, tap Clear Cache (the cache stores a copy of the page from the last time you visited).

Stopping a Wi-Fi Network From Joining

Your iPod touch remembers your Wi-Fi connections and automatically uses one when it detects it within your range. If you've used multiple Wi-Fi networks in the same location, it picks the last one you used. (For details on choosing a Wi-Fi network, see Chapter 4.)

But if your iPod touch keeps picking up a Wi-Fi network that you can't properly join, such as a private network that requires a password you don't know or a commercial network that charges for access, you can tell your iPod touch to *forget* this particular network, rather than turning off Wi-Fi itself. This is very useful if a paid service has somehow gotten hold of your iPod touch and won't let you move on to other Web pages without typing a password.

Choose Settings⤴Wi-Fi from the Home screen and tap the circled right-arrow (>) button next to the selected network's name. The network's information screen appears. Tap the Forget This Network button at the top of the screen so that your iPod touch doesn't join it automatically. Then tap the Wi-Fi Networks button at the top-left corner to return to the Wi-Fi Networks screen. You can always select this network manually, and you can still continue to use other Wi-Fi networks.

Ten Apps That Shook the iPod World

*1*t's not fair. Only ten apps? Hundreds of thousands of apps from almost as many software companies are competing for attention in the App Store. I could write an entire book about just the ones that have shaken *my* world — right down to the very routines I live by. (Maybe they'll let me write that book in the future.) Instead, the publisher dragged me kicking and screaming to the back of the book, and told me we'd run out of room and that we had to keep it to ten.

How did I pick these ten? I included apps I think are important as an introduction to the iPod touch experience, along with the apps that I use every day.

I left out of this list the ones I've already described in other chapters and on the Cheat Sheet of this book — Facebook, MySpace, Twitter, TweetDeck, Twitterific, Skype, and the messaging apps (Chapter 13); Google Earth (Chapter 12); Wikipanion and other wiki readers (Chapter 10); Pandora, Truveo, and other apps that stream video (Chapter 8); PocketGuitar and other apps that help you make music (Chapter 7); a variety of games that use time (Chapter 3) or the accelerometer (Chapter 2); and the apps for fun and travel (Online Cheat Sheet, available at www.dummies.com/ cheatsheet/ipodtouch2e). I also left out, of course, Apple's apps that are supplied with the iPod touch. And yet, all of these apps, and especially the ones from Apple, are responsible for shaking up the iPod world.

Remote

The Remote app from Apple (free) turns your iPod touch into a remote control for iTunes and Apple TV. That may seem like no big deal, but it was the first app to demonstrate how the iPod touch can control other Apple entertainment devices, which shows the direction Apple is heading — into the living room entertainment center. The Remote app works with your Wi-Fi network, so you can control playback from anywhere in and around your home.

Enigmo

Voted the best game at the 2008 Worldwide Developers Conference and winner of various awards, Enigmo (not free) is a unique puzzle game in which you direct animated flowing streams of water, oil, and lava, using your iPod touch to move and rotate the various puzzle pieces in order to divert the flow of the falling droplets so that they can reach their target. Engimo 2 expands on this theme by offering puzzles in 3D.

Tap Tap Revenge

With a name obviously inspired by Japan's megapopular Dance Dance Revolution, Tap Tap Revenge takes its cues from the addictive Guitar Hero, putting your rhythmic skills to the test. You tap through the beats of the music or shake left and right as the arrows fall. Version 3 offers lots of music tracks to download as well as an immersive 3D experience.

Angry Birds

This game has managed to stay at the very top of the charts far longer than other games. For only $0.99, Angry Birds offers many hours of gameplay in which you take revenge on green pigs who steal the birds' eggs and lay waste to their fortified castles. This powerhouse of a game offers 165 levels; find the golden eggs to unlock secret levels. At my last check there were over 39,000 customer reviews on the App Store, and its average rating is five stars! Angry Birds wins my prize for most influential game.

Ocarina

It would be remiss of me not to include the most famous of strange mobile apps that defy characterization. Ocarina (not free) turns your iPod touch into an ancient, flute-like instrument and lets you share the music you make with others. Without any musical training, you can touch the holes of the ocarina to make music or blow into an external microphone. Variations on this type of app include Leaf Trombone and one of my faves, Harmonica.

Dropbox

Dropbox has saved my, er, *reputation* a few times by giving me access on my iPod touch to documents and files on my computer at home — I could easily find a document and e-mail it. Dropbox makes your iPod touch an extension of your computer — you can view photos, videos, documents, and presentations on your computer, and share and send files by e-mail. You can also use your Dropbox account (free) to sync files across multiple devices, share large files, and maintain an online backup of your most important files.

Google Mobile

Searching with Google has always been part of Safari (see Chapter 10). Google Mobile (free) lets you search by voice, and provides instant access to Google Search, Gmail, Google News, Docs, Calendar, Talk, and other Google apps. You get relevant search suggestions as you type or speak, and you can use location search to find businesses, services, weather, and movie info, and then see these suggestions on Google Maps.

Shazam and SoundHound

Why am I listing two? Because if you're like me, and you hear a song in a store or restaurant, and you absolutely *need to know immediately* its title and artist, you might try both of these free apps. Shazam was the first to recognize songs using the internal iPod touch microphone or an external microphone (such as the Apple In-Ear Headphones with Remote and Mic). SoundHound also recognizes tunes it can hear, and you can also hum or sing into the microphone — and if you're good at karaoke, it may just find that song. SoundHound also provides lyrics and artist info, and both apps connect you to iTunes to buy the music. Both also provide premium versions for unlimited tagging, previews, and sharing music.

Stanza and iBooks

Okay, I have to list two again. The Stanza app (free) changed my reading habits — I not only read more classics now (which are mostly free), but I also read everywhere I go. You can download a vast selection of free classics and buy contemporary works, sort by title or author, and create custom collections to build reading lists and keep track of all your books. Although other readers have appeared (notably the Amazon Kindle Reader and Nook), Stanza was my favorite . . .

. . . until iBooks came along from Apple (I'm now dividing my reading time between both apps). iBooks, originally released with the iPad, offers the best reading experience — you flip through pages with a swipe or tap, and you can bookmark pages, add notes, find words and phrases, change the font size, and so on. It also offers access to Apple's online iBookstore. With the bookmark-syncing feature, I can keep my bookmarks, notes, and the current page in sync wirelessly with the iBooks app on my iPad and iPhone.

Tony's Tips for iPhone Users

Tony's Tips for iPhone Users Manual (not free), developed and published by yours truly, is an app that provides helpful tips for using your iPhone or iPod touch with iTunes and MobileMe. I add new tips and revise the information in Tony's Tips regularly as Apple updates the software — the app lets you search quickly for topics, bookmark pages, and save pages for offline reading.

Index